Reclaiming the Mainstream

Reclaiming the Mainstream

Individualist Feminism Rediscovered

Joan Kennedy Taylor

Prometheus Books • Buffalo, New York

A Cato Institute Book

Published 1992 by Prometheus Books.

96 95 94 93 92   5 4 3 2 1

Library of Congress Cataloging-in-Publication Data

Taylor, Joan Kennedy.
    Reclaiming the mainstream: individualist feminism rediscovered / by Joan Kennedy Taylor.
        p.   cm.
    Includes bibliographical references.
    ISBN 0-87975-717-5
    1. Feminism—United States. 2. Individualism—United States. 3. Women's rights—United States. I. Title.
HQ1426.T39   1992
305.42′0973—dc20   92-2807
                                                                          CIP

Printed in the United States of America on acid-free paper.

Contents

Contents

Acknowledgments

I want to thank a number of people for helping me in various ways to write this book. First and foremost is Roy A. Childs, Jr., who encouraged me not only in developing these ideas, but in deciding to write a book in the first place, and in navigating all the difficult shoals between preliminary idea and finished book. I would also like to thank psychologist Sharon Presley, the first National Coordinator of the Association of Libertarian Feminists, for introducing me to Roy Childs in 1977 and encouraging him to publish my first feminist article in his premier issue of *Libertarian Review*. And I mustn't neglect Edward Crane, president of the Cato Institute, who since 1979 has consistently supported my somewhat maverick feminist activities by employing me as a commentator and lecturer and promoting and encouraging me in ways too numerous to list here. It gives me great pleasure to be able to thank him and the Cato Institute publicly for this support. I would also like to thank William Hammett, president of the Manhattan Institute, for taking a chance on hiring me as publications director there in 1981, a job that put me in touch with many of the people who have helped me in putting together this book.

A number of people besides Roy Childs and Sharon Presley read an earlier version of the manuscript and offered invaluable advice and suggestions, really serving as surrogate editors. They are Barbara Abrash, Annelise Anderson and Martin Anderson of the Hoover Institution, David Boaz of the Cato Institute, Barbara Branden, Catherine Bly Cox, Elizabeth W. Kaplan of the Cato Institute, Charles Murray, Andrea Rich of Laissez Faire Books, Kay Nolte Smith, and Alysson Tucker of the Landmark Center for Civil Rights. I also would like to thank Nadine Strossen of the ACLU for pointing out that my reference to the Supreme Court *Beauharnais* case was misleading as I first wrote it.

I am especially indebted to the remarkable Kay Nolte Smith for persuading me to embark on a complete reorganization of the manuscript, which I believe has very much improved the book and clarified what I intended to say.

It was Roy Childs who influenced Bob Basil at Prometheus Books to take a chance on buying my proposal. Both Bob, who acquired the book, and Jeanne O'Day, who carefully edited it, have shown an understanding and enthusiasm that have gone far to make up for the difficulties inherent in having an exclusively long-distance relationship, and I want to thank them, too.

Finally, I would like to thank the long-term members of my former consciousness-raising group in the Berkshires: Sally Begley, Anne DeGersdorff, Gladys Flower, Virginia Sullivan Finn, Eleanor Lord, and Lois Rose, for opening my eyes to what feminism can be.

I think the contributions all these people have made to this book proves my point that the individual grows and flourishes best with the help of understanding and supportive communities.

CHAPTER ONE

So You Think You're Not a Feminist?

In October of 1991, an astonishingly large segment of the American television-viewing public was riveted by the hearings held by the Senate Judiciary Committee on the allegations by Anita Hill that Judge Clarence Thomas had sexually harassed her when she worked for him in the early 1980s. Various feminists were interviewed briefly by television reporters, and sometimes commented on the proceedings.

What did these feminists stand for? If the soundbites were all you knew of feminism, you would conclude that feminists were not only against sexual harassment (after all, nobody was for it) but considered that pornography was its direct cause and one of the worst social evils in our country. Some feminists stressed their allegation that there was a relationship between an interest in pornography and sexual harassment, even sexual crimes, while others who disagreed politely didn't mention the subject. You would have no hint that the issue of banning pornography has been a subject of deep division within the feminist community. You might conclude, from what these feminists said in opposition to the confirmation of Judge Thomas even before these charges, that they had a welfare-state agenda, perhaps leading them to be members of the left-wing of the Democratic Party.

But if you listened more carefully to what was going on, you might find evidence that didn't fit this simplistic picture of the agenda of contemporary feminists. Was Anita Hill a feminist? She had been a supporter of conservative Robert Bork. And what about the women who worked with and testified for Clarence Thomas, many of whom identified themselves as feminists? Did they share the views of the other interviewed feminists that Thomas's views—on affirmative action, for instance—or that his behavior toward Anita Hill were disastrous?

This is the age of feminism—or of post-feminism, depending on which issue of the *New York Times Magazine* you read. So obviously, since it has been so prominent, so important, so influential in our current society, we all know what it is. Or do we?

I am a believer in individualism and individual rights; in entrepreneurship and free enterprise; in civil liberties and minimal government. And I am a feminist. Does that surprise anyone? I am convinced that there are many people who would basically agree with me if they didn't have a soundbite image of what feminism entails.

The thesis of this book is that what we now call "feminism" began early in the nineteenth century as an individualist movement, and, further, that it is this individualism that has been the defining characteristic of the mainstream of that movement ever since. This does not mean that individualism has always predominated. Since the early days of the movement, there have been two philosophical strands of thought within it: individualism and collectivism, and from time to time one or the other strand has become dominant. When the collectivists predominate, the individualists become less active and return to cultivating their gardens.

Individualism and Collectivism

We have all been brought up in an era of big, powerful government, in which being "law-abiding" doesn't just mean refraining from theft and murder but may require such positive actions as wearing seat belts, cutting one's hedge if it exceeds a certain height, or separating one's trash. And society is also exacting in nonlegal ways. Too much "individualism" is not necessarily seen as a good thing today. It may be viewed as antisocial, since it is sometimes taken to imply antagonism to the interests of others or even the sacrifice of others to the self.

Western culture assumes the importance of the individual even when societies endorse political programs that may downgrade or jeopardize individual rights (the "war on drugs" comes to mind as an example). It may therefore seem to be tautological to say that feminism is individualistic. But in recent years there have been attacks on that very aspect of feminism. For instance, Sylvia Ann Hewlett's 1986 book, *A Lesser Life,* criticized American feminism's emphasis on consciousness raising, reproductive rights, and equality before the law on precisely that ground. In 1991 Emory University professor Elizabeth Fox-Genovese called her book *Feminism Without Illusions: A Critique of Individualism,* and she describes her thesis thus:

This book offers a critique of feminism's complicity in and acceptance of individualism. . . . Throughout, I am using "individualism" to mean the systematic theory of politics, society, economics, and epistemology that emerged following the Renaissance, that was consolidated in the great English, American, French, and Haitian revolutions of the seventeenth and eighteenth centuries, and that has found its purest logical outcome in the laissez-faire doctrines of neoclassical economics and libertarian political theory. The political triumph of individualism has led to its hegemony as *the* theory of human nature and rights, according to which, rights, including political sovereignty, are grounded in the individual and can only be infringed upon by the state in extraordinary circumstances.

. . . Here I am arguing that individualism actually perverts the idea of the socially obligated and personally responsible freedom that constitutes the only freedom worthy of the name or indeed historically possible.[1]

She goes on to suggest that individual rights should be seen as deriving from the community rather than as being "prior" to the claims of society. This she sees as a necessary underpinning for laws—her immediate example is laws against pornography—"that recognize liberties as interdependent and as inseparable from social responsibility."[2] When you speak of community in this way, you are downgrading the importance of individual legal rights.

But community remains important. The seeming contradiction that the individualist-centered women's movement keeps foundering on is the tension between the concepts of the individual and of the group. If you believe in the importance of the individual, does that mean you deny any importance to groups to which the individual belongs? Or, on the other hand, is group identification more important that individuality? As Elizabeth Fox-Genovese asked, which is prior? Do you view each individual as empowering the group by entering it, or do you view the group as bestowing rights that it can then take back?

The consistent individualist holds that the individual is the basic unit. An individual joins with others in various ways to achieve goals. An individual does not receive identity by being a member of a group. Nor should an individual's political and legal rights be decided by being born into a group.

When the group being referred to is the state, there is a real tension between it and its individual members because the state can use the force of law to require the behavior it wants from its members. It can draft people, jail people, outlaw their livelihoods. Individuals can try to take over the power of the state for their own purposes, to force *other* people to behave in a certain way, but that always has unexpected consequences

—the Prohibitionists didn't intend to foster the rise of mob gangsters or the social tolerance of public drunkenness, especially in women. Nongovernmental groups have less power than governments have, but they also can try to control by coercion.

When the group being referred to is a free association of people with a common goal uniting to achieve that goal, the group acts as an extension of its individual members and is no contradiction to individualism. A group formed by individual choices nourishes the individual—in fact, human nature is such that many life-serving goals can only be reached by people willing to act in concert. So the accusation that individualism means rampant and fragmented egoism is a misunderstanding of what individualism entails. Individuals need chosen groups of all sorts, and the existence of a multiplicity of such groups almost necessarily works to increase choices.

As I hope to show in this book, a number of women activists over the years have put their primary emphasis on the liberty of the individual and on the individual's freedom to make choices. Many of them have also felt that women could best be emancipated through various forms of communal action or communal living, which they sometimes thought of as utopian socialism, or "collectivism." That is not what I mean by collectivism. The real form of collectivism—of coercively subordinating and submerging the individual in the identity of the collective and looking at the individual only as a group member—has been present in some aspects of the women's movement, from the nineteenth-century days of social purity to contemporary Marxist feminism.

Classical Liberalism

It is, however, the individualist strand of feminism that has always reached a wider audience. My political view is the view called by some today "libertarian" or, more historically and formally, "classical liberal," but not many feminists since the actual classical liberal days in the eighteenth and nineteenth centuries share that view. So when I say that both the nineteenth-century Woman Movement (as it was called then) and the twentieth-century feminist movement are mainly individualist movements, I do not mean to imply that their members always, or even often, share my suspicion of the use of government power. I mean that they emphasize the importance of the individual woman's rights and happiness, even though they may think that this can be combined with some form of state power to enforce the policies they advocate.

Although I consider myself to be an adherent of classical liberalism, this book is not about classical liberalism or libertarianism. It is not about how libertarianism applies to women, or how all feminists should embrace the libertarian philosophy *in toto.* Rather, since I do not see feminism as a purely political philosophy or movement, my book has to do with the companion tradition of individualism in this country—understood to mean a tradition that holds it important to support the full flowering of the individual life.

Equal Liberty

Since I also want to recommend that a particular *political* stance be taken by feminists—that they concentrate on individual rights—I would like to bring up one preeminent principle of classical liberalism as enunciated in the writings of Herbert Spencer (before his name became synonymous with the concept of "the survival of the fittest"): the principle that he calls in his 1851 book *Social Statics* "equal liberty" or "equal freedom."

Spencer was interested in enunciating the importance of individual rights as a principle of government, as opposed to the utilitarian view of Jeremy Bentham, then in vogue, that government was meant to promote "the greatest happiness to the greatest number." The principle that Spencer proposed to substitute was "the general proposition, that every man may claim the fullest liberty to exercise his faculties compatible with the possession of like liberty by every other man."[3]

This equal liberty must be the province of women as well as men, said Spencer: "the word *man* must be understood in a generic, and not in a specific sense. The law of equal freedom manifestly applies to the whole race—female as well as male."[4] He went on to argue with those who defended the status quo in 1851. "Three positions only are open to us. It may be said that women have no rights at all—that their rights are not so great as those of men—or that they are equal to those of men."[5] He explodes the first two positions, explodes the argument of "mental inferiority," and concludes, "The extension of the law of equal freedom to both sexes will doubtless be objected to, on the ground that the political privileges exercised by men must thereby be ceded to women also. Of course they must; and why not?"[6]

This notion of equal liberty was suggested again in 1986 as the proper basis for a legal theory of gender in the book *Gender Justice,* by David L. Kirp, Mark G. Yudof, and Marlene Strong Franks, when they suggested "embracing equal liberty as the governing constitutional principle,"[7] rather than adopting the view that the law should put everyone in an equal position *or* that the law should reinforce differences between men and women. The authors of this book do not identify themselves as feminists, although the footnotes refer to many classics of feminist thought. I am suggesting, however, that the standard they present is an appropriate one for feminists to adopt, as the most consistent individualist standard. *Gender Justice* puts it this way:

> The Supreme Court has successively imposed different constitutional frameworks for reviewing legislation that draws lines between the sexes. In *Reed,* it demanded only that the state be "rational" in its gender-based distinctions. In *Frontiero,* it came close to converting into constitutional law the idea of equality as sameness. . . . The Court's lack of success is conspicuous: whether demanding sameness or accepting differentness, the decisions weaken the central idea of gender justice. It is neither equality as sameness nor equality as differentness that adequately comprehends the issue, but instead the very different concept of equal liberty under the law, rooted in the idea of individual autonomy.[8]

The authors elaborate later on an analysis close to Spencer's own, when they say,

> One person's liberty is sometimes felt by another person as a constraint, and so some way of choosing between competing liberty claims is required. It is acceptable, in classic understandings of liberty, to frustrate individual choices in order to prevent harm to others, since such activities diminish the ability of the would-be victims freely to select their own way of life.[9]

Finally, they conclude that "traditional assumptions about the proper behavior of men and women . . . dot the tax code, regulation of sexual conduct, and the social security laws. Equal liberty, if taken seriously, would change much of this society's gender policy."[10]

Contemporary feminists often invoke the classical liberal tradition of early feminism, even though few of them extend it consistently to apply to all areas of contemporary social policy. In a cover article in the *New York Times Magazine,* Vivian Gornick identified the essence of feminism with this recurring tradition of rights.

> The women's movement of the 70's was a moment akin to the one in the analyst's office when the patient says, "Now I see clearly." In reality, feminism saw clearly when Mary Wollstonecraft wrote "A Vindication of the Rights of Women" in 1792 and then again when Elizabeth Stanton organized the Seneca Falls convention in 1848, and then again when Alice Paul framed the equal rights amendment in 1923. The 1970's saw yet another rehearsal of fundamentals in this painfully long analysis. We

must believe that reiteration of the insight is the purge itself; that after each repeat the patient is, in fact, not the same as before—and neither is the world. I for one, do believe that.[11]

This book will examine all the events that Gornick mentions. At this point I would only add, if we fully understand the insight she speaks of, we may not need to repeat history again.

Cycles of Individualism and Social Feminism

There has been a pattern to the waxing and waning of feminist concerns. The individualist impulse brings women together. This is no paradox—once individuals set goals, they often find that supporting each other and taking joint action is necessary to achieve their goals. But, unfortunately, individuals in our society often don't distinguish between joining together to accomplish things themselves and joining together to get the government to support a specific legislative agenda. Nor do they distinguish between voicing a claim to the same negative rights as everyone else—to equal liberty, which no one feels comfortable in opposing—and voicing a claim to an agenda of positive rights, which the government would have to provide and enforce.

As the aims of the movement shift, from a stress on individualism, social cooperation, and negative rights to a stress on collectivism (not just any "collective" action, but in the sense of using government power) and positive rights, the movement becomes marginal and ineffective.

Books about the history of the women's movement often describe a movement that persisted relatively unchanged from the early nineteenth-century abolitionist days to 1920, when the Nineteenth Amendment finally allowed American women to vote; a period of complete inactivity from 1920 to shortly after 1960; and then the emergence of modern feminism. I will be discussing a somewhat different chronology, in which what might be called the "individualist feminist impulse" seemed to dwindle into a more general political activism, not once but twice, and may be on the road to doing so again.

Originally, in the early nineteenth century, the Woman Movement was a classical liberal, individualist movement, striving for legal equality, but also such social equality as the right to speak in public meetings without ostracism and the opportunity to gain an education and try to qualify for occupations traditionally reserved for men.

Gradually, after the Civil War, as an influx of immigrants to work in the new industries was accompanied by an interest in social reform and the passing of social legislation, the Woman Movement became less interested in individual rights and legal equality and more interested in collective action: the labor movement and the support of economic and "social purity" legislation.

In her 1982 anthology, *Freedom, Feminism, and the State,* Wendy McElroy details the individualist beginnings of feminism in the abolitionist movement and pinpoints the Civil War as the turning point of the first cycle in the movement, away from a concern with individual rights to a focus on gaining the vote. "The fundamental change, however," she writes,

> was feminism's attitude toward itself. Early feminism was a moral, pietistic crusade that refused to compromise an ideological context, which was broader than rights for women. . . . In contrast, post-war feminism seemed narrow and pragmatic. . . .
>
> Moreover, as feminism grew it became increasingly "respectable" in its attitude and goals. Eugenics and social purity reform, both popular causes, became a staple of mainstream feminism. Social purity campaigns included raising the age of consent, the reformation of prostitutes, censorship of obscenity, and the advocacy of birth control through restraint.[12]

Historian William L. O'Neill points out that around the turn of the century, "reformers, both men and women, gradually moved to combine woman suffrage with other reforms, a linkage that has often been called 'social feminism.' "[13] This new social feminism led to a demise of interest in the Woman Movement as such—all that held together the temperance movement, the social purity movement, and the settlement house movement was their support of woman suffrage. Women campaigned for suffrage actively from the end of the Civil War until the turn of the century with little effect, even abandoning their roots in the prewar abolitionist movement to make not-so-subtle appeals to racism, to try to achieve this political goal.

This progression seems to indicate that, in a period of a little less than a century, the Woman Movement was all going in the same direction, completely shifting its emphasis from rights to social programs. But what such an analysis leaves out is the rise of a countermovement, the movement that for the first time was called feminist, in which the individualist tradition seeking equal liberty remained. In the years before World War I, a revival of interest in individualist feminism came just in time to revivify the stodgy, moribund suffrage movement, to promote the accessibility of birth control, and to create a vital, self-centered feminism that challenged existing standards of sexual behavior and demanded to have both love and work. Wendy McElroy discusses the late-nineteenth-century efforts to reform the birth control and marriage laws, and points to the early periodicals, *Lucifer the Light Bearer, The Word,* and *Liberty,* all of which supported woman's natural rights, including the right to control her own sexuality. "Today," says McElroy,

> the activities of 19th-century libertarian feminists are virtually ignored by the current movement . . . despite the fact that the libertarians Moses Harman and Ezra Heywood were among the first to be arrested under the Comstock laws for distributing birth control information; Angela Heywood was virtually the only voice calling for legalized abortion in America in the 1890s; and Lillian Harman and E. C. Walker were perhaps the first couple to be imprisoned for violation of marriage statutes in America.[14]

These activities led to a more widespread individualist emphasis on women's rights in the decade after 1910, when the word *feminism* came into general use. Margaret Sanger coined the term *birth control* in 1914 and opened the first birth control clinic in New York in 1916. After the Nineteenth Amendment was passed, and women got the vote, feminists created the concept of an equal rights amendment in 1923.

But there were other forces that led once more to social feminism. There was an agitation to use the vote to campaign for a new set of legislative issues—the abolition of child labor, for instance.

The National American Woman Suffrage Association became the League of Women Voters and, according to a footnote in O'Neill's article, "during the 1920s . . . lobbied for food and drug legislation, prohibition of child labor, birth control, antilynching bills, compulsory school attendance, mother's pensions, government efficiency, and the repression of vice."[15] At the same time, the newly formed Women's Bureau of the Department of Labor began to lobby for protective labor laws. O'Neill goes on to say that "in 1921 Congress passed the Sheppard-Towner Act, the first federally financed health care program for mothers, a hard-won victory for social feminists."[16] As a result, says O'Neill, organizations like the League of Women Voters, the YWCA, and the Women's Bureau were smeared as "Bolshevist," and they lost widespread support from the general population.

The Great Depression downgraded the status of paid work for married women, who were accused of taking jobs away from the men who needed them. Finally, during the New Deal, activist women were disavowing any connection with feminism: they were political, but not feminists. Some few people and organizations kept thinking of themselves as feminist between the New Deal and the 1960s, but there was no general awareness of feminism until Women's Liberation came on the scene in the late sixties.

And, again, the first burst of feminist activity was individual. Consciousness raising was a profoundly individualistic activity, and the political issues that gained wide adherence were the reproductive rights to birth control and abortion, and the Equal Rights Amendment, which (at least in its initial support) was a classical liberal restraint on government.

Each time that feminism came on the scene, it was the message of individualism that captured the imagination of women. It is not a coincidence, I would argue, that both in the 1910s and the 1960s the newly self-identified feminists rediscovered Mary Wollstonecraft and her 1792 book, *A Vindication of the Rights of Women.*

Avoiding the State

The publication of Betty Friedan's *The Feminine Mystique* in 1963 was the impetus for the contemporary emergence of feminism in all its various guises. Friedan herself was never a radical, and her book was a psychological analysis of the negative impact of the mystique she had identified—that the truly "feminine" woman would find complete fulfillment in service to her husband and children—on contemporary marriage and on the children being raised in those marriages, as well as on the women themselves.

Feminism has had its greatest recent successes as a cultural movement. You might say that cultural feminism has always been dedicated to exploring and unravelling what may be emerging as the central problem of industrial society in the nineties—the relationship between the individual and the community, understood in its widest sense. Not many feminists have consciously and consistently identified that the state is the enemy of that relationship, but some of them, from different perspectives, have come close to doing so. Here are two examples, one from the perspective often called right, and one from that often called left.

Suzanne LaFollette, a cousin of the Progressive Senator Robert ("Fighting Bob") LaFollette, wrote for the journal the *Freeman,* edited by Albert J. Nock in the 1920s. Nock was an anti-collectivist who was to criticize Hitler, Stalin, Mussolini—and Franklin Delano Roosevelt. L. A. Kauffman, who often writes on women's issues for the *Progressive* (founded as *LaFollette's* in 1909), called it "the radical and iconoclastic *Freeman,* a political and literary journal of the early 1920s which regularly denounced social reform, liberalism, and American socialism."[17] LaFollette was also one of the *Freeman's* editors, and was encouraged by Nock to write a book on feminism, *Concerning Women,* that came out in 1926. In it she wrote,

It is evident from the very nature of the State that its interests are opposed to those of Society; and while the complete emancipation of women . . . would undoubtedly imply the destruction of the State, since it must accrue from the emancipation of the other subject classes, their emancipation, far from destroying Society, must be of inestimable benefit to it.[18]

She was also a critic of protective labor laws, writing,

They are sponsored by those well-meaning individuals who deplore social injustice enough to yearn to mitigate its evil results, but do not understand it well enough to attack its causes; by women's organizations whose intelligence is hardly commensurate with their zeal to uplift their sex; and by men's labour organizations which are quite frankly in favor of any legislation that will lessen the chances of women to compete with men in the labour market.[19]

Contemporary feminist Alice Rossi included an essay by LaFollette in her 1973 anthology *The Feminist Papers* and described her thus: "On issue after issue LaFollette comes down on the side of the least degree of state interference in the lives of men and women and a consistent belief that it is only through full economic independence and personal autonomy that sex equality will be achieved."[20] LaFollette did not continue to write extensively on feminism, but she went on to be the managing editor of the early *National Review* from 1955 until she retired in 1959.

In 1982, Jean Bethke Elshtain warned, in the now-famous essay, "Antigone's Daughters," that

feminists should approach the modern bureaucratic state from a standpoint of skepticism that keeps alive a critical distance between feminism and statism, between female self-identity and a social identity tied to the public-political world revolving around the structures, institutions, values, and ends of the state. The basis for my caution and skepticism is a sober recognition that any political order in our time which culminates in a state is an edifice that monopolizes and centralizes power and eliminates older, less universal forms of authority; that structures its activities and implements its policies through unaccountable hierarchies; that erodes local and particular patterns of ethnic, religious, and regional identities; that standardizes culture, ideas, and ideals; that links portions of the population to it through a variety of dependency relationships; that may find it necessary or convenient to override civil liberties and standards of decency for *raison d'etat* or executive privileges; and that, from time to time, commits its people to wars they have had neither the opportunity to debate fully nor the right to challenge openly.

> For feminists to discover in the state the new "Mr. Right," and to wed themselves thereby, for better or for worse, to a public identity inseparable from the exigencies of state power and policy would be a mistake.[21]

Elshtain has continued to assert the importance of family and communal values for women, and some social critics have considered that this constitutes a backlash against feminism on the left.

Families and Other Communities

There is a crucial distinction between a voluntarily chosen community and a community one feels one cannot escape, be it a religious discipline into which one has been born or a state organization like the Hitler Youth or the Russian Communist Party. The free individual, to be entirely happy and fulfilled, needs to feel in connection with some sort of community. And everyone's first community is the family.

In a 1981 book, *The Second Stage,* Betty Friedan wrote,

> "Family" is not just a buzz word for reaction; for women, as for men, it is the symbol of that last area where one has any hope of individual control over one's destiny, of meeting one's most basic human needs, of nourishing that core of personhood threatened now by vast impersonal institutions and uncontrollable corporate and government bureaucracies and the bewildering, accelerating pace of change. Against these menaces, the family may be as crucial for survival as it used to be against the untamed wilderness and the raging elements, and the old, simple kinds of despotism.
>
> For the family, all psychological science tells us, is the nutrient of our humanness, of all our individuality: our personhood.[22]

The family, point out Joseph Peden and Fred R. Glahe in their introduction to the anthology *The American Family and the State,* "begins in contract and, formally and informally, continues to be contractual, not coercive. (Even the child, though thrust into its midst by nature rather than its own will, gradually emancipates itself, and the child's continued membership becomes voluntary as soon as it is able to make such a choice.)"[23]

The family is where we all learn how to behave and how to relate to people. If one has a family in which there are no successful role models for how to work and have relationships, one may have to look elsewhere for such models. A thicket of communities and organizations—perhaps churches, perhaps neighborhoods, perhaps nurturing schools, perhaps scouting, perhaps lodges and fraternal associations—can enhance this search. In the absence of such a thicket of opportunities, contemporary feminism has provided one way for women to form a community in which they can learn from each other's experience of work and relationships.

Both men and women began in the middle of this century to call people with whom they had only superficial communication "friends," just because they shared activities. Feminism has attempted to fill the resulting void for women: encouraging women to talk to each other and creating a framework in which they could talk about what they felt was important, come together to support each other, and be positive about independence and achievement. Today, men's groups may be filling a similar void for men.

One of the consequences of big government is that it encourages the withering away of many cooperative associations and institutions that, in days of simpler government, stand in between the individual and the government so that the individual has many communities to choose from. As government enlarges, we see more and more that the functions of such groups are taken over by government or quasi-governmental big business, leaving the individual no one but bureaucracy to relate to. Charity and insurance, for instance, are social functions that used to be met in large part by a number of benevolent associations; in a 1990 article in *Critical Review,* David Beito details the importance of both secret societies, like the Masons, and fraternal insurance societies before the 1920s. "Only churches," he writes, "rivaled fraternal societies as institutional providers of social welfare before the advent of the welfare state. In 1920, about eighteen million Americans belonged to fraternal societies, i.e. nearly 30 percent of all adults over age twenty."[24]

These societies provided entertainment, help for the sick and bereaved, and sometimes orphanages and old-age homes as well as death benefits, and for a time they "dominated the health insurance market (at least among the working class)."[25] They were particularly valuable for immigrants and African Americans.

Americans in earlier times formed associations to, as Tocqueville put it, "found seminaries, to build inns, to construct churches, to diffuse books, to send missionaries to the antipodes."[26] They also built and ran hospitals, libraries, schools, and social centers, which are now run by governments.

An article in the *Journal of American History* by Anne Firor Scott deals with the importance of a multitude of voluntary associations for nineteenth-century American women. Ms. Scott writes,

> The records of some of those groups make it apparent that what we
> call "self-reliance" was often simply the habit of relying on groups of

peers to get things done. Cooperation—through the voluntary association—had at least as much to do with the rapid growth of the society
and the economy as did the more generally noted individual enterprise.[27]

She goes on to say, "One bemused observer remarked that it was as if
in the year 1800 a bell rang and all over the country women began coalescing
into groups,"[28] and that this tendency increased in the 1830s and 1840s,
after the Civil War, and again at the turn of the century. She concludes,

> No one has yet begun to trace in detail all the ways in which the work
> of women's associations shaped and changed society and social values
> over 120 years, but what we know so far suggests that when that detailed
> work is done, their influence will be seen to reach into every corner of
> community life as well as into state and national politics.[29]

The growth of government is not the only factor that has influenced
the downgrading of such community organizations, of course. Our society
has become so mobile that many people do not stay in the geographical
location in which they were born. Migration to large cities makes it hard
for neighborhoods to be cohesive. In many respects, society has become
fragmented, and a conscious effort to find a community to relate to has
to be made. Nationally identified membership organizations sometimes
make this search easier.

Today

Although the appeal of noncoercive, nongovernmental feminism has always reached a wider audience than collectivism has, it is often collectivism
that gets media attention. And various feminist theorists (and attackers
of feminism) have been happy to say that such collectivists speak for the
only true feminism.

This idea that all feminists are "socialists" seems very widespread today,
especially among conservatives, neoconservatives, and members of the
financial press. One reason for this impression may be that most of the
first theorists of the present wave of feminism in the seventies considered
themselves to be "left" in their politics, although these politics covered
a spectrum from modern liberals of the New Deal persuasion, like Betty
Friedan, to explicit Marxists, and included a group of radical feminists,
many of whom mistrusted government power at the same time that they
tried to wield almost total social power over their members.

People have allegiances, sometimes contradictory allegiances, to different terminologies. To some, Women's Liberation was a positive term. Virginia Postrel, editor of *Reason,* said in an editorial, "Because it evoked a fundamental sense of fairness and harkened back to basic American ideas of equality before the law, women's liberation won the heart of Americans who would never admit they'd been smitten." And she compares this to "the whine of feminism, with its invocations of victimhood and of woman's special status."[30]

On the other hand, Diana Trilling, when asked in a 1989 interview if she took "a feminist position" in the book she was writing about her marriage to Lionel Trilling, answered,

> "Feminist, perhaps yes; women's lib, perhaps no. This may be idiosyncratic of me, but I draw a distinction between the two."
> "In what way?"
> "I think of feminism as both firmer and gentler, less competitive, than women's lib. I was a feminist, if only by my own definition, long before women's lib was even dreamed of. But doing the best I could had nothing to do with being competitive with men."[31]

I don't think either of these definitions of feminism and women's lib is the "real" one—*feminism* is certainly the term that has been in use longer, and in the beginning of women's liberation the two terms were used identically. So I would say that Virginia Postrel is reflecting the fact that in the early seventies, the feminism one encountered was in large part an expansive, individualistic movement that emphasized how diverse its members were; but later, the most vocal, active feminists (who often seemed to be claiming to speak for the only true feminism) were either separatists or collectivist reformers through the political process, of one sort or another.

But the feminist movement is wider and more diverse than the "spokeswomen" presented to us by the media might indicate. There are women in small towns and cities all over the country who learned of feminism first in the seventies, from talking about books with friends and neighbors, and found they had internalized certain assumptions that they now questioned. Thousands, perhaps hundreds of thousands, of business and professional men and women consider themselves to be feminists, and still more would, if they hadn't accepted a narrow definition of feminism. Let me illustrate.

I had the privilege of knowing novelist-philosopher Ayn Rand in the 1960s. She epitomized what I would consider to be a feminist ideal. She never considered her ambitions to be limited by the fact that she was a woman; she was independent enough to leave the Soviet Union and come to the United States by herself after she left the university; she intended to become a writer in a language and a country that were foreign to her—and she became a best-selling author. Her heroines were independent, achieving women like herself—in many respects role models for feminists. And she went on to develop a philosophy based on the importance of reason and individuality and rights and human achievement.

In politics, Rand refused to support Ronald Reagan when he first sought the presidency even though he appeared to be a remarkable spokesman for her political views of opposition to communism and advocacy of free enterprise. Why? Because she said that anyone who didn't understand a woman's right to choose abortion didn't understand individual rights. If ever there was a woman whose life and thought should have brought her into the feminist movement, Ayn Rand was that woman. And yet, paradoxically, she considered herself an enemy of feminism and often wrote and spoke of feminists in pejorative terms.

Recently, I was at a gathering in New York attended by a number of people I often saw in the late sixties: former students of Ayn Rand's philosophy, Objectivism. Since Ayn Rand had not been a feminist, neither were most of her admirers. Since I am a self-identified feminist, I soon got into an argument with an old acquaintance about gender differences. He assumed I thought that men and women had no significant differences; I said there were probably a number of them, but I didn't believe we yet knew which were really innate and which were culturally determined (outside of the obvious primary and secondary sexual differences, of course).

"Well," he said, "take strength. I was raised to carry the suitcases in my family, because men are stronger than women. And it was true; I was stronger than my sisters."

"Look," I said, "this was true for you. So if your family said 'the strongest member carries the heaviest bag,' you would have carried it. But why can't everyone carry something? And why couldn't you have been carrying the load because of your strength, not because you were male?"

Now the interesting thing was that we were not alone; a group of friends and acquaintances were listening and joining in this discussion, and some of them could name woman wrestlers and other examples of female strength that I was not aware of. Most of the group came to be on my side in the argument, which ranged from gender differences to what had Betty Friedan really been saying in *The Feminine Mystique* to what is the definition of feminism anyway? And a group of articulate and knowledgeable people—mostly young women, but a few men—strongly disagreed with my friend's basic premise that the natural differences between men and women refute all feminist arguments.

All of us agreed that men and women have overlapping ranges of abilities, that those characteristics considered to be exclusively male or female will often coincide with reality, but occasionally may not. We all believed in diversity; we all resented stereotyping; we all saw his arguments as a wrong over-generalization that became a put-down of women. More than that, I was surprised to discover that most of us (with the exception of the man I was arguing with) knew the history of the nineteenth-century Woman Movement: knew of Mary Wollstonecraft's answers to Edmund Burke in England; knew of the growth of feminism out of the abolitionist movement in the United States; knew of the legal theories by which common law had deprived married women of individual rights; knew of the suffrage movement. What were we, if not feminists?

But I was the only one there who would admit to it.

This book, then, is an attempt to explore the tangled skein of individualist and collectivist ideas and theories that have led to today's rich diversities of feminisms, in the frank hope that I may persuade my reader of my particular view of what is important in this disparate heritage.

PART I

The Historical Cycles of Feminism

CHAPTER TWO

Inside Every Socialist is an Individualist Trying to Get Out

It all began with the idea that human beings, by their very nature, have rights. Man, said the classical liberals, is born into a state of natural freedom, and his rights to life, liberty, and property may be limited by governments only when his exercise of these rights infringes on the rights of others. But what about the rights of women? Aren't they human beings also? Between the turn of the nineteenth century and the turn of the twentieth, four books were written that became classics of the nineteenth-century Woman Movement. These books addressed similar themes: women as beings whose rights were not recognized, the limits of the education available to women, the restrictions on the occupations they were allowed to enter, and the legal subservience of married women. All but the earliest of these volumes also supported the issue of votes for women.

The authors had circumstances in common. Three women and a man, they all had unconventional love lives, and two of the four were subjects of educational experiments. Each lived and worked within a community of liberal thinkers who encouraged independent thought, and each felt in some way set apart from ordinary conventional society. All considered themselves to be champions of the individual, but two also thought of themselves as socialists.

Wollstonecraft's "Vindication"

The British statesman Edmund Burke had supported the American Revolution, but in 1790 he wrote an answer to a sermon advocating the right to revolution that had been preached by the distinguished liberal dissenting minister, Richard Price. Burke's book was *Reflections on the Revolution in France,* and in it he ridiculed belief in the rights of man. Dr. Price had a distinguished circle of literary friends; he was a close friend of Joseph Priestley and corresponded with David Hume, Benjamin Franklin, and Thomas Jefferson, as well as with French liberals. An answer to Burke, *A Vindication of the Rights of Men,* appeared in England five weeks after Burke's book, before the end of 1790. It was written by an anonymous member of Price's circle and challenged not only Burke's view of rights, but his view of the inferiority of women.

The book was itself written by a woman, Mary Wollstonecraft, a former school teacher and published author who was a friend, not only of Price, but of William Blake and Tom Paine. This book's general definition of rights was as follows: "The birthright of man . . . is such a degree of liberty, civil and religious, as is compatible with the liberty of every other individual with whom he is united in a social compact, and the continued existence of that compact."[1]

Mary Wollstonecraft's *Vindication of the Rights of Men* is not well known today; it has been overshadowed by the book she then wrote in 1792, *A Vindication of the Rights of Woman.* That book was dedicated to Talleyrand as an answer to a pamphlet he had written on education: "to induce you to reconsider the subject and maturely weigh what I have advanced respecting the rights of woman and national education."

A Vindication of the Rights of Woman may not be the very first book written in English on the subject of women's rights, but it is the earliest one that is generally available today. Its argument was the classical liberal one about natural rights that was assumed in our Declaration of Independence—and in the *Vindication of the Rights of Men.* In her "Dedication," Wollstonecraft says to Talleyrand:

> Consider . . . whether, when men contend for their freedom . . . it be not inconsistent and unjust to subjugate women, even though you firmly believe that you are acting in the manner best calculated to promote their happiness? . . .
>
> Let there be then no coercion *established* in society, and the common law of gravity prevailing, the sexes will fall into their proper places. . . .[2]

Wollstonecraft carefully analyzes and refutes the assumptions of her day about the nature and place of woman, paying particular attention to women of the middle and upper classes, who were supported by men and whose economic position would allow them to avail themselves of education. The shallowness that such women often exhibit is created by their treatment, she points out, for in order to preserve their innocence, as ignorance is courteously termed, truth is hidden from them, and they are made to assume an artificial character before their faculties have acquired any strength. Taught from their infancy that beauty is woman's sceptre, the mind shapes itself to the body, and, roaming round its gilt cage, only seeks to adore its prison. Men have various employments and pursuits which engage their attention, and give a character to the opening mind; but women, confined to one, and having their thoughts constantly directed to the most insignificant part of themselves, seldom extend their view beyond the triumph of the hour.[3]

Wollstonecraft took pains to refute the argument "reflecting the subjection in which the sex has ever been held," as she put it (that's the argument that if women stay in a subordinate position, that indicates an inferior nature), pointing out that men too have submitted to tyranny. And, she said, "till it is proved that the courtier, who servilely resigns the birthright of a man, is not a moral agent, it cannot be demonstrated that woman is essentially inferior to man because she has always been subjugated."[4]

Not only did Wollstonecraft argue that women should be considered "in the grand light of human creatures, who, in common with men, are placed on this earth to unfold their faculties,"[5] but she was probably the first person to point out that

the laws respecting woman . . . make an absurd unit of a man and his wife; and then, by the easy transition of only considering him as responsible, she is reduced to a mere cipher. . . . But to render her really virtuous and useful, she must not, if she discharge her civil duties, want, individually, the protection of civil laws; she must not be dependent on her husband's bounty for her subsistence during his life or support after his death— for how can a being be generous who has nothing of its own? or virtuous, who is not free?[6]

A proper education for women would fit them for various businesses, instead of their only being taught to please men.

How many women thus waste life away the prey of discontent, who might have practiced as physicians, regulated a farm, managed a shop, and stood erect, surrounded by their own industry. . . . Would men but generously snap our chains, and be content with rational fellowship instead of slavish obedience, they would find us more observant daughters, more affectionate sisters, more favorable wives, more reasonable mothers—in a word, better citizens.[7]

If this concern for the way families would benefit by the liberation of women sounds like a Betty Friedan speaking in somewhat archaic language, remember, this was all written at the end of the eighteenth century, in 1792, by a woman who had managed to take advantage of the few opportunities open to women.

Mary Wollstonecraft was the daughter of a weaver who later attempted to become a gentleman farmer. After working as a companion to a widow and then living with another family whose income Wollstonecraft helped augment with needlework, she helped her sister run away from an abusive husband and then, at the age of twenty-four, opened a school with the sister and a friend. Their first school failed; the second was a success and brought her into an intellectual circle of liberal thinkers. She began writing. Her first book, *Thoughts on the Education of Daughters,* was published when she was twenty-eight.

Her life was an unconventional one—not just because she wrote books and articles for the *Analytic Review*. She also had love affairs. She went to France after her *Vindication* was published where she lived with an American, Gilbert Imlay, by whom she had a child and while there wrote a history of the French Revolution. She tried to commit suicide when Imlay left her, returned to her old friends in London, and became involved with the love of her life, William Godwin.

She and Godwin married in March of 1797, after she had become pregnant with his child, but they continued to live and work in separate residences. Their daughter, Mary Godwin (who was to grow up to marry the poet Shelley and to write the classic *Frankenstein*) was born on August 30, 1797, and Mary Wollstonecraft died on September 10 from childbirth complications, at the age of thirty-nine.

Woman in the Nineteenth Century

The first American book to discuss the place of women in society and suggest ways of changing it was written by a woman named Margaret Fuller, who, like Mary Wollstonecraft, was the only woman writer in a group of similar-minded thinkers.

Man, says Fuller in her 1845 book, *Woman in the Nineteenth Century,* has not fulfilled his potential. "By Man I mean both man and woman; these are the two halves of one thought. I lay no especial stress on the welfare of either. I believe that the development of the one cannot be effected without that of the other."[8] She points out that as "the principle of liberty is better understood," it becomes clearer that the treatment of women is unfair. "As men become aware that few men have had a fair chance, they are inclined to say that no women have had a fair chance."[9]

Humanity is interconnected, according to Fuller. "Man can never be perfectly happy or virtuous, till all men are so."[10]

There are masculine and feminine attributes, but they are not evenly distributed in men and women: "the faculties have not been given pure to either, but only in preponderance."[11]

Man is the sex whose characteristic attributes are strength and energy and who "developed first," but rather than helping woman as a sex to develop, he held her back. "He did not clearly see that Woman was half himself; that her interests were identical with his; and that, by the law of their common being, he could never read his true proportions while she remained in any wise shorn of hers."[12]

Therefore, woman was placed at a legal and social disadvantage and usually not educated to develop her true talents. But these did flower when circumstances permitted and were demonstrated in "female authorship" and whenever men and women had marriages that rose above household partnership to intellectual companionship and joint spiritual pursuits. These examples showed the true possibilities of women.

> Whether much or little has been done, or will be done, whether women will add to the talent of narration the power of systematizing,—whether they will carve marble, as well as draw and paint,—is not important. But that it should be acknowledged that they have intellect which needs developing—that they should not be considered complete, if beings of affection and habit alone—is important.[13]

And it is also important that women develop their faculties and intellect, she adds, not merely to be better companions to men, but for themselves.

Throughout the ages there have always been women who showed what women were capable of, but now, in midnineteenth-century America, women had the possibility of removing the traditional barriers that had always held most women back. Fuller called for women to band together to achieve this goal:

> I believe that, at present, women are the best helpers of one another.
>   Let them think; let them act; till they know what they need.
>   We only ask of men to remove arbitrary barriers. Some would like to do more. But I believe it needs that Woman show herself in her native dignity, to teach them how to aid her; their minds are so encumbered by tradition.[14]

This is the proper action because we cannot predict what will happen after the barriers are removed.

> But if you ask me what offices they may fill, I reply—any. I do not care what case you put; let them be sea-captains, if you will. I do not doubt there are women well fitted for such an office. . . .
>
>   In families that I know, some little girls like to saw wood, others to use carpenters' tools. Where these tastes are indulged, cheerfulness and good-humor are promoted. Where they are forbidden, because "such things are not proper for girls," they grow sullen and mischievous. . . .
>
>   I have no doubt, however, that a large proportion of women would give themselves to the same employments as now, because there are circumstances that must lead them. Mothers will delight to make the nest soft and warm. Nature would take care of that; no need to clip the wings of any bird that wanted to soar and sing, or finds in itself the strength of pinion for a migratory flight unusual to its kind. The difference would be that *all* need not be constrained to employments for which *some* are unfit.[15]

Fuller speaks of the vote in passing, quoting an irritated man who said that an advocate of woman's rights wants "to take my wife away from the cradle and the kitchen hearth to vote at polls, and preach from a pulpit."[16] Later, she ridicules those opponents of her ideas who create pictures "of ladies in hysterics at the polls," but it's clear that she doesn't see the vote as the central issue in the revolution of society that she advocates.

Margaret Fuller was born in 1810, to a father who educated her himself and brought her up to believe that her mind was the equal of anyone's. In her youth she became friends with New England intellectuals. In 1836, she managed to get invited to visit Ralph Waldo Emerson and soon became a valued member of the Transcendentalists, a group of diverse thinkers who agreed on the importance of individualism, self-reliance, and self-determination. It included, besides Emerson, Henry David Thoreau, Bronson Alcott, and the Unitarian abolitionist minister, Theodore Parker. When the Transcendentalists decided to found a journal, the *Dial,* it was Margaret Fuller who was chosen to be its first editor from 1840 through 1842. (It was edited by Emerson for the next two years until it stopped publication in 1844.) From 1839 to 1844, she held "conversations" at the home of Elizabeth Peabody in Boston, discussing a number of topics, including her ideas on the role of women, which also appeared in the July 1843 issue of the *Dial,* in the essay, "The Great Lawsuit: Man *versus* Men; Woman *versus* Women."

In 1844 her first book, *Summer on the Lakes,* was published, and it attracted the attention of the editor of the New York *Daily-Tribune,* Horace Greeley, who gave her a job as literary critic. In 1845 *Woman in the Nineteenth Century,* an expansion on the ideas she had expressed in her conversation groups and in the *Dial,* was published.

She went to Europe in 1846 as a foreign correspondent for the *Tribune,* after an unhappy love affair. (Her letters to the man, James Nathan, were published in 1903 in *Love-Letters of Margaret Fuller.*) The reputation of *Woman in the Nineteenth Century* brought her introductions to George Sand, Thomas Carlyle, Robert and Elizabeth Barrett Browning, and the Italian patriot, Giuseppe Mazzini. Convinced of the cause of Italian independence, she went to Italy. There she became involved in revolutionary politics and a love affair with an Italian Marquis, Giovanni Angelo Ossoli. She converted him to the revolutionary cause, had a child by him in a secluded country village in 1848, and worked on a history of the Italian Revolution. She married Ossoli in 1849. She nursed the sick during the bombardment of Rome and was there when French troops overran it on July 4, 1849.

After the revolution failed, she planned to return with her husband, her baby, and the manuscript of her history of the revolution to the United States; but their boat was shipwrecked off Fire Island and they all died, on July 19, 1850. She was forty years old. The manuscript, which she had considered her best work, was also lost.

The Subjection of Women

The next of these important classics on the subject of women's rights, still influential today, appeared in England in 1869, written by a major intellectual figure, John Stuart Mill.

Mill wrote the first draft of *The Subjection of Women* in 1860 and waited to publish it until he thought it was politically opportune to do so. It is clear, however, that conditions had changed little since Mary Wollstonecraft's day. The book starts with a statement that "the principle which regulates the existing social relations between the two sexes —the legal subordination of one sex to the other—is wrong in itself," and a call to replace it by "a principle of perfect equality."[17] Like Wollstonecraft and Fuller before him, he said, "I deny that anyone knows, or can know, the nature of the two sexes, as long as they have only been seen in their present relation to each other."[18] But it seemed clear that legal and social constraints had created the existing situation.

The general opinion of men is supposed to be, that the natural vocation of a woman is that of a wife and mother. I say, is supposed to be, because, judging from acts—from the whole of the present constitution of society—one might infer that their opinion was the direct contrary. They might be supposed to think that the alleged natural vocation of women was of all things the most repugnant to their nature; insomuch that if they are free to do anything else—if any other means of living, or occupation of their time and faculties, is open, which has any chance of appearing desirable to them—there will not be enough of them who will be willing to accept the condition said to be natural to them.[19]

He considered that, under the condition in which women lived, one could not tell what a woman's "true nature" or talents were.

I consider it presumption in any one to pretend to decide what women are or are not, can or cannot be, by natural constitution. They have always hitherto been kept, as far as regards spontaneous development, in so unnatural a state, that their nature cannot but have been greatly distorted and disguised; and no one can safely pronounce that if women's nature were left to choose its direction as freely as men's, and if no artificial bent were attempted to be given to it except that required by the conditions of human society, and given to both sexes alike, there would be any material difference, or perhaps any difference at all, in the character and capacities which would unfold themselves.[20]

Women, he points out, although generally forbidden to vote for or to aspire to elective office, have shown themselves to be capable of outstanding achievement as political leaders.

It cannot be inferred to be impossible that a woman should be a Homer, or an Aristotle, or a Michael Angelo, or a Beethoven, because no woman has yet actually produced works comparable to theirs in any of those lines of excellence. This negative fact at most leaves the question uncertain, and open to psychological discussion. But it is quite certain that a woman can be a Queen Elizabeth, or a Deborah, or a Joan of Arc, since this is not inference, but fact.[21]

In the four parts of his book, Mill argues why subjection is wrong; examines in some detail the legal implications of the marriage contract and their injustice; addresses the limitations on women's activities, including their inability to vote; and outlines the ways in which equality of the sexes would benefit society. Since the subjection of women contradicts the liberal philosophy of merit, the true equality of women in the home would mean that a child would "for the first time in man's existence on earth, be trained in the way he should go,"[22] rather than being told to respect others by a mother not respected as an equal. The competition of women in occupations would double "the mass of mental faculties available for the higher service of humanity."[23]

Educated women would have a beneficial influence on public opinion. And, finally, marriages will be happier "when each of two persons, instead of being a nothing, is a something."[24]

> What marriage may be in the case of two persons of cultivated faculties, identical in opinions and purposes, between whom there exists that best kind of equality, similarity of powers and capacities with reciprocal superiority in them—so that each can enjoy the luxury of looking up to the other, and can have alternately the pleasure of leading and of being led in the path of development—I will not attempt to describe. To those who can conceive it, there is no need; to those who cannot, it would appear the dream of an enthusiast. But I maintain, with the profoundest conviction, that this, and this only, is the ideal of marriage; and that all opinions, customs, and institutions which favor any other notion of it, or turn the conceptions and aspirations connected with it into any other direction, by whatever pretences they may be coloured, are relics of primitive barbarism.[25]

Like Margaret Fuller, Mill called for women to join together to break down the barriers that restrained them.

John Stuart Mill (1806–1873), also like Margaret Fuller, had been the subject of an experimental education devised by his father; in his case, by James Mill, one of the founders of Utilitarianism. But whereas Fuller was brought up to consider herself the equal of any man, Mill was brought up to be a genius: he studied Greek at the age of three, Latin at eight, and began serious writing at eleven. By the time he entered his teens he was familiar with mathematics, philosophy, and scientific experiment. During his childhood he had no emotional life and no friends. When he was fourteen, he was sent abroad for a year to study music, French, and the sciences and then returned to work with the East India Company, directly under his father.

Mill almost immediately formed the Utilitarian Society to work for parliamentary reform and, soon after, started writing for Jeremy Bentham's *Westminster Review*. His closest associates in the 1820s were a group of men and women calling themselves the Philosophic Radicals, who agreed with his politics. But in the late twenties, after a long period of depression that led him to appreciate feelings, poetry, and literature as much (or more) than politics, Mill met another circle, the Unitarian Radicals who centered around a Unitarian minister, William J. Fox.

Sometime in 1830, Mill met a young married woman and mother, Harriet Taylor, at Fox's house. This was to be a relationship similar to the "ideal marriage" he later wrote of in *The Subjection of Women*. It has never been entirely clear whether or not their love blossomed into an actual affair; what is clear is that they soon became close intellectual companions, writing essays for each other, traveling together on many short trips, and declaring their feelings in correspondence. Many of their friends felt she was unworthy of him, but Mill considered her a collaborator on many of his books, especially his *Principles of Political Economy* in 1845.

In his *Autobiography*, Mill states that, by that time,

> our ideal of ultimate improvement went far beyond Democracy, and would class us decidedly under the general designation of Socialists. While we repudiated with the greatest energy that tyranny of society over the individual which most socialist systems are supposed to involve, we yet looked forward to a time when society will no longer be divided into the idle and the industrious; when the rule that they who do not work shall not eat, will be applied not to paupers only, but impartially to all; when the division of the produce of labour instead of depending, as in so great a degree it now does, on the accident of birth, will be made by concert, on an acknowledged principle of justice; and when it will no longer either be, or be thought to be, impossible for human beings to exert themselves strenuously in procuring benefits which are not to be exclusively their own, but to be shared with the society they belong to.[26]

They were finally married after her husband died in April 1851, after they had known each other for twenty-one years. Two months before this marriage, Mill wrote a statement about it.

> Being about, if I am so happy as to obtain her consent, to enter into the marriage relation with the only woman I have ever known, with whom I would have entered into that state; and the whole character of the marriage relation as constituted by law being such as both she and I entirely and conscientiously disapprove, for this among other reasons, that it confers upon one of the parties to the contract, legal power and control over the person, property, and freedom of action of the other party, independent of her own wishes and will; I, having no means of legally divesting myself of these odious powers (as I most assuredly would do if an engagement to that effect could be made legally binding on

me) feel it my duty to put on record a formal protest against the existing law of marriage, in so far as conferring such powers; and a solemn promise never in any case or under any circumstances to use them. And in the event of marriage between Mrs. Taylor and me I declare it to be my will and intention, and the condition of the engagement between us, that she retains in all respects whatever the same absolute freedom of action and freedom of disposal of herself and of all that does or may at any time belong to her, as if no such marriage had taken place; and I absolutely disclaim and repudiate all pretension to have acquired any rights whatever by virtue of such marriage.

6 March 1851   J.S. Mill[27]

In 1858 Harriet died. Two years later Mill began *The Subjection of Women.* He wrote that part of it "was enriched with some important ideas of my daughter's [actually Harriet's daughter], and passages of her writing. But," he went on, "in what was of my own composition, all that is most striking and profound belongs to my wife; coming from the fund of thought which had been made common to us both, by our innumerable conversations and discussions on a topic which filled so large a place in our minds."[28]

Women and Economics

The most ambitious of these four classic books, and the most modern, is *Women and Economics* by Charlotte Perkins Gilman, first published in 1898.

Human beings, says Gilman, like other species, are affected by their environment, but they are also uniquely affected by social conditions. The fact that, alone among the animal kingdom, women are supported by men has distorted the way in which women have developed. "We are the only animal species in which the female depends on the male for food, the only animal species in which the sex-relation is also an economic relation."[29] Therefore, women have developed exaggerated secondary sex characteristics. In other species, males and females search for food side by side and are similarly adapted for the search. "When both sexes obtain their food through the same exertions . . . both sexes . . . are developed alike by their environment," but when one is fed by the other, "the feeding sex becomes the environment of the fed."[30]

Gilman dissects the contention that women earn "partnership" with their husbands by the unpaid work they do, pointing out that no man divides his income with a paid housekeeper, even though she may free him to earn his living. "The labor of women in the house, certainly, enables men to produce more wealth than they otherwise could; and in this way women are economic factors in society," she admits. "But so are horses."[31]

Males have become more human than females have, because they have interests in "industry, commerce, science, manufacture, government, art, religion. . . . We have grown to consider most human attributes as masculine attributes for the simple reason that they were allowed to men and forbidden to women."[32] Women have had to concentrate on their sexual role and on a role as nonproductive consumers. Fortunately, these tendencies are checked by heredity, which "has set iron bounds to our absurd effort to make a race with one sex a million years behind the other."[33]

Only recently, said Gilman in 1898, has the rise of a group of working women who earn a wage begun to change this aspect of society, which has had centuries to pit the instinct of self-preservation (which in all species requires independent action) against the instinct of race preservation (which in all species develops sexual differentiation of certain organs and functions). Migrating birds or cattle cannot have a "weaker sex," she points out.

The human race's overemphasis on sex relationships is responsible for the rise of prostitution, which is merely another expression of the emphasis women must put on the economic value of their sexual functions. Gilman compares the attitude of a virtuous woman to a prostitute to "the hatred of the trade-unionist for 'scab labor.' "[34]

How did the situation develop? We needed it once to teach men to be loving and protective during the long period of human infancy. But now people are able to have wider circles of caring and have developed what Gilman calls "the social instincts." She finds great hope in the women's club movement, as well as in the labor movement and the women's movement itself. She sees the entry of women into the labor force as entirely positive; when productive work disappeared from the home, woman "followed her lost wheel and loom" to the mill.[35]

> Those who object to women's working on the ground that they should not compete with men or be forced to struggle for existence look only at work as a means of earning money. They should remember that human labor is an exercise of faculty, without which we should cease to be human.[36]

Gilman's socialism stresses the importance of ever-widening circles of caring, from the family to the community and, finally, to mankind. She feels that industrialization itself influences us in this direction: an industrial society promotes peace without any sacrifice, because it needs it. The only conflict she sees occurring is when the need of the individual man to support his family conflicts with his business ethic, and he therefore cuts corners, encouraged by his wife's consumerism. But these conflicts are created by the artificial situation that has imprisoned women. Free women, and as a consequence ethical behavior will again be the natural way to behave.

One of the most interesting aspects of Gilman's book is her semi-prophetic predictions of how society will have to change to accommodate women's work outside the home. She suggests apartments with communal kitchens that could provide meals either in a common dining room or in individual apartments; communal cleaning services, provided by the management; and "a roof-garden, day nursery, and kindergarten, under well-trained professional nurses and teachers, would insure proper care of the children."[37] Families could live privately, but without "the clumsy tangle of rudimentary industries that are supposed to accompany the home."[38] And there should be similar apartments available for single people without families, "who could live singly without losing home comfort." To help them to meet each other, there should be "common libraries and parlors, baths and gymnasia, work-rooms and play-rooms."[39]

None of this, however, should be provided by government. On the contrary, "This must be offered on a business basis to prove a substantial business success; and it will so prove, for it is a growing social need."[40]

Sometimes it is an effort to remember that at the time Gilman was writing, there were very few apartment buildings, and it was a new phenomenon that sometimes *families* as well as single people stayed in inns. She was aware that it was hard to predict "the precise forms which would ultimately prove most useful and pleasant,"[41] and in fact did not predict the move toward sharing housework that has developed in modern couples or the development of foods that take little or no preparation. She did correctly identify that in her day men and women did not work together, either in cleaning and cooking at home or in the workplace.

Charlotte Perkins Gilman was born in 1860, the year that Mill began writing his book on women, and died in 1935. The author's very name is indicative of a problem that women have had; that of being known by the name of a husband. She was born Charlotte Perkins, distantly related to the Beecher family (her paternal grandmother was the sister of Henry Ward Beecher and Harriet Beecher Stowe). An early first marriage brought her a daughter, Katherine Stetson, and led to a mental breakdown, which she later attributed to the unhappiness of her marriage and which was made worse by her treatment by Dr. S. Weir Mitchell. Later she turned this experience into a haunting short story about a woman driven mad by a stern husband and doctor, "The Yellow Wallpaper," which became a feminist classic. She recovered only after she left her husband and temporarily deserted her daughter (which caused some scandal). She later divorced and devoted herself to writing and lecturing, a career by which she was able to support her child. When the book was first published, the author was listed as Charlotte Perkins Stetson, but later editions were attributed to Charlotte Perkins Gilman, after she was able to combine her career with the kind of equal marriage she wanted. Her second husband was her first cousin, Houghton Gilman, whom she married in 1900.

She wrote four novels, including a feminist utopian novel, *Herland;* edited a feminist journal, the *Forerunner;* and was active in settlement houses, the campaigns for woman suffrage, and the early labor union movement.

Women and Economics established her reputation as a thinker and made her one of the most widely read and influential women of her day. She argued with other feminists, whose views were often more popular. In 1909, she told an audience of working women that they should support votes for women because suffrage would move them in the direction of economic independence and freedom from dominance by men. The audience overwhelmingly supported her opponent, who argued that, on the contrary, women suffrage would encourage women to stay home, by recognizing that a wife's work in the home made her an equal contributor to the family who should have political equality.

When the word "feminism" began to be used in the early twentieth century, Gilman engaged in a public argument with Ellen Key from 1912 to 1914 over its definition, which Gilman said was "quite outside of the Suffrage question." There were, she recognized, two conflicting schools of feminism. Gilman, the avowed socialist, was championing the more individualistic school. Her version intended to make women more human by entering the world of work that was dominated by men. This view Gilman called Human Feminism, as opposed to Female Feminism.

> The one holds that sex is a minor department of life; that the main lines of human development have nothing to do with sex, and that what women need most is the development of human characteristics. The other considers sex as paramount, as underlying or covering all phases of life, and that what woman needs is an even fuller exercise, development and recognition of her sex.[42]

And, indeed, Ellen Key felt that it was "socially pernicious" for mothers to work outside the home "and in contrast boosted 'motherliness' as women's personal and social contribution, the fount of altruism, unselfish ethics and social cooperation."[43]

Books to Change the World

The socialism of John Stuart Mill and Charlotte Perkins Gilman was of the nineteenth-century non-Marxist kind that labeled all sorts of communal activity as "socialism." Mill made clear that he repudiated any "tyranny of society over the individual"; Gilman saw industrialism for business profit, properly conducted, as a kind of socialism. What all these books had in common was the indignation their authors shared at the legal inequalities women were faced with and their conviction that, whatever the innate differences between men and women might be (Fuller thought there were many; Gilman, very few), the absence of legal compulsion would better everyone's life, man and woman alike.

The interesting question for us to ask is, why, when the most recent of these books was written almost one hundred years ago, is there *anything* relevant in them for us today? Yet we still hear voices in contemporary discourse raising the contentions that these books intended to refute: that women are not suited for certain occupations, that perhaps women and men should be educated differently, that the differences between men and women mean that woman's chief occupation should be marriage and motherhood. Apparently the argument still continues.

CHAPTER THREE

The Rights of Man—Are Women Included?

The classical liberal point of view holds that the basic unit of society is the individual and that the *only* legitimate function of government is to protect individual liberty by protecting the rights to life, liberty, property, and the pursuit of happiness. This was the tradition of eighteenth- and nineteenth-century British and French liberalism, which was transplanted to the American colonies and the United States.

Clearly, the institution of slavery violated the rights to life, liberty, and property of the slaves, but women are half of all races. In the early nineteenth century, some women were citizens, and those who were slaves were not. What led some people to think of women as a class in themselves, that needed to be granted "equal rights"?

Common Law Restrictions

The law did—that same common law that Mary Wollstonecraft had pointed out made of husband and wife "an absurd unit." In this country, the legal position of women had been defined by the common law of England, which became the basic law of the American colonies, and later, of the states of the Union (with the exception of Louisiana, which derived its similar law from France). Sir William Blackstone's *Commentaries on the Common Law* was the most influential interpreter of the British common law in the colonies, and his summary of the legal position of married women was, "By marriage the husband and wife are one person in law, that is, the very being or legal existence of the woman is suspended during marriage or at least is incorporated and consolidated into that of the husband."[1]

This meant that her property was his; if she earned wages, they were his; he was the primary guardian of the children; and she could not sign a contract, make a will, sue in court, or start a business. She also had certain "protections"; notably, she was not liable for a number of crimes if committed in the presence of her husband, as it was assumed that she acted entirely under his direction.

Single women had some legal rights, but they, too, did not have the political rights that men did. They could not vote, hold public office, or serve on juries. High-school public education was closed to them, and many occupations were forbidden to them by law.

Common law was state law; the states adopted the common law, either through their constitutions, or through court interpretation. So any change in the legal position of women had to come through a state-by-state fight.

The Right of Petition

Before such a state-by-state fight was even possible, however, the concept of taking part in the political process had to become real to women. And it did, through the antislavery movement. It was in this cause that women became politically active in the United States. There was only one political avenue open to them, and they discovered it—the First Amendment right to petition.

A compromise when the Constitution was framed left slavery as a state issue, not a federal one. Officially, the Constitution neither approved nor disapproved of slavery, but the federal government controlled Washington, D.C., and slavery was permitted there. When ex-president John Quincy Adams was elected to the House of Representatives from Massachusetts and gave his first speech to the House in December of 1831, he presented petitions from a group of Quakers, asking for the abolition of slavery and the slave trade in the District of Columbia. This was to become a major issue for him as a congressman.

This first petition was routinely sent to Congress's standing Committee on the District of Columbia, which didn't act on it. But more and more petitions against slavery began arriving in Congress.

There was a national crisis about the relation between the state and federal governments. President Andrew Jackson was committed to the idea of a federal government that would be more powerful than the state governments, and in 1832 he issued a Proclamation to the People of South Carolina (whose state legislature had invalidated a national tariff for that state) that declared that no state could disobey a national law or secede from the Union, because the United States was a sovereign and indivisible nation. He was backed up by Congress, which passed a bill allowing Jackson to use federal troops, if necessary, to collect the tariff. This had implications for the power of Congress over the issue of slavery that alarmed southerners. If Congress could force a tariff on the South that was against its economic interests, should it develop an antislavery majority it might vote to abolish slavery itself. Indeed, there might be a precedent in the fact that in 1833 the British Parliament proceeded to abolish slavery in the British West Indies, against the wishes of the British colonists there.

In December 1833, a national American Antislavery Society was formed, through the joining of the existing state societies. It promoted the sending of petitions to Congress.

By the end of 1835, petitions were coming in, not just from Quakers and other abolitionists, but from ordinary citizens in almost every northern and western congressional district. In May 1836, the House of Representatives passed a gag resolution to dispose of the petitions by resolving that petitions relating to the subject of slavery should be ignored and that no action was to be taken on them—they would neither be printed nor referred to committee.

This gag rule was in force from May 26, 1836, until December 3, 1842, over the opposition of Adams and a few others. Meanwhile, more and more petitions were collected and signed, even though they would be refused and unread. In the session of Congress that began in December 1837, more than 200,000 petitions were sent to Congress, signed by millions of citizens, at a time when the entire population of the North was only about ten million. The petitioning continued, and most of the volunteers collecting and signing these petitions were women.

The women who did this were widely criticized. Gilbert Hobbs Barnes describes the reaction:

> By nature and by divine command, woman was conceived to be for-
> ever subject and inferior to man, and her interference by petition in "the
> external and political duties of society," Caleb Cushing prophesied, would
> be at the sacrifice of "all that delicacy and maternal tenderness which
> are among the highest charms of woman." . . .
> In 1836, when Pinckney reported that on the petitions submitted
> to his committee women's names preponderated, it was considered a
> reproach even by some among the abolition host.[2]

Many women petitioners became aware for the first time of their subservient position. They, and some of the male abolitionists who were criticized with them, began to think and talk of woman's rights.

Woman as Man's Equal

Charles and Mary Beard, in *The Rise of American Civilization,* wrote (using the word *feminism* somewhat anachronistically, as it was not in use till the end of the nineteenth century) that, during this period,

> feminism came to the front as one of the disturbing factors that could not be ignored . . . the fruition of an agitation which began in the seventeenth century. Inevitably the discussion of the rights of man in America, France, and England raised the question of the rights of woman but, in the political reaction that followed the French Revolution, the hopes of women sank in the general disillusionment.[3]

In 1840 two antislavery workers, Elizabeth Cady Stanton and Lucretia Mott, went to London as delegates to a World Anti-Slavery Convention. They were horrified to find that they and the other female delegates were not allowed to sit in the meeting with the male delegates, but were required to listen to the proceedings from seats in the gallery. The American abolitionist leader, William Lloyd Garrison, was so incensed by their treatment that he refused to take his seat as a delegate and sat with the women.

The friendship that began between Elizabeth Cady Stanton and Lucretia Mott in London was continued by letter when they returned to the United States. The Stantons moved from Boston to Seneca Falls, New York, where Elizabeth Stanton felt isolated. Then two events occurred in 1848. In April the New York legislature passed a Married Woman's Property Act, for which Stanton had worked, and Lucretia Mott wrote later in the year that she was coming from Philadelphia in July to visit her sister Martha C. Wright in Waterloo, New York, a town within visiting distance of Seneca Falls. Together with two other Quaker women, the three decided to form some sort of women's society and to call a women's meeting, or convention, as Mott and Stanton had discussed in London. (The table at which the five sat when they wrote the announcement is now in the Smithsonian Institution.) They sent in an unsigned notice to the *Seneca County Courier* that was published on July 14, 1848.

> A convention to discuss the social, civil, and religious condition and rights of women will be held in the Wesleyan Chapel, at Seneca Falls, New York, on Wednesday and Thursday, the 19th and 20th of July current; commencing at 10 o'clock a.m.[4]

The notice said that the first day of the convention would be restricted to women, but the "general public" would be welcome on the second day.

Despite the fact that this was the only notice to appear, about three hundred people showed up on the first day, including forty men, and the rules of the meeting were changed. Wagonloads of women came from a radius of fifty miles around, according to Eleanor Flexner's *Century of Struggle.*[5] Over the weekend, Stanton drafted most of the "Declaration of Sentiments," which was to be read to the group attending the convention.

As the Beards described it, "In the strain of the eighteenth century document drawn by men, the Seneca Falls assembly issued a Woman's Declaration of Independence setting forth again the grand principles of liberty and equality."[6] But, whereas the tyrant Jefferson referred to was the British King, the tyrant that the Seneca Falls Declaration referred to was that generic Man who had created the laws and rules of contemporary American society. These are some of the points:

When, in the course of human events, it becomes necessary for one portion of the family of man to assume among the people of the earth a position different from that which they have hitherto occupied . . .

We hold these truths to be self evident: that all men and women are created equal; that they are endowed by their Creator with certain inalienable rights; that among these are life, liberty, and the pursuit of happiness. . . .

The history of mankind is a history of repeated injuries and usurpations on the part of man toward woman, having in direct object the establishment of an absolute tyranny over her. To prove this, let facts be submitted to a candid world.

He has never permitted her to exercise her inalienable right to the elective franchise.

He has compelled her to submit to laws, in the formation of which she had no voice.

He has withheld from her rights which are given to the most ignorant and degraded men—both natives and foreigners.

Having deprived her of this first right of a citizen, the elective franchise, thereby leaving her without representation in the halls of legislation, he has oppressed her on all sides.

He has made her, if married, in the eyes of the law, civilly dead.

He has taken from her all right in property, even to the wages she earns.

He has made her, morally, an irresponsible being, as she can commit many crimes with impunity, provided they be done in the presence of her husband. In the covenant of marriage, she is compelled to promise obedience to her husband, he becoming, to all intents and purposes, her master—the law giving him power to deprive her of her liberty, and to administer chastisement.

He has so framed the laws of divorce, as to what shall be the proper causes, and in case of separation, to whom the guardianship of the children shall be given, as to be wholly regardless of the happiness of women —the law, in all cases, going upon the false supposition of the supremacy of man, and giving all power into his hands.

After depriving her of all rights as a married woman, if single, and the owner of property, he has taxed her to support a government which recognizes her only when her property can be made profitable to it. . . .

In entering upon the great work before us, we anticipate no small amount of misconception, misrepresentation, and ridicule; but we shall use every instrumentality within our power to effect our object. We shall employ agents, circulate tracts, petition the State and National legislatures, and endeavor to enlist the pulpit and the press in our behalf. We hope this Convention will be followed by a series of Conventions embracing every part of the country.[7]

This Declaration was accompanied by a number of resolutions intended to implement it: When Elizabeth Cady Stanton read to her abolitionist husband a proposed resolution asking for votes for women, he refused to attend the meeting if she intended presenting it, and Lucretia Mott was afraid it would make them ridiculous. But, supported by the black abolitionist Frederick Douglass, Stanton presented it on the second day of the meeting, and it was passed by a small margin, making this the beginning of the woman suffrage movement, an attempt by women to gain legal rights through the right to vote on the laws that affected them. The other resolutions were all passed unanimously.

If such complaints could be made over seventy years after the original Declaration of Independence was signed, clearly the founding of the United States upon liberal principles hadn't done much for women. The speakers at this first Woman's Rights Convention were drawn from the abolitionist cause. How could one believe that slaves should have civil rights and still believe in denying those rights to the women who were championing their cause? Surely these supposedly free women were no less intelligent, no less worthy, no less human than these unfortunate members of another race enslaved on our shores. Yet, like the slaves, American married women in 1848 could not own property, could not sign contracts, could not vote, could not control their own earnings, could be physically beaten, and could be returned to their homes by force if they ran away.

Changing the Laws

The New York law that Stanton had supported in April 1848 was the first married woman's property law passed in the United States. It permitted a wife who inherited real estate to hold it in her own name rather than her husband's. This law encouraged women to hope that they might gain their rights by petitioning the legislature.

In 1851 Stanton met Susan B. Anthony, a young worker for women's rights who had previously been working in the temperance movement, which tried to wipe out drunkenness through preaching, writing, and campaigning for state prohibition laws. Anthony's mother and sister had been at the Seneca Falls Convention, and there was instant sympathy between her and Stanton when they met. Soon they became a team, working for temperance, the abolition of slavery, and especially, for women's rights. (In those days, many women became advocates of the Woman Movement through the temperance movement—the power that the common law gave to drunken husbands to abuse their wives and control their wages highlighted the unfairness of the legal subservience of wives.) In 1854 the two friends joined in a campaign to petition the New York State Legislature for a stronger married woman's property act. Anthony used her organizational talents to build a group that gathered signatures and presented a petition for a more extensive married woman's property bill to the New York State Legislature. Stanton, who after her maiden speech at the Seneca Falls convention was already beginning to be celebrated as a speaker, spoke to a joint session of the legislature in support of the bill.

According to Betty Friedan in *The Feminine Mystique,* "When Susan Anthony and her women captains collected 6,000 signatures in ten weeks, the New York State Assembly received them with roars of laughter. In mockery, the Assembly recommended that since ladies always get the 'choicest tidbits' at the table, the best seat in the carriage, and their choice of which side of the bed to lie on, 'if there is any inequity or oppression the gentlemen are the sufferers.' "[8]

Despite this setback, New York women continued to petition and lobby, and in 1860 Stanton was again invited to speak to a joint session of the legislature. This time, the amount of public opinion brought to bear by women resulted in the passage of a bill. It allowed a married woman to control inherited property of any kind, to own and control her own earnings, to make contracts and go into business, to sue or be sued, and to be the joint guardian of her children. It also gave a wife the same property inheritance rights upon the death of a husband that a husband had upon the death of a wife. This was the law in only one state, however, and the entire country was still riddled with common law restrictions of women's rights.

Sixteen years later, at the Philadelphia Centennial celebration of the Declaration of Independence in 1876, women organized to present a petition to the Vice President of the United States. They were thrown out of their lodgings because, as married women, most of them could not sign a contract under Pennsylvania law—in that case, a lease.

The Seneca Falls Convention was followed by a number of similar meetings in other parts of the country. Because of the growing tension between North and South, the last of these was held in Albany in 1861. After that, the almost impossible task of a state-by-state revision of the laws as well as the idea of campaigns for the vote were postponed with the advent of the Civil War in favor of war work and abolitionist aims. After Lincoln's Emancipation Proclamation became effective on January 1, 1863, Anthony and Stanton organized the National Woman's Loyalty League to collect signatures on petitions for Negro emancipation and collected almost 400,000 signatures in support of a Thirteenth Amendment to abolish slavery and involuntary servitude.

The Right to Vote

The men and women who had worked together for abolition and women's rights were champions of the right to vote, so, instead of disbanding after the passage and ratification of the Thirteenth Amendment in 1865, the American Antislavery Society began agitating for a suffrage amendment. Were women going to reap their reward for all the work they had done in the antislavery cause over the years? No, they were not.

As the Beards wrote, "champions of the colored man were declaring that no person's civil liberties were safe without the ballot. With a relevancy that could hardly be denied the feminists now asked why the doctrine did not apply to women, only to receive a curt answer from the politicians that sent them flying to the platform."[9]

A Fourteenth Amendment was proposed and introduced in Congress. Its original purpose was to give the vote to slaves and to take it away from southerners who had fought against the Union, and, for the first time in the history of the Constitution, it was suggested that the word "male" be used to characterize voters.

Women activists were alarmed. Susan B. Anthony collected ten thousand signatures on a petition asking that women also be given the vote. Although these advocates of woman suffrage hoped to remove the word "male" and specifically include women, the male abolitionists (and some female ones) who had championed woman's right to vote in the abstract were unwilling to make it a concrete political issue. When the Fourteenth Amendment was under consideration in the Senate, Senator Charles Sumner, a former advocate of women's rights, presented the petition for woman suffrage "apologetically," says Katherine Anthony in her biography of Anthony, "remarking that it was 'most inopportune.' "[10]

The petition was rejected and the Amendment was passed. It was ratified in July of 1868.

In 1869 Congress decided to strengthen it with a Fifteenth Amendment, specifically concerned with the denial of the right to vote on the basis of race. Women campaigned to add the words "or sex," but again were not successful. The Fifteenth Amendment passed Congress in February of 1869. In March of that year, according to Katherine Anthony, "George W. Julian of Indiana introduced a joint resolution in Congress proposing a sixteenth amendment for the enfranchisement of the women of the United States."[11]

This began a half-century fight for the right of women to vote. Two national suffrage associations were formed, a conservative one, the American Woman Suffrage Association, which accepted men as members, and a more radical one formed by Anthony and Stanton, the National Woman Suffrage Association, which excluded men. They both kept the issue alive and asked every Congress for the next fifty years to pass an amendment.

There was some thought that perhaps the Fourteenth Amendment had *inadvertently* given women the right to vote. Its second section provided that the basis of representation in Congress should be reduced for any state that denied the right to vote to any "male inhabitants" who had reached the age of twenty-one. (The provision has never been invoked.) Although this section inserted the world "male" into the Constitution, it also provided a possible presumption that the right to vote was a privilege of citizenship that no state could deny. Two members of the House Judiciary Committee in 1871 signed a minority report holding this view. Susan B. Anthony not only adopted the view as her own but, after waging a vigorous campaign in support of the Republican Party and the reelection of President Ulysses S. Grant in 1872, led sixteen women to vote the straight Republican ticket in the fall election.

This is how Katherine Anthony described it.

> When they first appeared, headed by Susan, the inspectors hesitated; but not for long. Susan had brought along the Fourteenth Amendment and the state election law, which she read aloud to them, pointing out that nothing in the text expressly prohibited women from voting. She repeated her request to be registered as a voter. The inspectors obliged.[12]

On election day, the women were allowed to vote. Susan B. Anthony was arrested for the federal crime of illegal participation in a national election, tried, and convicted in what Katherine Anthony makes clear was a rigged trial. It ended with a directed verdict of guilty—illegal in a jury criminal trial—at which the jury stood mute and refused to act. Her trial was presided over by Justice Ward Hunt of the Supreme Court, who rejected Anthony's constitutional claim. Hoping to be able to make this a constitutional test case, Anthony never paid her fine. Had she been jailed for this defiance, she would have been able to appeal her case. But she was never jailed.

But a voting rights case did get to the Supreme Court, in 1874. The case was *Minor* v. *Happersett*.[13] Virginia L. Minor brought a civil suit against a Missouri election official, claiming that a state that limited the vote to males violated the privileges and immunities of its female citizens, in violation of the first section of the Fourteenth Amendment. Chief Justice Morrison R. Waite ruled that the Fourteenth Amendment hadn't given the right to vote to anyone, and that, with the exception of the limitation on racial exclusion in the Fifteenth Amendment, the states had a complete right to set the requirements for voting. This case ended attempts to win votes for women through a Supreme Court ruling.

Those Who Never Married

Activists in the Woman Movement have sometimes been given the name of "manhaters," even though most of the well-known women activists in the movement were married—many of them to abolitionist men also committed to women's rights. There were James and Lucretia Mott, Henry and Elizabeth Cady Stanton, Lucy Stone and Henry Blackwell, and Angelina Grimké and Theodore Weld. The one outstanding spinster activist was Susan B. Anthony, and Barbara Deckard, in her book on *The Women's Movement,* says, "In fact, the women's movement was run mostly by married women in their few moments of spare time, after doing all the housework and child care. . . . Unmarried, Anthony bore the brunt of the traveling and lecturing when her married friends could not get away from home."[14] Where did the identification of women's rights with manhating come from?

Could it be that some people felt so threatened at the idea of overturning the common law legal prerogatives of men that they decided that the idea of seeking any sort of legal equality for women was an attempt to change the very nature of men and therefore had to be an expression of hostility toward men? Perhaps. But there was another more visible explanation—the fact that most of the pioneers in the struggle of women to work in the professions did not marry.

The Search for Higher Education and Professional Careers

It's not clear whether there was a single reason for this; probably not. The general assumption, held until World War II, that married women didn't need to work often resulted in discrimination. (As late as 1929, according to Barbara Deckard, a woman dean at a midwestern college was fired because she got married.) In the nineteenth century it took a great deal of dedication for a woman even to obtain an education. The requirements of marriage were often restrictive, and it probably was sometimes extremely difficult for a woman dedicated to an unusual life to find a man who wanted to marry her. Robert Smuts, examining the ata collected in the 1890 census, says that, at that late date, "very few women prepared for professional work by going to college. . . . It was often viewed as evidence of strongminded and unfeminine disregard for social convention." He goes on to say,

> The few young women who did prepare for professional careers other than teaching and nursing were distinguished by their disrespect for convention and determination to override all obstacles. If not active feminists, they were often deeply affected by the feminist revolt. Many of them could see no hope of freedom in marriage, and remained single. More than one fourth of the women who graduated from college around the turn of the century never married. Of those who went on to establish professional careers, even fewer married. More than half the women doctors in 1890 were single. About one fifth were widowed or divorced, and only about one fourth were married.[15]

Most of these women, of course, came from relatively well-off families who could afford to pay to educate their daughters—and were open enough to new ideas to be willing to. Education for women had been gained in small increments over the course of the nineteenth century. When Emma Willard founded her "woman's seminary" in Troy, New York, in 1819 there was no public higher education for women in the United States, only private seminaries. Free public high-school education for women did not exist until after the Civil War, when the first free high schools for women opened in Boston and Philadelphia. The first college to admit women was Oberlin, in 1833, but at first they were only admitted to special courses; it was not until 1841 that the first women graduated from Oberlin's regular program. In 1834 Wheaton College for Women was established in Massachusetts. In 1852 Antioch College joined Oberlin as a coeducational institution. Iowa in 1858 was the first state university to admit women, followed by Wisconsin in 1863 (to normal training courses);

Michigan, Ohio, and Illinois admitted women in 1870. And several women's colleges were founded in the second half of the century in the East: Vassar in 1865, Sage College (part of Cornell University) in 1874, Smith and Wellesley in 1875, the Harvard Annex (later Radcliffe) in 1879; and Bryn Mawr in 1885.

All these institutions had to battle against the assumption that too much education for women was hazardous to their health. A book called *Sex in Education,* by Edward H. Clarke who was professor of Materia Medica at Harvard for seventeen years, detailed the dire consequences he saw produced in women's systems from "constrained positions, muscular effort, brain work, and all forms of mental and physical excitement."[16] These bad conditions, he said, "pervade" schools. Robert Smuts says that when the Associated Collegiate Alumnae was formed in 1882,

> One of the first tasks undertaken by the newly formed organization was a study to determine whether college education had, in fact, damaged the health of women. A list of questions was drawn up with the help of a panel of physicians and sent to all 1,290 women college graduates in the United States . . . 77.87 percent of the respondents were in good health, while only 17.02 percent were in poor health—which seemed to give college women a good margin of healthiness over other women.[17]

But if it were considered by experts that the brain work and mental and physical excitement of going to college might injure women's health, what about the brain work involved in the exacting work of the sciences or the professions? How would a woman who did that sort of work be viewed by the society in which she lived? Perhaps the surprise is that there were outstanding women at all and that they did receive recognition from their peers.

One of the earliest was Maria Mitchell (1818–89), the companion and coworker of her astronomer father, William Mitchell, in Nantucket. In 1847, when she was twenty-eight, she discovered the comet that is named after her: as a result of this discovery she became the first woman to be elected to the American Academy of Arts and Sciences in 1848 and, with the sponsorship of Louis Agassiz, to the Association for the Advancement of Science in 1850. In 1865 she became the first woman professor of astronomy in the U.S. at Vassar College and in 1873 was a founder of the Association for the Advancement of Women.

Elizabeth Blackwell (1821–1910) was not only the first American woman to become a doctor of medicine (although not the first woman to *practice* medicine when credentials were not as important as they are today), but was also the first woman medical school graduate in *the world* when she received her M.D. (at the head of her class) from Geneva College in New York in 1849. She had been turned down by twenty-nine medical schools and was only admitted to Geneva when the idea was submitted to a vote by the student body, who thought it would be amusing. She went to Paris and London for further study and returned to New York City in 1851. She couldn't find a house or an office to rent, or a hospital that would admit her to practice, so in 1857 she started her own hospital, the New York Infirmary for Women and Children, staffed entirely by women, including her sister, Emily, who had followed in her footsteps to become a doctor, too. After the Civil War, she started a medical school for women in 1868 and then returned to England to practice medicine there.

Myra Bradwell (1831–94) was the first notable woman lawyer, but she never actually practiced law. She was also one of the few women pioneers who combined marriage with her career. She lived in a period when most lawyers qualified by studying in an existing law office; Myra married lawyer James Bradwell and studied law in his office. He became a judge and a legislator. In 1868, with invaluable help from her husband (who lobbied a special charter through the Illinois legislature), she founded the first weekly law periodical published in the West, the *Chicago Legal News,* and became its editor. Myra Bradwell then, with the encouragement of her husband, took the bar exam and passed with distinction, but was denied admission to the bar by the State of Illinois.

Although a special charter had enabled her to head her business despite the common law handicaps imposed on married women, the Supreme Court of Illinois decided the common law legal handicap prevented her from practicing law because she, "as a married woman would be bound neither by her express contracts nor by those implied contracts which it is the policy of the law to create between lawyer and client."[18] In other words, the fact that a married woman at that time could not legally sign a contract meant that no married woman could practice law.

Myra Bradwell appealed to the Supreme Court of the United States, and in 1872 it decided that common law restrictions on married women rest on the fact that "the paramount destiny and mission of woman are to fulfill the noble and benign offices of wife and mother," and, therefore, neither common law nor the ruling of the Illinois court that Bradwell could not be a lawyer abridged her "privileges and immunities" protected by the Fourteenth Amendment.[19] She led a successful campaign to reform Illinois law, but never again asked for admission to the bar for herself. In 1890, four years before she died, the state supreme court finally reversed its earlier position and admitted her to the bar without being asked. Her publication had become highly successful and profitable, and she made it a vehicle to influence and improve the operation of the courts. Says

Caroline Bird in *Enterprising Women,* "since as a woman she could not serve private individuals for a fee, she took the profession itself for her client and improved the practice of the law for clients and lawyers alike."[20]

The general assumption that women were not strong enough to be fitted for the professions had a certain amount of hypocrisy to it as well, since low-income and farm women were routinely engaged in heavy work. A contemporary observer, Jane Swisshelm, one of the first women to publish a newspaper (whose book, *Letters to Country Girls,* was published in 1853), is quoted in Eleanor Flexner's *Century of Struggle*:

> It is well known that thousands, nay, millions of women in this country are condemned to the most menial drudgery, such as men would scorn to engage in, and that for one fourth the wages; that thousands of them toil at avocations which public opinion pretends to assign to men. They plow, harrow, reap, dig, make hay, rake, bind grain, thrash, chop wood, milk, churn, do anything that is hard work, physical labor, and who says anything against it? But let one presume to use her mental powers— let her aspire to turn editor, public speaker, doctor, lawyer—take up any profession or avocation which is deemed honorable and requires talent, and O! bring cologne, get a cambric kerchief and feather fan, unloose his corsets and take off his cravat! What a fainting fit Mr. Propriety has taken![21]

According to Robert Smuts, most of the active proponents of women's rights were professional women, and they had to contend with the explicit argument that "women were destined by nature for the home." They did this, according to Smuts, by appealing to "the essential equality of all human beings, the dignity of the individual, the right to self-determination," but they also agreed that maternity was "woman's highest function."[22]

Many economic changes, however, were having their impact on the family. The divorce rate rose, the number of children in a family was shrinking, and young people left home and went to the city to work and to live alone. The growing employment of women was also viewed by some as a problem. Says Smuts, "In 1911 the report of the Chicago Vice Commission expressed the suspicion that the decay of the family, the employment of women, the entrance of women into politics, and prostitution were all reflections of the impact of modern urban life on the 'tastes, the possibilities [and] the opportunities' of women in general."[23]

Women who graduated from college were no longer considered freaks by the turn of the century, and the necessity to choose between education and career on the one hand or marriage on the other gradually disappeared from the scene.

Changes in the Lives of Women

In the last quarter of the nineteenth century there were a number of changes in American society that particularly changed the lives of women. Household technology became entirely different; by 1870 cooking stoves had almost entirely replaced open-hearth cooking, and men's clothing was no longer made in the home but was almost entirely factory made. Cities constructed sewer lines and water-supply systems; breakfast cereals and canned foods became available beginning in the 1880s.

As work in the home grew less arduous, there was an expanding job market for women. Clerical jobs and jobs as telegraph operators were open to women who had graduated from school, and in rural districts, since boys were needed to work the land, more girls than boys were able to finish school. According to Barbara Deckard, "in 1870 there were 90,000 women teachers; by 1890, the number had increased to 250,000—and they also formed organizations."[24] Women formed clubs: literary clubs, self-improvement clubs. The Women's Christian Temperance Union (WCTU) was formed in 1874, and when Frances Willard became its president in 1879 she increased its membership to over 200,000 and brought it actively into the fight for woman suffrage.

Immigrants congregated in the cities, and more and more immigrant women went into poorly paid factory work. Some of them became active in the labor movement. A settlement house movement began, inspired by the establishment of Toynbee Hall in London in 1884. Educated men and women set up a "settlement" in the slums where they could work with the poor to reform the area. All over the United States settlement houses were established in working-class neighborhoods, where idealistic, upper-class women lived and worked with people of the neighborhood, giving classes and lectures, organizing local clubs, supporting legislation, helping union organization, and bringing in labor leaders to speak. Philip Foner in his first volume of *Women and the American Labor Movement* says there were six U.S. settlements by 1891, over one hundred by 1900, over two hundred by 1905, and over four hundred by 1910.[25] Some settlement houses actively fomented and supported strikes for better wages and working conditions.

The National Suffrage Movement

Meanwhile, Anthony and Stanton had begun trying to interest working women in the cause of suffrage. As early as 1866, Anthony said that "the working women of the country are with us. Say to them that with the ballot in their hands, they can secure equal pay for their work, and the demand for the ballot will be as strong as that of the black man today."[26]

George Francis Train offered to finance their publication, the *Revolution*; its first issue on January 8, 1868, pledged to support not only votes for women but also, says Philip Foner, "equal pay for equal work; the eight hour day; the abolition of party despotism; currency reform; unrestricted immigration; and the regeneration of American society."[27] The paper also reprinted as serials two books that were not widely available in the U.S.—Mary Wollstonecraft's *Rights of Women* and John Stuart Mill's *Subjection of Women.*[28]

A National Labor Union had been formed in Baltimore on August 20, 1866, and, although most of the labor leaders who formed it felt that woman's place was in the home, not the labor market, some of them saw that women were in the labor market to stay, and, if they were not to take jobs away from men, they must be unionized at equal pay levels. The Union pledged "individual and undivided support to the sewing women, factory operatives, and daughters of toil" and called for equal pay.[29] They asked individual trade unions to admit women workers, and one, the Cigar Makers International Union, did so in 1867.

Every issue of the *Revolution* supported unions and strikes and argued that, in Foner's words, "without the ballot workingwomen would never be able to resolve the two major disadvantages from which they suffered: inequality of wages with men and inability to enter the trades and professions."[30]

> The *Revolution* analyzed and then endorsed every one of the NLU planks: the eight-hour day, land reform, opposition to monopolies, producer and consumer cooperatives, currency reform, and support of trade unionism. "The principles of the National Labor Union are our principles," the editors proclaimed. "We see on the surface of this great movement the portent of bright days and hear a voice that shall be heard by all the people's servants in Washington, and by the selfish, hard-hearted oppressors everywhere."[31]

When the National Labor Union had a convention in 1868, Anthony formed the Working Women's Association #1 from among the *Revolution*'s typesetters and clerks in order to accredit herself as a delegate to the convention. Stanton came with credentials from another organization that had just been formed, the Woman Suffrage Association of America, and there was some difficulty over seating her. At the convention, Anthony chaired a Committee on Female Labor, but was not able to get the convention to endorse votes for women. By the 1869 Convention, however, it came to the labor leaders' attention that Anthony had encouraged women typographers to replace striking union members in order to "gain experience," and the National Labor Union would not seat her. This was the end of the alliance between the *Revolution* and the National Labor Union. The Working Women's Association moved from supporting unionism to investigating working conditions for women in various industries as its membership became entirely middle-class, and, says Foner, "the last recorded act of the association before its formal dissolution in November, 1869, was to drop the descriptive word 'Working' from its title."[32] The *Revolution* folded in June 1870. From then on, the National Woman Suffrage Association devoted itself exclusively to woman suffrage. It supported Virginia Minor's lawsuit when it began in 1872 and introduced a suffrage amendment, the Anthony Amendment, each year in Congress.

Meanwhile, the more conservative American Woman Suffrage Association was working to change state laws. It campaigned successfully in the Territory of Wyoming, which was almost refused statehood in 1889 because of it. When the legislature was asked if Wyoming would drop woman suffrage in order to get statehood, it telegraphed back, says Barbara Deckard, "We will remain out of the Union a hundred years rather than come in without the women."[33] Wyoming thus became the first state in which women could vote in 1890. Utah Territory also gave women the vote in 1870, but Congress revoked it in 1887. When Utah became a state in 1896, its state constitution gave women the vote again.

In 1890 the National and the American Woman Suffrage Associations merged to form the National American Woman uffrage Association (NAWSA), with Stanton as its first president. She had become increasingly interested in issues other than suffrage: divorce reform and the responsibility of organized religion for the view that woman was an inferior being. Anthony succeeded her friend as president of the Association in 1892, but could not stop the weakening of its support of a federal amendment. Gradually it restricted its activities to supporting state referenda. By the turn of the century, NAWSA was willing to pass a resolution supporting educational qualifications for the ballot, which would have kept many immigrants and poor people from voting.

At the end of the nineteenth century, the influence of the suffrage organization seemed to be waning. After 1893 the federal amendment had not been favorably reported on by Congress. Between 1896 and 1910, the movement made no gains. The state campaigns had been disappointing, and the liquor industry had responded to the activities of the WCTU by successfully entering the fray against woman suffrage. Also, the old leaders were passing from the scene. Anthony resigned her presidency of the Association in 1900; Stanton died in 1902; Anthony, in 1906. With these deaths it seemed for a time as if the movement had come to an end.

When Stanton's daughter, Harriot Stanton Blatch, returned to the United States after her husband of twenty years had died, she said that the suffrage movement "bored its adherents and repelled its opponents."[34] She had seen the British suffrage movement galvanized into success when it decided to provoke police violence. In January 1907 she persuaded thirty-nine women to form a new organization that would dramatize the suffrage struggle in the United States and reach out both to women in the labor movement and to women in business and the professions. It was first called the Equality League of Self-Supporting Women and later became the Women's Political Union.

By October 1908 the League had 19,000 members. It presented working women as witnesses in legislative hearings; it held open-air meetings, campaigning against legislators opposed to woman suffrage; and it brought labor leaders to hear British suffragettes speak. Also, it held parades to support suffrage. By 1909 the movement had spread from its origins in New York State to a number of other states, and other suffrage organizations were springing up. Carrie Chapman Catt, a former president of the NAWSA, helped form a Woman's Suffrage Party.

In 1910 a state referendum was finally won in the state of Washington, and in 1911 California was won. In 1912 two young women who had both worked with militant suffragettes in England offered their services to the Board of the National Suffrage Association to work for a federal amendment. Their names were Alice Paul and Lucy Burns.

They organized a spectacular campaign, beginning with a parade of 5,000 held the day before Woodrow Wilson's inauguration. In April 1913 they organized a national Congressional Union to work only on a federal amendment. The Union also campaigned against Democrats in 1914 and formed a National Woman's Party in 1916 to run candidates against them. For three years the Congressional Union and its successor, the Woman's Party, was waging the only effective campaign for an amendment, getting it to the floor of Congress twice.

In 1917 the Union began copying their British sisters' tactics: picketing, lighting bonfires, and staging hunger strikes. Meanwhile, Carrie Chapman Catt became the president of the NAWSA and breathed new life into that organization. Rather than confronting Wilson, as the Congressional Union was doing, she invited him to address the NAWSA convention during his campaign for reelection. Eleanor Flexner tells us that Carrie Chapman Catt believed that Wilson decided to support a federal amendment at this convention after a NAWSA leader replied to his address, "We have waited so long, Mr. President, for the vote—we had hoped it might come in your administration," and the audience stood up and turned silently to him. "Although it was another year before Wilson took the position . . . that Congress should act on woman suffrage, he never thereafter refused to grant the National aid when asked, and he gave it in ways the public never learned."[35]

During World War I, American women went into the work force to replace the soldiers who had gone overseas, giving them a strong moral argument for the vote. By the beginning of 1918, there had been several state victories, but Congress had been in a special war session from April to October 1917 and was forbidden to do any business not connected with the war. It reconvened on December 3, 1917 and scheduled a vote on the Anthony Amendment on January 10, 1918. On January 9 President Wilson declared his support of the measure. Four supporters left sickbeds to attend the vote in the House, and the amendment passed with exactly the two-thirds majority that it needed. Carrie Chapman Catt summed it all up.

> To get the word "male" in effect out of the Constitution cost the women of the country fifty-two years of pauseless campaigns. . . . During that time they were forced to conduct fifty-six campaigns of referenda to male voters; 480 campaigns to get Legislatures to submit suffrage amendments to voters; 47 campaigns to get State constitutional conventions to write woman suffrage into State conventions; 277 campaigns to get State party conventions to include woman's suffrage planks; 30 campaigns to get presidential party conventions to adopt woman's suffrage planks in party platforms; and 19 campaigns with 19 successive Congresses.[36]

The Decline of Liberalism

The classical liberal spirit was alive in the Woman Movement as late as 1876. When Susan B. Anthony read a Declaration of Women's Rights to an audience at the Philadelphia Centennial in 1876, it was couched in classical liberal language:

> We ask of our rulers at this hour no special favors, no special privileges, no special legislation. We ask justice, we ask equality, we ask that all the civil and political rights that belong to the citizens of the United States be guaranteed to us and our daughters forever.[38]

But forces had been at work to produce special legislation on a number of issues. When in 1840 President Martin Van Buren established a ten-hour day for federal employees by executive order, people assumed, writes Philip Foner, that "to do the same thing for employees of private concerns involved the state legislatures that had chartered them."[38] The temperance movement found state prohibition laws entirely proper. The settlement house movement was to use its influence to campaign for social welfare legislation. In 1903 reformers formed a National Women's Trade Union League to organize women workers and join middle-class women and trade unionists in one organization, to educate unions about women workers and women workers about unions. By 1908 this league dropped its other activities to concentrate on campaigning for protective labor legislation for women. This was the year that the constitutionality of such legislation was endorsed by the Supreme Court in the case of *Muller* v. *Oregon.*[39] The Court decided that although state protective legislation to limit the hours that men worked was a violation of their right to contract, an Oregon law limiting the working hours of *women* was constitutional because "woman has always been dependent upon man."

On the intellectual front, socialist theories were in the ascendancy. The complexities of industrialization posed social problems that seemed controllable only through government action. John Stuart Mill was not the only classical liberal who came to call himself a socialist.

In *Race Relations in American Law,* Jack Greenberg summarizes this modification of liberal theory.

> English liberals at first held that the highest degree of liberty would be achieved if government kept hands completely off individual conduct. Later—John Mill personally underwent the transition in belief—they concluded that restricting the state alone was not enough and that in some situations government should restrict private action in the interest of greater freedom . . . holding that in a given case government's failure to limit private freedom to some extent could mean subjecting others to the constraint of powerful private forces which might stifle liberty as effectively as might government.[40]

Mill, of course, had no idea of the extent to which government might grow, as he eloquently expressed in *On Liberty.* "If the roads, the railways, the banks, the insurance offices, the great joint-stock companies, the universities, and the public charities, were all of them branches of the government," he cried, attempting to stun his audience by this vision of an impossible extension of government power, " . . . not all the freedom of the press and popular constitution of the legislature would make this or any country free otherwise than in name."[41] And he went on to speculate,

> If every part of the business of society which required organized concert, or large and comprehensive views, were in the hands of the government,

and if government offices were universally filled by the ablest men, all the enlarged culture and practiced intelligence in the country, except the purely speculative, would be concentrated in a numerous bureaucracy, to whom alone the rest of the community would look for all things: . . . Under this regime . . . no reform can be effected which is contrary to the interest of the bureaucracy.[42]

But no one expected such a situation to come to pass at the end of the nineteenth century, and social reform was considered to be part of the progress we could expect. Economic regulation was part of that agenda.

In July of 1901, the Socialist Party of America was founded in Indianapolis, devoted, among other goals, to "equal civil and political rights for men and women."[43] Ten percent of its founding members were women, and it was the first political party to call for votes for women. It also, says Philip Foner, expected women to put pressures on "legislators to draft measures regulating woman's employment."[44] Whatever liberal ideals the Woman Movement had started with, it seemed to be entering the twentieth century with a mandate to expand government regulation and government power.

CHAPTER FOUR

The Rise of Feminism

The fact that the woman suffrage movement became revivified in 1910 was part of a new emphasis in the Woman Movement that began to be called "feminism." In the fifteenth-anniversary issue of *Ms.* magazine, Catharine R. Stimpson wrote, " 'Feminism' entered the English language in 1895."[1] Nancy F. Cott tells us, in her excellent 1987 book, *The Grounding of Modern Feminism,* that the word only came into general use in the 1910s. (Says Cott, "The appearance of Feminism in the 1910s signaled a new phrase in the debate and agitation about women's rights and freedoms that had flared for hundreds of years. People in the nineteenth century did not say feminism."[2])

When people in the Woman Movement added other issues to their attempts to securing the vote, these were not only inspired by voices for government regulation in the labor movement, the settlement houses, and the temperance movement. All along there had been other issues with which individual women in the movement identified, often providing individualist voices for change. We have seen that there were early agitators in support of birth control and reproductive rights. There was also the movement to reform women's dress in the 1850s, which women like Elizabeth Cady Stanton and Susan B. Anthony finally abandoned after one or two years because the ridicule the "bloomer" costume inspired was just too much for them. There were continuing attacks on the position of women in marriage, from the marriage contract of Lucy Stone and Henry Blackwell in 1855, repudiating the common law position of wives, to Victoria Woodhull's advocacy of free love in *Woodhull & Claflin's Weekly* in the early 1870s. Stanton was a lifelong agitator for more liberal divorce laws and a lifelong critic of the role of organized religion in the suppression of women, an interest that led to her last major project, a massive two-volume commentary on the Bible, *The Woman's Bible,* which was published from 1895 to 1898. She also attacked the WCTU in a meeting of the National American Woman Suffrage Association, as potentially violating the separation of church and state.

The nineteenth-century Woman Movement, according to Cott, was made up of different movements whose support overlapped, each of which had a different ideological background—service and social action (supported by Evangelical Protestantism), woman's rights (supported by Enlightenment rationalism and bourgeois individualism), and woman's emancipation (supported by utopian socialist visions like those of Charles Fourier). All of these trends changed under feminism. Feminism "severed the ties the woman movement had to Christianity and conventional respectability," says Cott.[3]

> When the woman movement of the 1910s stressed woman's duties, Feminists reinvigorated demands for women's rights. They took as a mentor the democratic theorist Mary Wollstonecraft and revered her for her norm-defying sexual life as well as for her vindication of the rights of women.[4]

And although "born in an era of social tumult as an ideology of women's social awakening, [feminism] was nonetheless inward looking and individualistic."[5] Cott attributes to Katherine Anthony the idea that "feminism in the 1910s had *two* 'dominating ideas': 'the emancipation of woman both as a human being and as a sex-being.' "[6]

The Feminist Search for Identity

It was the rebellious spirit of the flapper, who cut off the trailing skirts of the nineteenth century at her knees, threw away her corsets, left home to support herself in the big city even after she married, and drank the bathtub gin her older nineteenth-century sister had helped to outlaw that became the image of the feminist during the 1920s. Her social movements were birth control, companionate marriage, the Lucy Stone League, and sometimes radical art and politics. Sometimes they were professional organizations, too. Her feminist creed was the ability of women to "Do Anything," perhaps better than men did, and she didn't much care whether this was justified because women were identical to men or radically different from them. Once the vote was won, there was no "woman's vote," as some had predicted; women voted in as many ways as men did, for similar reasons. But there was no feminist vote either.

There was an active group of women who called themselves feminists in the 1920s and 1930s. They had become aware of their status as women and were concerned with personal and artistic freedom, keeping their own identities and careers after marriage, using their newly won vote to better the world in amorphous ways (such as "ending war"), and often proselytizing for birth control.

Their husbands usually called themselves feminists, too, which meant to them encouraging the use of separate names and sometimes separate studios, but which carried none of the demands for their time and energy in the house that married male feminists face today. Some of these feminists were agitating for utopian schemes like communal housekeeping for professional women, but the economics of the times were such that household help was fairly generally available for those with even moderate means: concerns about child care for working mothers and sharing housework didn't exist in its current form. Domestic service was so low paid that in many parts of the country most American mothers had hired help to care for their children and households at least some of the time. It certainly wasn't a personal concern for the actresses, writers, and artists that predominated in the feminist circle. The question was merely, what did the mother do with her time? Did she pursue a professional interest, or did she spend it on social and community activities—on "wifely" rather than "individual" pursuits?

They wanted to have it all, these feminists, to be sexually *and* professionally liberated. They married for love; they divorced more easily than they had ever done before. Some were lesbians, and it was acknowledged privately that lesbians existed, although they were hardly out of the closet. Instead of being women in the Woman Movement, the feminists encouraged everyone to call them "girls," because they thought of themselves as eternally young.

Since the passage of the Nineteenth Amendment in 1920 had guaranteed votes for women, there was little general emphasis on political activity in the feminism of the day. The main political feminist organization was the Lucy Stone League, whose slogan when it was founded was "Keep Your Own Name." Early members of the executive committee included Anita Loos and Fannie Hurst as well as a sprinkling of men, notably Heywood Broun and public-relations expert Edward L. Bernays (in the early 1950s, his daughter, novelist Anne Bernays, became "Junior Adviser" to the League).

Children of Lucy Stoners, instead of growing up on slogans like "the personal is the political," grew up on the saying, "How can you bear to be tagged with a man's name, as if you were his luggage?" In its early days the League publicized the case of Helena Normanton in England, who in 1922 established her right to become a barrister under her own name as a principle of common law, which *allowed* women to take their husband's surnames upon marriage, but also allowed people to be known by any names they wished as long as it was without criminal intent. In 1924 Miss Normanton won a second victory; she got a passport. According to Bulletin No. 2 of the Lucy Stone League, edited by Ottilie Amend,

> When she applied in her own name she met with the usual opposition and was advised that married women often wanted the privilege of use of their maiden names on passports, but for reasons of public policy it was invariably refused. It had never been granted by the British Foreign Office. Miss Normanton thereupon prepared a brief, used her same argument as before the Joint Council of the Four Inns of Court and cited the same cases and text books as authority. The Foreign Office considered her case and on September 26 advised her that her right was incontrovertible and so issued her passport in the name of Helena Normanton.

This helped American women to gain the same right to a passport in their own name. When she arrived in this country in December 1924 (using the controversial passport), she testified at a hearing before the Secretary of State on a petition for a passport for a Washington newspaper woman, Ruby A. Black. The Secretary quoted one of his predecessors, who had refused a similar request, saying it was "contrary to the customs of Christian countries."[7] Because of Miss Normanton's testimony that England was Christian and had still issued her a passport, Secretary Kellogg did issue an "emergency passport" to "Ruby A. Black, wife of Herbert Little." Within two months another professional woman was allowed to use her old passport after her marriage, merely by stamping the name of her husband in the back, and a third was given a passport in her own name. From then on, the custom gradually became established.

The original Lucy Stone was an abolitionist who did not take the name of her husband, Henry Blackwell, when they were married, and at the time she had gotten legal advice that she was not required to do so from no less a person than Salmon P. Chase, then the Chief Justice of the Supreme Court. The League consulted a number of lawyers in the twenties to ascertain that this legal right still existed, publicized their findings, and intervened in legal cases and proceedings, from the issuing of library cards to challenging a 1924 order of the Comptroller General of the United States that married women must use their husband's surnames on the government payroll. (Clearly, by the time that Frances Perkins, who was married to Paul C. Wilson, took office as Secretary of Labor under Franklin D. Roosevelt, the order had been rescinded.)

A Changing National Woman's Party

The suffrage movement provided an environment that kept women with very different interests together, but the split in tactics between the National American Woman Suffrage Association and the National Woman's Party at the time of World War I was reflective of a difference in ideology. The NAWSA was the more conservative organization and supported the war; the National Woman's Party was militant and dedicated solely to suffrage. Its focus on that single issue kept it open to socialists and pacifists during World War I, attracting many socialist feminists who opposed war, while the NAWSA was excluding them from its platforms. This gave women of widely differing political persuasions a place to go within the suffrage movement.

After the war, however, the left came to dislike this same single emphasis of the National Woman's Party on feminism. With the founding of the Communist Party in 1919, feminism was considered to be a "reformist" tendency by CP members and gradually fell out of favor with the left in general. Barbara Deckard tells us that the National Woman's Party had only 8,000 members by 1923, "down from 50,000 in 1920."[8]

Two things that happened in 1920 affected the legal status of women. The passing of the Nineteenth Amendment gave them the right to vote, and the Department of Labor established a special bureau devoted to the "interests" of working women. Its predecessor had been a wartime agency, the Women's Division of the Ordnance Department, which dealt with women workers in munitions plants, and became, in June 1918, the Woman in Industry Service of the Department of Labor. Mary Anderson, who was the head of the Woman in Industry Service in 1919, became the first director of the Women's Bureau in 1920.

Judith Hole and Ellen Levine write, "In 1920 the Women's Bureau was established and, among other things, became central in the continuing drive during the subsequent decades for protective laws for women. The Women's Bureau and the organized labor movement worked in concert around this issue."[9]

Many idealistic socialists had been supporting such legislation for years, as had some working women and women's rights advocates, but the National Woman's Party did not. According to Hole and Levine, the Party considered disbanding after the vote was won.

> After a series of meetings with an organization called Wage Earning Women, however, the Woman's Party became convinced that the 19th Amendment, limited to voting rights, was not sufficient to correct the social and economic inequalities between men and women written into

the law. Therefore, in 1921, the group reorganized as a permanent body to work for the removal of all legal distinctions based on sex.

The group directed its initial political efforts on the state level. . . . However, the time and expense involved in a state-by-state campaign were prohibitive. . . .

In 1923, at the 75th anniversary conference of the Seneca Falls Convention, the Woman's Party decided to turn its efforts to the national level and lobby for constitutional reform. The group drafted an equal rights amendment. . . .

Shortly after the Amendment was first introduced, the Woman's Party locked horns with the Women's Bureau (established under the Department of Labor in 1920), primarily over the Amendment's potential impact on protective legislation. For over forty years, the Woman's Party and the Bureau fought bitterly."[10]

The first constitutional amendment considered by the National Woman's Party was as follows: "No political, civil or legal disabilities or inequalities on account of sex, or on account of marriage unless applying alike to both sexes, shall exist within the United States or any place subject to their jurisdiction."[11]

Florence Kelley, director of the National Consumer's League, which had been promoting state regulation of working conditions for years, asked Alice Paul to remove the words *civil* and *legal* and also asked her not to propose the amendment until a way could be found to safeguard protective labor legislation. Alice Paul refused, saying the amendment had gone through twenty-six drafts, and she saw no wording that could not be applied against such legislation. By February 1922 another wording was introduced at the meeting of the National Woman's Party Executive Council: "Equality of the sexes shall not be denied or abridged on account of sex and marriage,"[12] and the position of the Party was hardening into a positive opposition to protective laws. Finally, the language adopted officially was: "Men and women shall have equal rights throughout the United States and every place subject to its jurisdiction."[13] This was the wording that was introduced in Congress on December 10, 1923.

Nancy Cott summarizes the National Woman's Party position thus.

In its emphasis on the "human" outlook and its aim for women no longer to face discrimination through special treatment, the NWP upheld an essential legacy of feminism. But . . . the NWP position on sex-based labor legislation also sounded suspiciously like a laissez-faire ideology which would overlook industrial exploitation and oppose any state regulation of the employer-employee relation. The NWP took the language of liberal individualism to express its feminism.[14]

There was some suspicion of the National Woman's Party because it never mounted campaigns to extend existing protective labor legislation to men, which the wording of the amendment it supported would supposedly allow. Although a number of women's groups and clubs continued to exist, the group that succeeded the NAWSA, the League of Women Voters, did not support an Equal Rights Amendment, instead taking the position that women had won their rights when they won the vote. The League preferred to try to organize women in support of many issues that it had been supposed, in the late nineteenth century, women would support: the abolition of child labor, protective labor legislation, pacifism, and the general political reform of ward politics. As a result, says Barbara Deckard, "Whereas NAWSA had about 2 million members in 1920, the League of Women Voters was down to about 100,000 by 1923."[15] The Women's Trade Union League and the National Consumer's League died off in the 1920s, and the women's associations that did survive tended not to be primarily political or even to emphasize feminism: the General Federation of Women's Clubs, the DAR, the YWCA, the American Association of University Women, and professional associations of women who had been excluded from primary professional associations, such as the Women's National Book Association, formed in 1917 by a group of fifteen women booksellers who had been refused membership in the Booksellers League.

Even though there was less and less support for it, the National Woman's Party was able to get its Equal Rights Amendment introduced in every Congress from 1923 on. In 1931, the Senate held hearings on it. The National Woman's Party, says Barbara Deckard,

> argued that the ERA is necessary because of discrimination against women in wages, employment, education, and numerous laws. It listed at least 1000 discriminatory state laws, including laws in 11 states giving control over a wife's wages to her husband, laws in 16 states forbidding a wife to make a contract, laws in 20 states barring women from jury service, and a law in Minnesota allowing a husband—but not a wife—to collect damages from a lover for adultery![16]

This was at the height of the Depression, when there was great pressure on women to "solve" the unemployment problem by going back to the home and stop taking jobs away from men.

Meanwhile, the National Woman's Party continued to introduce an Equal Rights Amendment in Congress after Congress, but it never came to a vote until 1946, when it failed to gain the required two-thirds majority in the Senate but did get a simple majority. Just as there was support for woman suffrage after World War I in recognition of the work women had done during the war, there was support for an Equal Rights Amendment after World War II in both major parties. It was still opposed by the Women's Bureau, however, because of the effect it would have on protective labor legislation, and was also opposed by a number of prominent women in politics, especially by Eleanor Roosevelt.

The Triumph of Social Feminism

In 1950 and 1953 the proposed ERA was amended, to include a rider that would leave protective legislation intact by providing that the amendment "shall not be construed to impair any rights, benefits, or exemptions now or hereafter conferred by law upon persons of the female sex." In this form it passed the Senate in 1950 and 1953 but was not acceptable to the National Woman's Party, which helped to keep it from coming to a vote in the House. It was rumored that the rider was adopted largely at the urging of Eleanor Roosevelt.

The Lucy Stone League persisted through the 1950s, although it changed its bylaws along the way. A suggested wording sent to members was:

> The original object of this League to encourage those women who wish to continue their own names after marriage has been broadened to include activities to safeguard and extend all civil, legal, social and political rights of women in the fields of professional, commercial and labor occupations; property rights; family responsibilities; jury duty and other activities which limit and discriminate against women in their status as full citizens.

The League also had a committee in the late fifties that awarded scholarships to young women. At first there was just one scholarship to go to Lucy Stone's alma mater, Oberlin College, but later the League was able to add a scholarship to the Wharton School of the University of Pennsylvania and one to Mount Holyoke.

In 1961 President John F. Kennedy appointed a Commission on the Status of Women, chaired by Eleanor Roosevelt, which decided not to support the ERA but instead, in the words of Mary Dublin Keyserling, former director of the Women's Bureau and a consistent ERA foe, "counseled that we seek amendments of state laws to extend benefits now applicable only to women to men as well."[17]

This was the conventional liberal (as opposed to classical liberal) philosophy of the time—government regulation of working conditions was an unmitigated good and was the only way to get powerful private business interests to modify their pursuit of profit in order to benefit the working class. Early labor union leaders such as Samuel Gompers of the A.F. of L. had opposed the regulation of the hours, pay, and workplace conditions of male workers by government, holding that they should be determined by collective bargaining. Such a position at least allowed a majority of the workers to decide whether having a certain number of jobs available to them was of more value than having the wages allotted to some of those jobs spent instead on certain benefits or improved working conditions for those who were hired. After the courts approved the Fair Labor Standards Act in 1941, however, legislation of working conditions for men as well as women was constitutionally permitted and became routine. But special legislation for women was still being pushed by the Women's Bureau and supported by labor unions.

There was so little vocal allegiance to feminism that historians were able to overlook its strong upsurge in the 1920s and to assume that all interest in it had ended in 1920 with the passing of the Nineteenth Amendment. Barbara Deckard has a chapter in *The Women's Movement* called "Forty Years in the Desert: American Women, 1920–1960." Supporters of the Equal Rights Amendment had become a classical liberal remnant within the National Woman's Party.

And supporters of the right to keep your own name had become a classical liberal remnant within the Lucy Stone League. Its original intention had become so little known by 1958 that the head of the Scholarship Committee had to write to the Dean of Women at Oberlin that "Lucy Stone *never* used the form 'Mrs. Henry Blackwell,' " and it should therefore not be used in publicity for the scholarship!

It looked as if the feminist heritage had been completely forgotten. But, in just a few years, feminism was due to be reborn. In the early sixties, Betty Friedan's *The Feminine Mystique* was published (1963), women were included in the Civil Rights Act of 1964 (as a joke by southern senators, says Friedan), and the National Organization for Women (NOW) was formed in 1966. There was going to be a feminist movement again, and equality before the law was about to become a national issue. But first there was a movement called consciousness raising.

CHAPTER FIVE

What Does a Woman Want?

The strongest impact of contemporary feminism has been social, not political. Feminism has changed commonly accepted social expectations as well as the behavior and relationships of individuals. When it came upon the scene in the late sixties, it was an idea whose time had come.

What does the concept of "an idea whose time has come" really mean? I think it means that an ideal of behavior becomes widespread at a time when social and economic conditions allow behaving that way. The idea that woman's fulfillment does not come from motherhood or marriage but from her individual actions, goals, and purposes could not change society until it was articulated in an economic and political context in which such actions, goals, and purposes were possible. When John Stuart Mill wrote about this idea in 1869, only a small fraction of privileged women could manage to educate themselves, and only a smaller fraction could find a congenial circle of like thinkers willing to talk to them.

Authorship has been the first refuge of a liberated woman for some centuries now. It takes little or no capital investment, can be done in solitude, can be combined with many other life activities, can be easily hidden (Jane Austen supposedly covered her novel-in-progress with a piece of needlework when friends or family stopped by), and, if the climate is really uncongenial to women, can still find an audience under a masculine pseudonym. Consider the great nineteenth-century woman novelists: Charlotte and Emily Brontë had *Jane Eyre* and *Wuthering Heights* accepted by publishers who assumed that these books' authors, Currer Bell and Ellis Bell, were men; Mary Ann Evans made her pen name, George Eliot, so famous that few readers remember her real name today.

Published writing is also a form of advertisement that can attract whatever kindred spirits exist to form a community of sorts. It was a long, hard process by which women writers and then women speakers converted men and women to the cause of equal rights in principle, during the nineteenth century; it was another long hard process by which legal and social barriers to professional education and employment were breached enough to make careers other than writing open to women. *Work* has always been open to women, but it was usually marginal and low paid: domestic work, work in factories, unpaid work in the home or on the farm, and, of course, prostitution.

It was the work involved in the most productive and prestigious life of the community that women had to pry open.

After World War II

Women had made a lot more progress by the 1950s than appeared on the surface. Although many social institutions had conjoined in sending most (but not all) women back to the home after their explosive entry into the work force during World War II, these institutions were not all completely closed to women; they merely didn't expect very many women to be interested in anything outside the home. The Army and state universities and law and medical schools had quotas for women, but at least that meant that some women were able to get in. Employers generally didn't expect women to be serious about their jobs, but there were always some exceptions. Also, it made a difference that the United States was an industrialized, capitalistic economy in which the customer was always right. Where there was a strong demand, sooner or later someone would supply it.

So when, as a result of social and economic changes, large numbers of women decided to change their lives in the sixties and early seventies, it was relatively easy for them to make a social revolution. Entry level jobs opened up for educated articulate women willing to work for little more than what they needed for child care and carfare. Training courses became available for women whose education had been interrupted by marriage. Peripheral household services became more available as less time was spent at home by the lady of the house.

If people believe things that are not so about their lives, sooner or later reality will make at least partial converts of them. When a woman's well-being was defined by her being a mother, that was an incentive for her to have a number of children so that she could continue in that occupation over the years. A woman on the frontier found having many children was also an economic asset—they helped bring in the crops and do the many tasks of the household. The entire family was a productive economic unit. But when the frontier closed, when children no longer produced economic assets but consumed them, and when urban child rearing, spacious housing, and education were all becoming more and more expensive, there was a contradictory incentive to have fewer children. So women did. This meant, however, that instead of being in charge of a home that was a productive economic unit, a woman was now in charge of consumption and a term of child rearing that was only a fraction of her life expectancy. Even her husband wondered disparagingly what she did all day.

For many women who tried valiantly to be "creative" homemakers after World War II, this life turned out not to be satisfying. They knew they were unhappy, but they couldn't make the imaginative leap that would allow them to see themselves changing their lives in a way that would be both meaningful and, at the same time, preserve what they valued in the situation they had. They couldn't visualize it, so they couldn't do it.

What helped many of them to start to do it was a process that, ironically, was developed primarily by a very small group of left-wing Marxist women who had been trained in the New Left Student Movement, but who had not been allowed to be "creative" there.

Consciousness Raising

The men of the New Left had generally treated women as sex objects and servants, a treatment that was all the more galling because the women in question were generally student colleagues who were their social, educational, and intellectual equals. New Left women finally began to get together in "rap groups" to talk about their anger, and these sessions gradually began to range over their entire lives and experiences in a process they called *consciousness raising*. In the words of Barbara Deckard,

> The male Left ridiculed women's problems as trivial and CR groups as bourgeois therapy. Feminists countered that CR was highly political because it aimed at fundamental change, not at adjustment. Theory and analysis, if it is to be valuable as a guide to action, must stem from personal feelings and experiences. In a CR group, women discuss their own feelings and experiences. In discussing how similar these are from woman to woman, women discover the political nature of their problems. The individual woman learns that she is not a misfit, a kook, or sick but rather that society is sick.[1]

Gradually, for a number of these women, their socialism and their feminism came into conflict. They split off from the New Left, and called themselves radical feminists rather than socialist feminists, because they felt that sexism and sexist oppression were more fundamental than economic exploitation in explaining social injustice. They wanted a feminist analysis of social problems, focusing on male dominance and emphasizing personal change as political, instead of calling for the usual forms of political action.

One such group, the New York Radical Women, developed the consciousness-raising technique and presented a paper about it as part of a debate between socialists and feminists at a national women's conference held in Chicago in 1968. The technique was further developed by the Redstockings, an offshoot of the New York Radical Women that was founded in 1969. The Redstockings were formed to take militant political action, but became so involved in consciousness raising that they ultimately did little else. But then a new group, the New York Radical Feminists, set up hundreds of consciousness-raising groups in New York City, offering guidelines for discussion and acting as a sort of clearing house for women who wanted to find other interested women in their own neighborhoods.

There was a communist revolutionary precedent for consciousness raising. Leah Fritz's *Dreamers and Dealers* says the technique has several origins and lists

> the practice, developed by women in China in the 1940s, of "speaking pain," that is, of getting together in groups to bear witness against the oppression by the men who ruled over them, usually their husbands. The Chinese male revolutionaries, assuming the oppression of women was a problem of capitalism, approved of this practice as a good tool for organizing women against the system. Variations on "speaking pain" were later used by Che Guevara to organize peasants, both male and female, in Latin America, and by the Student Nonviolent Coordinating Committee in the United States in the 1960s.
>
> Other precedents for consciousness-raising, as it is practiced by feminists today, might include Quaker meetings . . . and group psychotherapy.[2]

But because of the nature and structure of consciousness raising, it was a technique that couldn't be ideologically controlled. It spread to all corners of the movement, and feminism became grassroots. Small-town housewives picked it up from magazine articles and books. By 1972 the establishment of consciousness-raising groups was a primary objective of NOW, and within a year NOW had brought together an estimated 100,000 women into groups all over the country. One was described in the *New York Times Magazine* by Anita Shreve in 1986.

> Every Tuesday night they divulged their thoughts, feelings and fears about issues prescribed by NOW as being pertinent to consciousness-raising:

body image, first sexual encounters, marriage, sexism in the work place, aging, abortion, to name a few. . . . A topic from the prepared list was selected for each meeting; topics were also introduced by the women themselves. Each woman was allowed "free space" to talk for as long as she liked, without interruption. Women who were by nature reticent, therefore had as much opportunity to speak as women who were inclined to run the show.[3]

The women in this particular group all eventually became high-profile women: a pianist, a restaurant owner, a research scientist, an opera singer, and an actress. Other groups were formed by women with less glamorous lives: office workers in particular companies or high-school and college students. Barbara Deckard describes a working-class group in the East Flatbush section of Brooklyn that Susan Jacoby observed for the Riverside (California) *Press-Enterprise* in 1973.

The women are in their forties; most graduated from high school, married soon thereafter, and quickly had children. . . . Following the advice they got from a copy of *Ms.,* the women decided on regular weekly meetings, agreeing that only a true emergency would be allowed to interfere. . . .

Many of the women had joined because, with their children grown, they saw 20 or 30 empty years ahead of them with little idea how to fill them. The groups gave some the confidence to try something new. Ruth Levine, who had never held a job, became the first to begin working. Lacking training, she became a file clerk in an advertising agency; but for her this opened the door to a whole new world. . . . Initially opposed, her husband, a taxidriver, has gradually begun to cut down on his 14-hour workday. They spend more time together and their sex life has improved. . . .

A year after its founding, the group will take in five new members to replace those who have dropped out because they are too busy with jobs and college courses. "All of the women call that progress," Susan Jacoby reports.[4]

This kind of consciousness raising was the individualist heart of the Women's Movement that began in the late 1960s. I myself joined such a group in a small town in western Massachusetts in 1972. It was an exciting experience.

Women from three nearby towns had decided they would like to explore Women's Liberation and each other. They were divided, at their first meeting, as to whether they wanted to form a politically active group or a consciousness-raising group, and so for a while they decided to form two groups. It then developed that Group A, dedicated to political action, spent its time discussing books and personal experiences. The members of Group B, committed to consciousness raising, became very restless because they felt that they should *do something*. Finally, remnants of both groups met jointly and coalesced into a single consciousness-raising group at the end of January.

The group grew so fast that it was hard for us all to fit into an ordinary living room. (In February it spun off a related group: some husbands, including mine, and close male friends formed a men's group.) After a long time and a number of meetings with varied personnel, a core group of six or seven (the seventh was from a neighboring town) coalesced; all were women with children, some with husbands, some without. We had grown up in different parts of the country (one of us was born in Cuba) and had different religious upbringings; some were from large families, some from small; some rich, some poor.

We got together in each other's houses once a week to talk. We talked about ourselves, how we felt about our jobs, our houses, our husbands, our children, and our life decisions. Sometimes we discussed books and articles about what impact being female had on our lives. We talked about marriage, bringing up children, and housework (one of the best suggestions was that we should all get together and clean each others' houses, but we never did implement that one). And we talked about possible new ways of living.

We found out more than how similar our experiences had been. We found that we had all made similar *assumptions* about our limitations and about what was expected of us. In other words, although some of us might have experienced discrimination or sexism, far more pervasive and disturbing was the way in which we had internalized what society expected of us.

One of us, later to become a minister, found it hard to remember why she had dropped out of theological school (within months of graduation) when she became pregnant, even though her husband encouraged her to stay and get her degree. No one besides her husband, however, no teacher, no advisor, no relative, gave her similar encouragement. They all said, "You mustn't miss a moment of this glorious experience of having a baby," and she had listened to them.

Another of us had a great deal of concern about marrying a younger man. (She is happily married to him now, about twenty years later.) Another had difficulty in leaving an abusive husband. I myself had a lot of conflict with my mother and found a new perspective in looking at her as a "sister"— that is, a woman who had needed to cope with some of the same problems we were all identifying—as well as a mother.

There wasn't any one concrete issue on which we all agreed. Not the right to abortion. Not whether it was right to be both a working woman and a mother. Not whether child-care centers should be provided by government. Not whether Freud's influence had helped women or hurt them. Clearly it was the talking, the questioning, the realization of how many assumptions we had never questioned before that was valuable and kept us coming back, week after week.

An unsigned article in *Women: Berkshire Women's Liberation Newsletter,* described an eleven-member group that decided not to accept any more members this way:

> Our first experience together was one of relief, comfort, and a sense of community—almost unanimously acknowledged as a very pleasant beginning. We recognized that none of us had been able to feel a sense of "sisterhood" in groups of this size before. We recalled what mixed blessings real sisters sometimes can be, and how often we felt alienated from more traditional women's groups in churches, schools, etc. . . .
>
> Many of us are bothered by the name "women's liberation," but we are certainly interested in building on our common experiences as women. It's going to take more than just a few weeks to make sense of such concepts as "oppression" and "victimization." . . . There are many unspoken and unanswered questions about what we are looking for in our personal lives.[5]

There was a surprising spectrum of support for consciousness raising. Ursula Niebuhr, the widow of the Protestant theologian Reinhold Niebuhr and a professor of religion in her own right, wrote a letter to the *Berkshire Eagle* (Pittsfield, Mass.) in the midseventies, protesting that she had been misquoted in a newspaper story so as to appear hostile to the women's movement. "I am both a believer in and supporter of the women's movement . . ." she wrote.

> The purpose of consciousness-raising groups, or sensitivity sessions, is for people of common concern to come together to share problems and insights. There is—and must be—mutual trust, as well as interest in each other as individuals and as egos.
>
> Such groups have of course also existed in other milieux, as in the religious world. The Christian fellowship of the early church was to be a true community (*Koinonia*). . . .
>
> Today, groups in the women's movement exist for those deprived of voice and status even in the Christian community. Consciousness-raising groups "build up, stimulate and encourage" our sisters. Had this happened earlier, many women would have felt neither so frustrated, nor lonely nor isolated from their own kind.

Activists (whether radical or liberal) hoped, of course, that consciousness raising would lead to political organization and action, but often the action taken was to change one's own life. Ronnie Feit, a lawyer who was the coordinator of the organizing conference of the National Women's Political Caucus in 1971 and in 1979 was the Executive Director of the Interagency Committee on Women's Business Enterprise in the Carter Administration, wrote,

> Feminists showed women that much of what they blamed themselves for as due to character or personality defects was the result of societal conditions and structures. The women's movement is based on the famous "click" of perception that something happening to an individual woman has to do with her being a woman and not with her individual being.[6]

The reference is to a famous 1972 article that appeared in the Preview Issue of *Ms.,* "The Housewife's Moment of Truth," by Jane O'Reilly. In it, O'Reilly makes a case for the importance of women freeing themselves from the sole responsibility for housework. She starts by gathering together a number of instances of women being looked at as "housewives" rather than as persons who may have a variety of interests and important things to do. Their sudden realizations of their status are symbolized by "Click!"

> Last summer I got a letter, from a man who wrote: "I do not agree with your last article, and I am cancelling my wife's subscription." The next day I got a letter from his wife saying, "*I* am not cancelling *my* subscription." Click! . . .
>   In New York last fall, my neighbors—named Jones—had a couple named Smith over for dinner. Mr. Smith kept telling his wife to get up and help Mrs. Jones. Click! Click! Two women radicalized at once. . . .
>   In an office, a political columnist, male, was waiting to see the editor-in-chief. Leaning against a doorway, the columnist turned to the first woman he saw and said, "Listen, call Barry Brown and tell him I'll be late." Click! It wasn't because she happened to be an editor herself that she refused to make the call.[7]

O'Reilly's article hit a nerve and rapidly entered the feminist lexicon. Surprisingly, all over the United States—to some extent all over the world— women who had seemed to be extraordinarily different found, through feminism, that they were not so different after all. Not that disagreements, even fights, didn't occur between members of consciousness-raising groups; they did. But women became intoxicated with the idea of remaking their lives and supported each other in doing it. Suddenly, the housewife who had been so isolated in her suburban home, when her children went to school and her husband went to the office, was no longer alone.

Consciousness raising persisted for a good ten or fifteen years. By 1979 my Berkshire consciousness-raising group had dwindled down to a hardcore five members, and we behaved in many ways like an extended family, bringing our husbands and children to celebrate holidays together. In April of 1979, my husband suddenly died of a heart attack just as we were about to move across the country because I had accepted a job on the *Libertarian Review* in San Francisco. I went alone, ten days after his death ended a twenty-year marriage, to a new job in a strange city.

What made the transition possible for me was my connecting almost immediately with three women's groups. One was a consciousness-raising group of libertarian women, all of whom were younger than I. Another held periodic meetings in the house of Louise Lacey, the editor of a newsletter called *Woman's Choice,* at which a single topic was discussed (Depression, Competition); the discussion was then recorded, transcribed, edited, and published.

There was also a professional networking organization called Women's Success Teams, which had been originated by Barbara Sher, coauthor of *Wishcraft,* on the East Coast. For a fee, this organization provided me with a seminar on setting goals and developing action plans, a follow-up support team to join, a computerized network of contacts, and a newsletter. The support teams were much more structured than consciousness-raising groups. We met in a different home each week and rotated the role of "facilitator," who not only ran the meeting but kept notes in the team notebook, which had a section for each member. A timer was used to ensure equal time for each member, and the meeting was to last exactly two hours. We were urged to be sure to begin and end on time.

Through these three groups, I met a wide cross section of women in my new city and was plunged into intimate conversation with them. I was told where to shop and eat and go for recreation. I was given furniture for my new home. I had people giving me advice on career goals and libertarian activism and how to cope with depression. I had a community. No, I had three communities, each with a different emphasis. The people in my office were helpful and friendly, and I soon made a number of friends among my colleagues there, but the sense I had from the women's groups of being rooted in the larger life of the community was invaluable.

The communication between women that consciousness raising had started may have been changing over the years, but it had not been broken. And the emphasis on remaking one's life went on. It had become clear that just getting a job and talking to one's family about helping with the chores was not salvation. In 1981, two books came out that explored some of the problems that still existed. They were *The Cinderella Complex,* by Colette Dowling, and *The Second Stage,* by Betty Friedan.

Emphasis on Self-Responsibility

Women had discovered that they faced similar problems and were treated in similar ways. They also discovered that if "society" had certain false attitudes and norms about what women wanted and what abilities they had, women themselves had internalized these same attitudes. *The Cinderella Complex* was written by a self-professed feminist who was appalled to discover her own psychological dependency, and she spent several years interviewing women around the country, finding that many of them, too, had a deep-seated desire to have others make decisions for them. She concluded,

> We have only one real shot at "liberation," and that is to emancipate ourselves from within. *It is the thesis of this book that personal, psychological dependency—the deep wish to be taken care of by others—is the chief force holding women down today. . . . Like Cinderella, women today are still waiting for something external to transform their lives.* (Emphasis in original)[8]

Many feminist reviewers criticized the book for emphasizing psychological dynamics rather than external factors such as discrimination in the labor market. Despite this the book became a best-seller and was translated into ten languages. A lot of women in consciousness raising had apparently also realized that they had internalized some of the attitudes that they deplored.

Betty Friedan's *The Second Stage* was also given a hard time by some feminist reviewers. The first feminists, she says, were fighting to escape from the feminine mystique, but in 1981 there was another malaise, this time inside the feminist movement—an antifamily "feminist mystique," which said that the women's movement was for women alone. That phase, says Friedan, is over. Now it is time for the second stage of liberation.

> *The second stage cannot be seen in terms of women alone, our separate personhood or equality with men.*
> *The second stage involves coming to new terms with the family— new terms with love and with work.*
> *The second stage may not even be a women's movement. Men may be at the cutting edge of the second stage.*

The second stage has to transcend the battle for equal power in institutions. The second stage will restructure institutions and transform the nature of power itself.

The second stage may even now be evolving, out of or even aside from what we have thought of as our battle. . . .

I and other feminists dread to admit or discuss out loud these troubling symptoms because the women's movement has, in fact, been the source and focus of so much of our own energy and strength and security, its root and support, for so many years. (Emphasis in original)[9]

Friedan believes that the enemies of feminism who see it as a movement to destroy the family as well as those feminists who are still separatist and radical are reactive, and she holds that each position denies a truth about human nature. People need work *and* relationships. She discusses studies that have found that women cannot be easily divided into supporters of feminism or supporters of the family—perhaps a majority of women are both. One 1979 study in Michigan, for instance, in which white mothers between the ages of 28 and 45 were interviewed, reported that "None of the women we spoke with subscribes completely to one ideology or the other; they all expressed some combination of the two, in their words and in their lives."

And Friedan concludes,

They were moving, with varying degrees of conscious feminism or individualism, into their own personhood with utmost concern for, and no conflict over, its foundation in the family. It is the same kind of political mistake for feminists to abandon the family to reaction as it was for liberals and radicals to abandon individualism to the right.[10]

The second stage, she says, is human liberation, a sex-role revolution.

Many feminists were appalled by what they saw as an abandonment of sexual politics on the part of one of the founders of the contemporary women's movement. But, of course, Friedan had never subscribed to separatism or radical feminism. In 1970 when a celebration took place in New York to mark the fiftieth anniversary of woman suffrage, Betty Friedan collaborated with songwriter Jacquelyn Reinach on a song, "Liberation Now," to be sung at the festivities in Bryant Park. The connection to the sound amplifying system was mysteriously broken (presumably by radical feminists) while the song was being sung, because it contained the words, "It's time for woman and man/To walk hand in hand."

It's not just radical feminists who deplore Friedan's idea of a sex-role revolution. Conservatives, too, often misunderstand the idea as implying either the death of romance, or an insistence that men and women be totally androgynous, or a denial that biological differences exist. On the contrary, questioning sex-*roles* is the way to find out, through experience, what biological differences there may be. All that a sex-role revolution implies is that *no one is required to take on a role he or she dislikes because it is supposed to be the masculine or the feminine thing to do.* The Man does not have always to appear to be strong, reasonable, or courageous— sometimes he can feel weak, or emotional, or afraid. And the Woman does not have always to be caring, understanding, or gentle. Experiences that came out of consciousness raising often reveal that the process *strengthened* marriage and romance. Susan Jacoby reports that many of the women she observed in Brooklyn had never discussed sex with their husbands until after they talked about it in the group. Anita Shreve quoted one of the five women in "The Group: 12 Years Later" as crediting feminism with saving her marriage, because she continually shared the insight she gained with her husband. " 'He was smart enough and insightful enough to listen to the issues and to see the justice. . . . My marriage has succeeded because of that—because he heard and he understood.' "[11]

If discussing what each person in a marriage *really* wants makes them understand each other better, romance is enhanced, not killed. What a sex-role revolution can do in a marriage is to make friends and partners out of people who were almost strangers and turn what were grudgingly accepted as duties into voluntary commitments.

Are Men Next?

Men are beginning to understand that sex-roles can hamper them, too. I mentioned that when I joined a consciousness-raising group in the seventies, my husband joined a men's group. He was ahead of his time. Now, in the nineties, poet Robert Bly has attracted national attention with his "Wildman" movement, aimed at helping men to get in touch with their inner wildman—a forceful, spontaneous, *emotional* being. In a *New York Times Magazine* article in October 1990, Trip Gabriel reports on one such meeting that he went to in the hills of North Texas. He speaks of "a loosely organized but rapidly growing phenomenon known as the men's movement" and estimates that 50,000 men have attended Wildman Gatherings, at which they drum and dance around bonfires and also speak to their absent fathers and weep. "The men's movement," according to Gabriel, "says it's not a reactionary response to feminism. Rather, it sees itself as a parallel development. While feminism has often dealt with politics and the outward conditions of women's lives, the men's movement is about internal issues, about men's psyches."[12] He seemed to echo Betty Friedan's view of the need for a sex-role revolution that includes men.

> What emerged in the testimonies of men was a deep confusion at having to live up to conventional expectations of masculinity. Men said they'd tried to be fearless, invulnerable, all-knowing. Their fathers and their culture had taught them this was the way to act manly. But no one had prepared them for real life, for the breakup of a marriage and the sadness they would be unable to express. . . .
>
> . . . What most men seem to want are more forums in which they can talk directly to one another, a kind of recovery program for victims of errant notions of masculinity, a sort of Men's Anonymous.[13]

Consciousness raising for women doesn't seem to be very big in the world today. Perhaps one reason is that as women moved into the Superwoman mode, trying to combine demanding jobs with family concerns, they didn't have as much time as they did in the seventies. Perhaps it's that feminism is no longer new, and women think they have nothing to learn from each other in this way. It is in some ways an expression of success, but in others, it's a loss. Consciousness raising formed a connection between many women that will never be broken.

A 1989 book by Anita Shreve, *Women Together, Women Alone: The Legacy of the Consciousness-Raising Movement,* is the result of interviews with sixty-five women who had been through the experience. Shreve recounts that all the women felt consciousness-raising had changed their lives for the better, and they missed the support of their groups but no longer had time to revive them. As a consequence, "isolation" was a feeling that they reported.

As women are abandoning consciousness raising, men are starting to see its value. But who knows? Women may take it up again. Anita Shreve reprints the New York Radical Feminists' description of consciousness raising in an appendix and suggests that readers may want to use it to form their own groups. When Alix Kates Shulman reviewed the book in the *New York Times Book Review,* she endorsed that suggestion, saying "assemble your friends, select a topic from the New York Radical Feminists' handout . . . or from Ms. Shreve's own loosely updated version in the afterword, form a circle and begin."[14]

CHAPTER SIX

The Workplace:
I'm Not a Woman's Libber, But

The exodus of women from the home changed the face of American society. In an astonishingly short period of time, we became a society that asks women, "What do you do?" before asking "Are you married?" In 1960 only 19 percent of American married women with children were in the labor force. By 1970 the figure was 28 percent. By 1986, not only was a majority of women with children in the labor force, but a majority with children as young as one year old; the percentage of all American women in paid employment rose from 35 percent in 1960 to 55 percent in 1986.

Where They Went

Where did all those housewives go when they left the home? We saw in the last chapter that a lot of women took entry-level jobs; others were breaking new ground, as the world of work began changing, too. Old assumptions that certain occupations could and should be closed to women, and that others should be closed to married women because they didn't need the jobs as much as men did, were strongly questioned. Some of the barriers were legal, and some social; some were the legally enforced policies of organizations like unions, but they all came into question.

In 1973 the first officially recognized woman miner was hired in West Virginia.[1] Local 659 of the International Photographers Guild admitted Brianne Murphy as its first woman member in the same year. (By 1986, according to *TV Guide,* she was still the only female director of photography in the union.)[2] Women became telephone installers, bus drivers, real estate developers, accountants, bartenders, construction engineers, motion picture directors, presidents of colleges, firefighters, and members of police forces. (Elizabeth Watson, who became Houston's first female police chief in 1990, said that when "she joined the Houston police department 17 years ago, she was handed a dress pattern and told to sew her own uniform."[3]) In 1985 the Cherokee Indians installed Wilma P. Mankiller as the first woman chief of a major American Indian tribe.[4] And women were entering the prestigious professions in increasing numbers. Dr. Perri Klass wrote in the *New York Times Magazine* in 1988,

> In 1969, 9 percent of the first-year medical students in America were women; in 1987, it was 37 percent. In 1970, women accounted for 8 percent of all the physicians in America and 11 percent of all residents. In 1985, they made up 15 percent of all physicians and 26 percent of all residents.[5]

Women were going back to college to gain the education they needed in order to qualify for nontraditional jobs. Some universities, such as the University of Massachusetts, instituted "University Without Walls" programs that gave academic credit for "life experience," including job history. Pam Mendelsohn, author of *Happier by Degrees,* wrote in 1980 that "nearly 40 percent of the students in college these days are over the age of twenty-five. In California, the average age of students at public two-year colleges is twenty-six—and rising."[6] A 1982 front-page *Wall Street Journal* article by Sue Shellenbarger called the expanding ranks of working women "a transformation in society" and quoted the managing vice president of an executive-recruiting firm who estimated that "more than one-third of the 15 million women who joined the labor force since 1970 entered traditionally male-dominated fields."[7] Of course, this means that two-thirds of these women had entered female-dominated fields, but it was a large enough percentage to create a social revolution of sorts.

Changing Expectations

As early as 1979 Caroline Bird (author of *Born Female* and *The Two Paycheck Marriage*) gave an interview that was headlined, "Full-Time Homemaking Is Now 'Obsolete'."[8] Steve Curwood of the *Boston Globe* staff reported in 1983 on how women's expectations had changed.

> As recently as 1968, 62 percent of women aged 14 to 22 told researchers at Ohio State University they expected to be housewives at age 35. By 1979, just 20 percent of young women said they expected to be full-

time homemakers, and that proportion will likely continue to decline.

Many women say they want to work in the better-paying positions now dominated by men, and at least one study indicates that by the 1990s very few college-educated women will prefer a traditionally female job.[9]

In 1983 an article in the *Christian Science Monitor* discussed the Seven College Study, which had recently been done of 8,000 women at "seven of the most prestigious universities in America," in which *"only two women* out of those thousands surveyed plan to be full-time homemakers."[10] (emphasis added)

The expectation that one would automatically have children declined for a while, along with the expectation that one's career would be to get married. As reported on the front page of the *New York Times* in 1983, a 1970 Virginia Slims poll had "53 percent of the women surveyed" saying that motherhood was "one of the best parts of being a woman"; a *New York Times* 1983 poll found just 26 percent agreed with that statement.[11] I can still remember the shock I felt the first time I heard a newly married woman say casually at a party that she wasn't sure she wanted to have children; this happened sometime in the late sixties or early seventies.

Problems and Solutions

For those who still wanted to have children, a whole world of new concerns opened up: child care, flexible time, new roles and responsibilities for fathers.

When it became the exception and not the rule for a woman with children to stay home in order to care for them, young families faced a problem: who *would* care for the children? There were several alternatives: some sort of day care, some sort of live-in help, or some sort of change in the nature or timing of a woman's work (flexible time, job sharing, home office, entrepreneurship, alternating going to work and staying home). All of these required some sort of change in the nature of the father's work, too.

Day care seemed to many people to be an obvious solution. But provided by whom? Organizations like NOW called for federal financing, but as early as 1981 Betty Friedan's *Second Stage* warned that it was being "locked into the first stage" for feminists to propose "massive, federally financed child-care programs that imply more bureaucracies taking more money out of everyone's pocket and invading the final sphere of privacy, where women, and men, don't want to lose a sense of personal value, meaning and control."[12] She also pointed out that such programs were so expensive that they were impossible in a practical sense; a judgment that seems even more cogent ten years later.

So it seems to be up to private persons and organizations to fill the demand. Business began to see that providing child care could be profitable. In 1982 Sue Shellenbarger reported in the *Wall Street Journal* that an estimated "500 employers nationwide, perhaps double the number of two years ago" provided day-care assistance to employees.[13] By 1985, the *New York Times* reported, "About 2,000 corporations . . . now underwrite some form of child-care assistance," including some business giants like IBM and Proctor & Gamble.[14] By 1989, another *Times* story reported the number as "3,300 companies with more than 100 employees," and said that "half of all American companies are currently considering offering child-care benefits."[15]

The benefits offered range from on-site child-care centers (still, at this writing, a rare option), to off-site consortiums run by several companies in a downtown area, to information about existing local facilities coupled with cash subsidies for child care, to such things as sick leave to care for a sick child. A growing number of companies offer unpaid maternity leaves; a lesser number also offer paternity leaves to new fathers.

The business of child care has become so lucrative that there are now a number of chains of for-profit child-care centers plus a growing number of consulting firms that design family benefit programs for corporations. There also are state programs in which states work in partnership with industry. California in 1985 instituted the California Child Care Initiative to train day-care providers. Illinois had a two-year project to develop a statewide child-care referral network. Minnesota began awarding grants to individuals and companies who were starting day-care operations in 1988. Even some localities are supporting child care in various ways.

Many of these efforts were sparked by large companies that wanted to get government into the act. The 1989 *New York Times* article quoted above also quoted Rosemary Mans, a vice president at the BankAmerica Corporation who was instrumental in starting the California program, as saying, "If the private sector went ahead on its own, it would be seen as capable of solving the day-care problem on its own."[16]

But more and more employers *are* going ahead on their own, realizing that child-care assistance is a valued benefit that helps them recruit and keep employees. There is speculation that the growing number of women managers with children in American business has helped that realization.

High-income women are increasingly using another option—child care in the home by a housekeeper or nanny. In an attempt to professionalize the field, a group called Household Technicians of America suggests the use of a standardized contract to its members. There is also an American

Council of Nanny Schools, which by 1987 knew of one hundred nanny schools nationwide, as well as an International Nanny Association. But most "caregivers," as they like to be called, are immigrants, often illegal immigrants. A *Washington Post* column by Lynda S. Zengerle in 1982 complained bitterly that the Department of Labor demanded proof that a live-in housekeeper was a "business necessity" before issuing labor certification; "That is, the family hiring the alien must show work-related or extraordinary household conditions to justify their desire for live-in help." Similar documentation was not required, the author said, for taxi drivers, busboys, or parking-lot attendants. Ms. Zengerle concluded:

> Live-in help is, of course, not the answer for everyone. But for those who want it and can afford it, should Uncle Sam be able to say "Buy American or Do Without"?
>
> The last time I advertised for a housekeeper, I had *one* American respondent. Her first question: "How old do you have to be for the job?" I replied with an inquiry of my own, "How old are you?" Her answer: "I'm 12."
>
> I rest my case.[17]

The new immigration law in the mideighties didn't help this situation, with its threat of fines for hiring illegals, although now it is possible to sponsor a household worker for legal status under certain circumstances. The demand, however, far outreaches the legal supply.

Changing the Nature or Timing of Work

A number of companies have included more flexibility in working arrangements among the "child-care benefits" they offer. These include job sharing, part-time schedules, "flextime" and "telecommuting" programs, as well as time off to care for sick children. Some maternity leaves are as long as six months.

"Flextime" is short for flexible working hours. It was originally a program in which all employees were at work for a core period of hours in the middle of the day, but the beginning and ending times of the working day could be arranged to suit individual schedules. A mother who wanted to be home when her children got out of school might work from 7:00 A.M. to 3:00 P.M., while one who could not get child care early in the morning might work from 11:00 A.M. to 7:00 P.M.

The newest of these options for flexibility is "telecommuting," an option first explored by an innovative engineer for an insurance company in 1973.

People worked at home on computers instead of driving to work. In 1988 *Insight* magazine estimated that by the midnineties "as many as 15 million corporate employees could be working out of their homes."[18] The growing catalogue-shopping industry often hires home-based people to take incoming telephone orders, equipping them with company owned computers. In 1985 Pacific Bell began a work-at-home program for "some 100 engineers, analysts, public relations personnel and others at the managerial level."[19] Many working mothers work at home in this way for a period after their maternity leave is over, or they may use telecommuting to stay at home periodically, some on a scheduled basis.

A significant number of ambitious, professional women have recently begun to decide to take several years off from their careers and become full-time mothers for that period. In 1985 one such mother, Deborah Fallows, wrote a book called *A Mother's Work,* which was about her decision to do so. "Neither the women's movement nor the pro-family movement offers an adequate, or even honest prescription for mothers," she wrote. ". . . The women's movement, with which I sympathize much more than I do with the right, defines success in terms of professional achievement, thereby implicitly downgrading the idea that parents should care for their children themselves."[20] Fallows suggests a new approach to parenthood, emphasizing four points: the importance of parents caring for their own children if they can, a recognition that "the parenthood/ career balance" is the business of fathers as well as mothers, "practical protections" such as pension reform and enforcement of child-support orders to help women who stay home, and the importance of more quality day care. She also asks some "second stage" questions that, she complains, feminists are not asking:

> Why stay at home? How can I find satisfaction there? How does life at home fit with important things in my family's life or the fabric of a larger community? . . . The exhortations feminists direct at careerists— to bring out the best in themselves, to be responsible, independent, and strong—should also be issued as challenges to women at home."[21]

In January of 1989, the president of Catalyst, an organization that for several years had been actively researching women in the work force and advising companies on how to advance women's careers, put into words what had been happening and created a furor. Felice N. Schwartz wrote an article for the January-February issue of the *Harvard Business Review* called "Management Women and the New Facts of Life" in which she said that employing women costs companies more than employing men because of their high turnover in management positions and because of the interruption of women's careers when they have children. She suggested that companies should make efforts to identify two classes of women: "career-primary" women, who put their careers before family considerations, and the majority of working women, who put their families on an equal or even preferred basis with their careers. For these women, companies should plan even more for maternity, with greater flexibility and more day-care benefits, but should not count on them as heavily for advancement as they count on the career-primary women, who would be put on a fast track.

The track that the article suggested for the majority of women was immediately called the "mommy track." The *Harvard Business Review* received so many critical letters about this article that a selection of them was published in the Sunday *New York Times*. There, four women and one man agreed that the two-track idea was based on an old-fashioned concept of what business success required. Faith A. Wohl, director of a division of Du Pont, Deborah Biodolilio, a vice president of Apple Computer, and Michael Maccoby, president of the Maccoby Group, agreed that, in Ms. Wohl's words, "The workplace must be flexible enough to allow both men and women to balance work and family commitments as they choose, without artificial assumptions by employers." Betty Friedan also felt the mommy-track approach was based on an "obsolete model" of corporate life, but hoped the ensuing controversy would build support for parental leave legislation. (It didn't.) Nancy Evans, president and publisher of Doubleday & Company wrote,

> During the last few weeks of my pregnancy, we set up a fax machine at my house, brought in an assistant and held meetings at my home. There are ways of doing things so that business doesn't stop and women don't become exhausted. . . . Integrating family life and work isn't just good for people; it makes good business sense.[22]

And indeed several 1990 *New York Times* articles discovered trends in the business world that made it clear that analyzing corporate life was not quite as simple as mommy-track theorists might suggest. A January 28 article found companies keeping women on the fast track and promoting them, even though they worked part time. One on April 29 explored a discovery that a lot of companies were making—that many professional women cared more about career satisfaction and promotion than they did about family benefits. Finally, two articles, one on April 15 and one on December 16, discussed the new phenomenon of "temporary executives," both men and women, who prefer coming into companies as hands-on troubleshooters to carving out conventional corporate careers. Agencies in New York, San Francisco, even Stamford, Connecticut, have handled hundreds of such executives, paid them as much as $500 a day for several months, but hired them only to see a specific job through. These executives are willing to give up benefits, bonuses, and salary in exchange for the freedom of not having a regular job.

The "Glass Ceiling"

Although women were entering American business in droves (in 1979, 20 percent of the MBA graduates were women; by 1986 that number was 40 percent), they soon discovered that there was more to learn about the way American businesses were run than could be taught in school. Women found that, although they were recruited and hired as managerial employees and did subsequently advance within their companies, they seemed to hit what came to be called a "glass ceiling" above which they could not advance. Was this pure discrimination, or was it more complex?

As early as 1977, the book *Games Mother Never Taught You: Corporate Gamesmanship for Women* (which is still being read as a valuable resource), by Betty Lehan Harragan, set out the thesis that corporate advancement was based on two models that women had little experience with and therefore did not understand: team sports and military hierarchy. Some rules, which were not explicitly articulated because so many corporate men were so familiar with them, needed to be spelled out for women, because many of these rules wouldn't coincide with assumptions that most women were likely to make. Women expect loyalty and hard work to be rewarded, expect chain-of-command to matter less than the inherent justice of a complaint, expect office politics to be unimportant, and assume that avoiding mistakes is more important than quick decisions. All of these, assumptions, said Harragan, are wrong.[23]

This book was just one of a growing number of advice books, magazines (like *Executive Female* and *Working Woman*), and seminars for women in business. (As Barbara Ehrenreich wrote in a 1986 article in the *New Republic,* "The continuing boom in the advice industry is in itself an indication of some kind of trouble."[24]) Another adviser, Lawrence D. Schwimmer, who held seminars for businesswomen, said in a 1982 interview in *U.S. News & World Report* that women were less skilled at playing the corporate game, more apt to expect the business world to be fair, handicapped because they didn't participate in after-hours activities with "the boys," less willing to take risks, and too willing to push for affirmative action. "If management perceives you to be a boat rocker," he said, you may never get the opportunity to move up into the higher ranks. If they see you as a team player, there's a greater likelihood of their viewing you as a professional with a future at the top. If they see you as somebody who needs to get special help and consideration, there's a tendency for them not to view you as an equal.[25]

By the time of the Ehrenreich article, the advice to corporate women was, she wrote, becoming contradictory:

how to be more impersonal and masculine (*The Right Moves*) or more nurturing and intuitive (*Feminine Leadership*); how to assemble the standard skirted suited uniform (de rigueur until approximately 1982) or move beyond it for the softness and individuality of a dress; how to conquer stress or how to transform it into drive; how to repress the least hint of sexuality, or alternatively, how to "focus the increase in energy that derives from sexual excitement so that you are more productive on the job" (*Corporate Romance*). When we find so much contradictory advice, we must assume that much of it is not working.[26]

In 1986, too, Andrew Hacker's *New York Review of Books* article quoted a *Wall Street Journal* article on "The Glass Ceiling," which appeared earlier that year.

A *Wall Street Journal* supplement on corporate women cited the biggest obstacle to advancement: "Men at the top feel uncomfortable with women beside them." Forming friendships and offering advice take place informally in all-male preserves, notably golf courses and squash courts, not to mention clubs that exclude women. Nuances and humor draw on athletic allusions, mingled with sexual and military overtones. Women entering such circles cannot help sensing that they are seen as outsiders, if not out-and-out intruders.[27]

Taking the Clubs to Court

It's perhaps not surprising that, beginning in the mid-1980s, there was a concerted attack on men's clubs. It began with undergraduate clubs in Ivy League schools that had begun to admit women undergraduates. In 1986 one of Princeton's three all-male "eating clubs" decided to admit women, in the face of a sex-discrimination suit brought by a 1980 woman graduate. Also in 1986 a controversy arose in California over whether lawyers and judges should belong to private clubs that discriminate against women (or on the basis of race or religion), and the Supreme Court ruled that Rotary International could not oust chapters that decided to admit women. In February of 1987, the New York Court of Appeals upheld a New York City law that said clubs not "distinctly private" were subject to antidiscrimination statutes; under this legal pressure, by the end of 1988, the Century Association and the University Club had voted to admit women, as had the show-business-oriented Friars Club.

It was also becoming clear that it was more and more ridiculous for all-male clubs to have the rules they did about women on the premises, whether or not they admitted women as members. A year before the Friars Club admitted women as members, it decided to hire a woman decorator, Elaine Lewis, to redecorate its premises. When she showed up one morning for her first meeting, however, she was barred from the building (whose rules excluded women until 4:00 P.M.) and sent across the street to a coffee shop to wait for management to allow her in to do her job.

Similarly, when Vice President George Bush was first running for president, he was scheduled to speak at the Burning Tree Country Club outside of Washington, D.C. His appearance had to be postponed because Burning Tree would not admit the head of his Secret Service detail to inspect the premises, because that person was (you guessed it) a woman. Even though exclusionary policies were looking increasingly ridiculous by the beginning of the nineties, there are reasons why this practice should not be forbidden by law, as we will examine in a later chapter of this book.

Networking

It was in the seventies that women attempting to advance in the business world consciously tried to devise a substitute for the "old-boy networks" that operated in the world of private business clubs, athletic clubs, and informal contacts cultivated by male executives. It started with some very serious and high-level professional groups such as the New York Women's Forum, which was conceived of by Elinor Guggenheimer, a former New York City Commissioner of Consumer Affairs. A story on such groups in the "Style" section of the *New York Times* in 1979 said that among the 155 members of the forum at that time were Bess Myerson, Bella Abzug, Carol Bellamy, Barbara Walters, Erica Jong, the president of Marymount Manhattan College, an assistant vice president of Equitable Life Assurance, a special assistant to Governor Carey, a screenwriter, the chairman of Dell Publishing Company, a senior vice president of R. H. Macy & Co., a vice president of Johnson and Johnson, and the president of a department store. Other similar forums existed at the time in Los Angeles, San Francisco, Colorado, and North Carolina, all limited in membership and requiring sponsorship, like the best men's clubs.[28]

Anna Quindlen wrote an article for the *New York Times Magazine* in 1981, detailing a number of groups that she called "new girls' networks," with such diverse interests as the California Elected Women's Association, Women in Mining, the National Alliance of Homebased Working Women, and the New York-based Women's Media Group. "While many women say the usefulness of these networks will inevitably dwindle as younger women become more and more integrated into male groups and organizations," she wrote, "at the moment the all-female groups are thriving."[29] Quindlen also interviewed women who had the opportunity to join men's networks, as well as women's, who said that the one thing that was special about the women's networks was the support women gave each other.

Almost ten years later, in April 1991, the *Times* reported on the eleventh annual conference of the American Woman's Economic Development Corporation (AWED), held at the Jacob K. Javitz Convention Center in New York. There, "Networking seemed to be the order of the day," wrote Deirdre Fanning.

> Networking? Now there's a throwback to the early 1970's when working women buzzed with talk about relying on their connections. . . . Surely, some 20 years later, there should be new points of focus, new strategies, fresh points of concern.
>
> Yet the women at this conference seemed unanimous in their view that the importance of networking had not diminished.[30]

Consciousness raising may officially be no more, but networking has in many ways become its substitute for many business and professional women. And it has become a recognized resource. Groups like the Women's Forum are approached when companies are looking for women directors for their boards and political administrations are looking for women for appointed political office. Companies that in the early seventies might have spawned consciousness-raising groups now have company sponsored "women's groups," "women's action teams," and "women's management associations"—budgeted by management, which is coming to rely on such groups to recommend strategies to promote women.

Entrepreneurship

Still, there is one alternative that more and more women are choosing as the option to deal with both the glass ceiling and their family scheduling problems. That is, starting their own businesses. The American Woman's

Economic Development Corporation (AWED) is a national nonprofit organization dedicated to training entrepreneurial women, which held its first training group in 1977; by 1984 over 20,000 women had taken their courses. A 1986 article in *Inc.* said that women owned "more than a quarter of the nation's sole proprietorships" and were "starting new enterprises at more than three times the rate of men." But it quoted a woman who worked with AWED in St. Paul as saying, "Most of the women represented by the statistics are in microbusinesses that are going to stay small." The article continues,

> Mostly, these women are just trying to support themselves, to bring balance and flexibility to their lives in ways that the corporate world can't. And won't. They are out to redefine work, not to restructure the economy. What they are doing has much more to do with self-employment than enterprise.[31]

The National Association of Women Business Owners (NAWBO), founded in 1974, which had twenty-two chapters by 1984, urged the Congressional Women's Political Caucus in 1991 to support privatization of government functions, because it would "open up more opportunities for women-owned businesses and small businesses in general."[32] This organization has long been both oriented to the needs of its members and critical of goals that many feminists were adopting. In 1984 I interviewed Sharon Poindexter, the past president of NAWBO, on the subject of comparable worth, and she said that, although NAWBO had taken no official position on the issue, and some newer members supported the concept, "those of us who have been in business a lot longer realize that woman-owned firms are labor-intensive. Therefore it would just be a real untenable position."[33]

In February 1987, the magazine *Inc.* selected Betsy Tabac, a forty-four-year-old who had been active in the feminist movement before getting a master's degree in public administration and starting her "policy research and writing firm," Tabac & Associates, as its "Hottest Entrepreneur in America." The article said, "Tabac is the hottest just because she embodies so many of the characteristics and motives that typify this next generation of entrepreneurs," because she is a woman, because she uses technology for leverage, and because she started her business for the life it gives her. Says *Inc.,*

> A lifestyle entrepreneur . . . the new autonomy . . . the enterprise ethic . . . new wave . . . post industrial.
> By any name, the sizable group that Tabac represents are the hottest entrepreneurs of the year.[34]

The percentage and the rate of women-owned businesses have both increased since 1986.

The Daddy Track?

American business has realized that it needs an increasing number of women employees in management in order to continue to expand. This realization has changed the workplace in irrevocable ways, as we have seen. But male employees have changed their expectations, too. If women are finding that they are no longer willing to move from city to city at the drop of a hat or put in unlimited hours at the office, as men used to be expected to do, men are now bringing family obligations to office attention, too. The two-career family also means that sometimes it is the man who has to adjust to the demands of his wife's career.

A growing number of married women are being named as ambassadors to foreign governments; a Foreign Service training session for new ambassadorial couples in Washington in 1989 had six men in the diplomatic spouse training course, learning how to redecorate an embassy and pack and ship household belongings. Brandon Grove, director of the Foreign Service institute, was quoted by the *New York Times* in 1989 as saying that because this was the largest number of male spouses they had ever had to train, "we've asked some spouses who have had similar experiences to come in to meet with them and answer such questions as, 'What is it like to go into receptions very much behind your wife?' "[35]

Commuter marriages are on the rise (when one spouse relocates and the other is reluctant to), but when a couple decides to move together, it is no longer always the woman who will be what Deirdre Fanning of the *New York Times* calls "the trailing spouse." In one of her "Executive Life" columns she tells the story of Colette Murray, who agreed to move from Texas to be the newly appointed corporate vice president of philanthropy at the Henry Ford Health System in Detroit. "When Colette Murray was being wooed by her new employer," Fanning writes,

> a cocktail party was thrown for her and her husband, the Texas Tech athletic director. Included among the guests was a carefully assembled group of prominent Detroit business executives who had ties to sports organizations in the city.
>
> "This has given me a foundation to start off with when I come to Detroit looking for a job," Mr. Murray said. "The fact is, both people in a marriage work these days, and the organization that is recruiting one of them needs to see that both are happy."[36]

Gail Gregg did a long *New York Times Magazine* piece in 1986 on the balancing act that modern fathers often feel called upon to make. It starts with an anecdote about an investment banker and a magazine editor with one child. The investment banker decided to give up a potential six-figure income in order to spend more time with his family. Gregg quotes him as saying: "I told them I was happy with my title and salary but unhappy with the unpredictability of the hours. . . . The response was they gave me a better title and more money. They really didn't seem to understand what I was saying." So he left the job, and the senior partner told Gregg, "I wish I had him back."[37]

This article came out the day before the opening of a big Labor Department conference in Washington, D.C., on "Work and Family: Seeking a New Balance," for union officials, government managers, and corporate executives to explore how such issues affect both men and women. Men have been slower than women, says Gregg, to make family-related demands, "but employers now report that men increasingly are speaking out about their new home responsibilities."[38]

Do Women in Business Still Need Feminism?

The media are quick to pronounce that feminism is outgrown, unnecessary, or dead. But has everything changed so much, by 1991? Sexism hasn't ended, as the resignation of Dr. Frances K. Conley of Stanford Medical School in May 1991 attests. A highly acclaimed neurosurgeon who said she had endured what the *New York Times* called "a quarter-century of subtle sexism,"[39] including some uninvited fondling by male colleagues, she received more than three hundred letters of support from people who agreed with her (mostly women doctors and nurses). She later was persuaded to return to Stanford when the medical school made some changes.

Let's look at some polls and surveys. In 1983 when the *Christian Science Monitor* reported on the Seven College Study, it called the women surveyed

perhaps the best and brightest of the young, "postfeminist" generation: women who have grown up with a more complete sense of themselves as capable people, and don't carry the bitterness of the battle for equality. They do not see themselves as a minority group, nor as feminists.

"Feminism has a bad image," says study director Diana Zuckerman.[40]

That was in 1983. In 1988 a *New York Times* article quoted a number of young women around the country on their hopes and expectations. Two of them were planning a conference in Washington, "to get more women thinking about issues of career and children in the context of the women's movement. . . . They are calling it 'I'm Not a Feminist, but . . .' and plan to invite 500 young women from the East Coast."[41]

On August 20, 1989, the front page of the *New York Times* reported on its latest poll on the women's movement. The poll and its follow-up interviews found a major concern about balancing work and family. It found that 71 percent of women between the ages of eighteen and twenty-nine said the United States still needed "a strong women's movement to push for changes that benefit women." At the same time, "big majorities" of both men and women said "the women's movement had helped make all sorts of relationships between men and women more honest."[42]

So it seems that the vanishing women's movement keeps reappearing, year after year, just as "networking" does. First of all, the question of what feminism is and can be is more complex than the media usually allow. Does the fact that women are willing to be interested in frills and decorating and entertaining mean they are no longer feminists? Betty Rollin, NBC correspondent and author, doesn't think so. In a 1991 "Last Gasp" column for *New York Woman,* she writes:

> We were soldiers in the early days of the women's movement and we'll be in the reserves for life, but we don't have to wear the uniform any more or show off our medals. We know who we are and what we've done. And now we want to do some of that domestic stuff we fought against, because now that we don't *have* to do it, it's fun.

But its not just Betty Rollin and her generation of feminists who enjoy "domestic stuff." I think that the new feminists are right under the media's noses, hidden in the hearts of all those women—and their spouses—who are still trying to find the right individual balance between work and family, still finding glass ceilings and even sexism in the workplace, and wanting to talk to each other about it. They've got the game; there's no reason they shouldn't be proud of the name.

CHAPTER SEVEN

A Funny Thing Happened to Us on the Way to the ERA

It was a group of feminists from NOW, led by Wilma Scott Heide, who disrupted a session of the Subcommittee on Constitutional Amendments of the Senate Judiciary Committee in 1970 and demanded that the subcommittee hold immediate hearings on the Equal Rights Amendment. The hearings were held, chaired by Senator Birch Bayh, in May 1970—the first formal legislative testimony on the amendment since 1956. The wording of the amendment that had been submitted, a wording that had been first introduced in 1946, was as follows:

> Section 1. Equality of rights under the law shall not be denied or abridged by the United States or by any State on account of sex.
> Section 2. The Congress shall have the power to enforce, by appropriate legislation, the provisions of this article.
> Section 3. This amendment shall take effect two years after the date of ratification.

It should perhaps be pointed out that several parts of this amendment had become standard procedure for constitutional amendments. The enforcement section, giving Congress the power to enforce the amendment through legislation, had been included in amendments ever since Congress passed the Thirteenth Amendment to end slavery at the end of the Civil War. The postponement of when the amendment took effect was one year for the Eighteenth Amendment and until "the 15th day of October following the ratification" for the Twentieth Amendment. The joint resolution in which the amendment was submitted to the states had the provision that it should be "inoperative" unless it was ratified within seven years— a provision that had been in the text of amendments since the Eighteenth.

The amendment was needed, in the opinion of feminists, because the Supreme Court had ruled consistently that the Fourteenth Amendment did not apply to women, since at the time of its ratification, women had asked to be included and had been turned down. As I write this in 1991, the Court has still never stated unequivocally that it does.

There were three hearings before Congress voted to pass the ERA in 1972. Bayh's subcommittee reported favorably on the amendment on July 28, 1970. Senator Sam Ervin, an opponent of the amendment, chaired additional hearings before the full Senate Judiciary Committee the following September, and, after his committee's negative recommendation, the ERA, which had been previously passed by the House, failed to come to a vote in the Senate. In March and April of 1971, there was another House Judiciary Committee hearing, which ended in a favorable report, and the House passed the ERA again the following October 12, by a vote of 354 to 23. On March 22, 1972, the ERA also passed the Senate, by a vote of 84 to 8, and was sent to the states for ratification. Three-fourths of the state legislatures had to ratify the amendment by March 22, 1979. But they did not manage to do so.

What is the Legislative History?

Constitutional scholars take very seriously the *legislative history* of a law or an amendment to the Constitution—that is, what interpretive arguments were made consistently by the proponents of the legislation? They are generally considered to represent what was intended by those who framed it and by the majority that passed it. Also, dire predictions of the consequences of the legislation that were exhaustively argued by opponents but dismissed by proponents are considered to have been rejected, since a majority was not convinced by the arguments.

What did the members of Congress who passed the ERA think that its consequences would be? A reasonable guide would be the assumptions held in common by *every* legal expert who spoke either for or against the ERA in the various hearings.

First of all, and most important, every legal expert agreed with the statement made by Rep. Martha Griffiths in introducing the ERA on the floor of the House in 1970: "This amendment would restrict only government action and would not apply to purely private action." Legislators and lawyers and university professors stated this, and committee members made sure that nonexpert witnesses understood it.

Rep. Charles Wiggins, a member of the Judiciary Committee, stressed this point to a witness.

> *Wiggins:* I did not wish to interrupt your presentation, but I think it
> is generally true that there is discrimination in private employment. We
> all have to understand that, and that is not a matter that this amendment
> is addressed to.
> *Mrs. Faust:* You are absolutely right. Yes, I understand that, too.[1]

Even though all the legal experts who supported the ERA agreed that
it applied only to governments, many supporters also expressed commitment
to egalitarian legislation that *would* apply to private businesses. (This was
all happening between 1970 and 1972, remember, and the Civil Rights
Act of 1964 had already made private employment discrimination against
women illegal.) *No one who testified, either for or against the ERA, felt
that this amendment was necessary in order to enact such legislation.* On
the contrary, all supporters of the ERA saw any such goals as requiring
legislation unconnected to the ERA or its enforcement clause, and spoke
of amending already existing legislation in order to achieve them.

Another issue that all witnesses agreed on was that the ERA meant
that women as well as men would be subject to the draft. Some witnesses
deplored this possibility (notably Senator Ervin), some considered it only
fair, and there was an interesting third view, introduced as an objection
to the ERA by Professor Paul Freund of Harvard.

Professor Freund speculated,

> Actually as I have read the debates, the proponents are quite literal and,
> for example, acknowledge very freely that women would be subject to
> compulsory military service, though they add that the appropriateness
> of the particular branch of service would be left, of course, to be decided.
> . . . In effect *it might be a constitutional bar for practical purposes to
> future compulsory military service,* and some people might welcome that,
> but I think that is an issue that would be put before the appropriate
> committees of the Congress . . . and not be a conclusion that would be
> an almost unnoticed incident of the adoption of a constitutional amend-
> ment. (Emphasis added)[2]

In the House debate on the ERA on August 10, 1970, Rep. Griffiths
said that, although women would be subject to a draft, they would not
have to serve in ways for which they were not fitted any more than men
do. In her testimony before the Ervin Committee she added, "I myself
don't believe that in the immediate future they [women] would be drafted
because I think we are moving toward a volunteer army. The equal rights
amendment would only require that women be permitted to volunteer
on the same basis as men, and I assure you they do not now have such
rights."[3]

Another issue on which the intent of the framers was forcefully presented was the effect on rape laws. Ervin, who kept reading into the record definitions of "sex" that he insisted would confuse the Supreme Court, raised the possible nullification of rape laws as a problem. No one agreed with him. His suggestion was either ignored or emphatically denied by the other legal experts who testified. (Nevertheless, as we shall see, Ervin and his conservative supporters later found a way to use this and other arguments against the ERA.)

The issue of unisex toilets in public buildings and the sexual integration of prison facilities was not considered a serious problem, although it was later made much of in popular campaigns against the ERA. Law Professor Thomas I. Emerson said,

> Finally, it should be noted that the equal rights amendment fits into the total framework of the Constitution and should be construed to mesh with the remainder of the constitutional structure. One particular aspect of this is worth brief attention. That concerns the constitutional right to privacy. . . .
>
> Thus, I think the constitutional right of privacy would justify police practices by which a search of a woman could be performed only by another woman and search of a man by another man.
>
> Similarly, the right of privacy would permit, perhaps require, the separation of the sexes in public restrooms.[4]

As for the specter of homosexual marriages, the only comment made on this issue by the amendment's proponents was a quip by Griffiths: "I will admit that if any State were silly enough to sanction marriage between two men it would have to sanction it between two women."[5]

Everyone agreed that two general areas of law would be affected by the ERA, and there was strong disagreement as to whether or not the effect would be beneficial. These two areas are protective labor legislation and domestic and family law, which includes the legal rights and responsibilities of husband and wife. As might be expected by looking at the history of the Equal Rights Amendment, the heart of the struggle between its proponents and its opponents was the issue of protective labor legislation for women.

Protective Labor Legislation Would Go

During the May 1970 hearings, six witnesses testified against the ERA and eight statements in opposition to it were submitted, six from organized labor and one each from the National Council of Jewish Women and the National Council of Catholic Women. *All of these witnesses and statements without exception cited their support of protective labor legislation as a reason for opposing the ERA.* It is the only single reason that they all agreed on.

In the hearings the following September, nine witnesses testified against the amendment, including constitutional lawyers. With the exception of one woman who identified herself as a housewife and opposed the ERA on the ground that all men think objectively and all women think subjectively, again every witness who spoke against the ERA feared that it would do away with protective legislation.

When the House held joint hearings the following year on *both* the ERA and on H.R. 916, "The Women's Equality Act" (a piece of federal legislation against private discrimination), of the six witnesses who testified against the ERA, all six favored both the retention of protective labor legislation and the passage of H.R. 916. So much for the later emphasis the Stop ERA campaign put on the dangers of federal legislation! Federal legislation was what their predecessors wanted.

All these witnesses agreed that state protective labor legislation as it existed would be unconstitutional if the amendment were passed. They disagreed as to whether courts and legislatures would extend it to both sexes or nullify it. Opponents uniformly were convinced that such legislation *wouldn't* be extended to men, reasoning that such extension would be opposed by both employers and employees. Proponents seemed generally to postpone evaluating labor regulation in itself.

The points made for and against protective legislation might be dialogue from a political play.

Marijana Relich, attorney from Detroit: "There are approximately thirty million working women in the United States, the majority of whom are unorganized. . . . These women must, therefore, turn to their State legislatures to protect them from the exploitations of employers."[6]

Aileen Hernandez, president of NOW: "It is my considered opinion that the State protective laws which apply only to women are an anachronism and should be changed. . . . It is clear to me that the amendment is needed because some courts are still affirming ancient taboos and stereotypes which affect the ability of women to move throughout society."[7]

Statement by Bernard Schwartz, included in the record of the 1971 House hearings by Sam Ervin: "If we follow the traditional police-power approach . . . we may say that the protective statutes dealt with thus far may be justified as legislative attempts to protect the health, safety, and welfare (primarily the economic welfare) of women. The same approach should also sustain comparable legislative efforts to protect the morals of women."[8]

Marjorie C. Leonard, speaking for the National Woman's Party, referred to Sir William Blackstone's *Commentaries on the Common Law,* the eighteenth-century authority on which most interpretation of U.S. common law is based: "Blackstone went on to say that the husband has the right to beat his wife . . . for her protection. This appears to be the first use of the phrase 'protection of women.' "[9]

A letter from Judge Susie Sharp, Associate Justice of the Supreme Court of North Carolina, was included in the record by Sam Ervin: "Laws which bar women from operating saloons, engaging in professional wrestling, and which impose weight-lifting restrictions on them do not offend me. I am satisfied that the majority of women do not feel enslaved by them and that if they are repealed the exploitation of women will result."[10]

Lawyer Marguerite Rawalt of Washington, D.C.: "On the subject of occupations barred to women, I know of no law which *compels* any male to work in a mine. There is certainly none which denies him permission to do so, none which denies him permission to work anywhere, at any job he can do. The Equal Rights Amendment would *not compel* any female to work in a mine; it would permit her the choice to do so, as any male worker has that same choice."[11]

Libertarians would point out, of course, that this political play understood much of the issue as far as it went, but still didn't come to grips with the fact that *all* "protective legislation"—minimum wage laws, hours laws, the works—is at the expense of the workers it purports to protect. None of the champions of women's rights who came to the realization that this was the effect of such legislation on women would go further and cite economist Walter Williams's analysis of how the minimum wage reduces the employment of black teenagers, for instance.

Domestic Chaos?

The impact of the ERA on domestic law was generally expected to be "chaotic" by ERA opponents. For instance, Myra Wolfgang, vice president of the Hotel and Restaurant Employees and Bartenders International Union, after she voiced her union's opposition to jeopardizing "existing labor laws and standards that apply to women," added that "it would create endless confusion in the wide field of laws relating to property, personal status, and marriage. This will adversely affect the women of America and their families."[12]

As Thomas I. Emerson said to the Senate Judiciary Committee, this sort of objection to the Equal Rights Amendment acknowledged "that widespread discrimination against women persists throughout our society."[13]

Conservatives took an exactly opposite interpretation of what the ERA would do from the one they were to take in their successful later campaign to oppose the ERA. That campaign was to try to arouse fears of a "federal power grab" by which the enforcement section of the amendment would, as one pamphlet put it, "transfer to the Washington politicians, bureaucrats and judges vast new power." But Senator Ervin, in his opening address to the Senate Judiciary hearings, quoted a speech he had made on the floor of the Senate on August 21, 1970, in which he had said that he feared the ERA would bring "legal chaos" because it would "merely abolish all laws making any distinction between men and women. It would not bring into existence any new laws giving us a discrimination free society."[14]

He expounded on his own private version of Natural Law, in true nineteenth-century language:

When He created them, God made physiological and functional differences between men and women. These differences confer upon men a greater capacity to perform arduous and hazardous physical tasks. Some wise people even profess the belief that there may be psychological differences between men and women. To justify their belief, they assert that women possess an intuitive power to distinguish between wisdom and folly, good and evil. . . .

From time whereof the memory of mankind runneth not to the contrary, custom and law have imposed upon men the primary responsibility for providing a habitation and a livelihood for their wives and children to enable their wives to make the habitations homes, and to furnish nurture, care, and training to their children during their early years.[15]

He went on to state that in order to ensure this division of labor by sex we need laws "to exempt or exclude women from certain arduous and hazardous activities in order to protect their health and safety."[16]

And besides, Ervin was to say later on in the hearing, it's *convenient* to have the law make sweeping assumptions about men and women.

If you are going to pass this amendment, it would be a question of fact in every case whether the wife has got the most money or whether the wife has borrowed to get more money working a job than the husband or whether the wife is more energetic and could come nearer supporting a family than the husband because of her energy. At the present time, all you got is the law which says it is the primary duty of the husband and father to support the wife and children. And all you got to prove is that he is the husband and the father and that he has failed to support the children. And then you can get an order of the court for support, or you can put him on the chain gang or in prison if he doesn't support them.

But this amendment would open the door to litigate every question whether the wife is stronger than the husband, whether the wife is more intelligent than the husband, whether the wife is richer than the husband, and then leave the court without any guide, so keep the law simple. Keep the law responsible where the good Lord put it—on the man to bear the burdens of support and the woman to bear the children.[17]

Ervin suggested his committee recommend an amended version of the ERA, which would add to the text: "This article shall not impair, however, the validity of any law of the United States or any State which exempts women from compulsory military service or which is reasonably designed to promote the health, safety, privacy, education, or economic welfare of women, or to enable them to perform their duties as wives and mothers."[18]

The answers given to such arguments by proponents of the ERA were in terms of principle, echoing the classical liberal angers of feminism. They made it clear that discrimination enforced by law was not tolerable.

Sister Margaret Ellen Traxler of the National Coalition of American Nuns said,

One would have to have the viewpoint of a woman in order to understand what it means to be denied a categorical statement of her human rights. Human beings simply do not premise their freedom upon restrictive limitations and qualifications. . . .

What women ask for in the Equal Rights Amendment is in fact already the right of women. . . . Our rights are in fact not anyone's gift to give, but ours inherently. We have the moral obligation to fight for them.[19]

Dr. Elizabeth Farians of Loyola University said that Catholic women who had formed a coalition to support the ERA understood the amendment and were tired of waiting for it to pass. "I want my rights. I want everybody in the country to have their rights. And rights are indivisible. Nobody can have their rights at the expense of everyone else. I want to walk free and I want everyone else to also."[20]

Virginia R. Allan, former chairman of the President's Task Force on Women's Rights and Responsibilities, testified to the House Committee: "A century ago Susan B. Anthony declared, 'Men, their rights, and nothing more. Women, their rights, and nothing less.' Essentially this statement reflects the position of the proponents of the equal rights amendment today."[21]

The National Woman's Party statement to Senator Ervin's committee said, "The purpose of the Amendment is to lift the women of the United States out of the state of inferiority imposed by the English common law and the French and Spanish civil law brought here by the colonists."[22]

The statement of the District of Columbia Commission on the Status of Women said: "Time and again women's assertion of their right to equal protection of the laws under the Constitution has been denied by the Courts on the ground that under the common law of England women were not entitled to the equal protection of the laws.

"The purpose of the Amendment adopted by the House of Representatives is to free the women of the United States from the application to them by the Courts of those outmoded principles."[23]

In answer to Senator Ervin's proposed amendment to the amendment, Wilma Scott Heide, then Chairman of the Board of NOW, retorted, "I can hardly believe the backward step of allowing for laws for women to 'promote' our privacy and enable us to perform our duties as homemakers and mothers. First, any laws addressed to our duties as homemakers and mothers would be a gross invasion of our privacy. Who is to say what our 'duties' as homemakers and mothers are? . . . In short, Senators, we will define our own life styles and whatever duties thereof to combine parenthood, career, marriage, friendship, recreation, citizen action. We don't need the State to invade our private pursuit of happiness."[24]

What the ERA Wouldn't Do

The arguments given in opposition to the ERA may seem to people concerned about government invasion of individual liberty suspiciously like arguments *for* it.

Thus, Mary Dublin Keyserling, the former director of the Women's Bureau of the Department of Labor, said:

> This amendment wouldn't put a single law on the books. It wouldn't require equality of pay in States now lacking statutes toward this end. It would not require Yale, or Harvard, Princeton or Notre Dame to add a few women full professors to their staffs. Nor would it change policy with respect to women seeking admission to law or medical schools or any other private institutions of higher learning. It wouldn't put more women in top jobs, nor supply a single day care center to enlarge the opportunity of a welfare mother to obtain a job.
>
> The inequality of women does not arise out of constitutional defect— but rather out of economic, social, political, and legislative default.[25]

Katherine Ellickson, speaking against the amendment on behalf of the National Consumers League, complained,

> It would not provide maternity benefits nor liberalize tax deductions for child care expenses. It would not provide day care centers, or the many other positive programs needed. But adoption of this amendment would wipe out all the special State labor legislation for women that has been built up over many years to safeguard low-paid working women, such as minimum wages, maximum hours, mandatory rest periods, seating provisions, et cetera. . . . The league would not be opposed to extending the same safeguards to men, but State legislatures are not likely to do this and the Equal Rights Amendment would not force them to do so.[26]

Many witnesses who opposed the ERA preferred working against *private* discrimination and suggested that the Equal Employment Opportunity Commission (EEOC), the agency charged with enforcing the Civil Rights Act of 1964, should be given stronger powers. Keyserling said,

> Let's take the case of a law that restricts the opportunity of 10 women but benefits 10,000, one would presume from the arguments of the proponents of the amendment that it would still be unconstitutional. All laws, they say, must apply identically. . . . The proposed amendment wouldn't affect private employment but Title VII of the Civil Rights Act does so. It rules out discrimination in employment on the basis of sex. But the words on the book haven't brought about equality. If discrimination is, in fact, to be eliminated there must be funds sufficient to employ an adequate number of enforcement officers. The Equal Employment Opportunity Commission which administers the title must be given the power it now lacks to issue cease and desist orders where there is clear violation. These are goals we must work for. They are legislative, not constitutional goals.[27]

What the ERA Was Intended to Do

It seemed clear that the opponents of the ERA were ready and anxious to increase the laws affecting and the legal supervision of the private sector with respect to women. Legislation that already existed or was shortly to be passed included, besides the Civil Rights Act of 1964, the Equal Pay Act of 1963, the Health Manpower Training Act of 1964, the Education Amendments of 1972 to the Civil Rights Act and the Equal Pay Act, and the Higher Education Act of 1972.

What areas were left for discrimination against women? The whole discussion reminds me of a card shark forcing the mark to take the card he's supposed to. Every time a complaint is made against government, it is diverted into a complaint against society in general, and a legislative remedy is proposed that affects private parties. Well, such legislation did not affect the actions of government.

One woman who identified herself as a career civil servant who had been the highest woman in her bureau said that she was dropped without a hearing when she came up for promotion. She read to the committee a memorandum circulated by her superiors that said, "There is no statute applying to the Department of Labor which requires it not to discriminate against women."[28]

And indeed, although Title VII of the Civil Rights Act prohibits discriminatory employment on the basis of sex, the national, state, and local governments and agencies were exempted.

In the words of Thomas I. Emerson,

Discriminations occur in Federal legislation, they occur in the administration of various Federal agencies, such as HEW, they occur to a great degree in State legislation, legislation which affects a score of different areas ranging from marriage and divorce to criminal laws; they occur in dozens of State bureaucracies which are governed by their own regulations; they occur in Federal institutions of various kinds. . . . I realize that Congress has more powers now than it had at the time of the 14th amendment. The expansion of the commerce power, particularly, has put Congress in a position where it can do more than it could a hundred years ago. But that has not put Congress in a position where it can by legislation solve this problem. It can't do anything about the discriminations that appear in State legislation, and in State official practices.[29]

It was clear. The politicians didn't want to give up their power to legislate as they pleased in a certain area—gender-based distinctions. They tried to substitute the forced card of private discrimination, but advocates of the women's movement had done their homework and weren't buying it. There were restrictive laws affecting women in fifteen major categories, including laws prohibiting women from entering certain occupations, laws mandating heavier sentences for women than for men committing the same crime (although a federal and a state court overturned such laws in 1968),[30] laws restricting the legal capacity of married women, and dual pay schedules for male and female public school teachers. It was time for an ERA, and everyone really agreed on what it would do. The majority report for the House Committee ended by saying that the Committee estimated that passage of the amendment would result in no costs to the federal government.

The vote was considerably more than was needed. Within a few hours of passage in March 1972, Hawaii became the first state to ratify, and twenty-one other states also ratified in that same year. There were only seventeen to go, and in 1973 pro-ERA forces got an official endorsement from the AFL-CIO, perhaps the major opponent of the amendment up to that time. The amendment picked up eight more ratifications in 1973, but then things slowed down. Only three more states ratified in 1974, one in 1975, and one in 1977. And, although it was a procedure of dubious constitutional validity, three States tried to rescind their ratifications, in 1973, 1974, and 1977. Try as ERA supporters might—even by persuading Congress to extend the deadline (by a simple majority, not the two-thirds required for the original amendment) from March 22, 1979, to June 30, 1982—those thirty-five ratifications were it, and the Constitution requires three-fourths of the states (currently thirty-eight states) to ratify an amendment.

So What Happened?

In the Senate before the vote, Sam Ervin tried to establish some spurious legislative history by introducing a number of amendments to the ERA that he knew would be voted down as irrelevant. In the words of an August 1979 *Phyllis Schlafly Report,* he "offered nine amendments, variously exempting from the absolute-equality mandate compulsory military service; combat duty; the traditional rights of wives, mothers, widows and working women; privacy; punishment for sexual crimes; and distinctions made on physiological or functional differences."[31] The hearings had clearly established that women *would* be subject to a draft but not necessarily to combat duty; that no one wanted special laws "protecting" wives, mothers, widows, and working women; that privacy, punishment for sexual crimes, or physiological differences (laws affecting sperm banks, for instance) *would not* be affected.

Nevertheless, Schlafly claimed that the mere *introduction* and voting down of these amendments forced "the legal conclusion that the Federal ERA is designed to accomplish precisely what Senator Ervin and his supporters wanted to exempt,"[32] although the record makes clear that there were great differences in the subject matter of his various amendments. The majority report of his own Judiciary Committee had said that amendment on these subjects was in part unnecessary and in part undesirable.

At first, supporters of ERA made it very clear that what they wanted was the abolition of special privileges for women. Lawyer Karen DeCrow, then president of NOW, wrote in a book that set forth in detail the "thousands" of discriminatory laws that affected women—"When opponents of free choice in occupations call up the specter of women working in mines or digging ditches, the only reasonable response must be that women should have the same opportunity as men to work at (perhaps) less-than-dainty occupations for the same reason that men do—because they pay well."[33]

Ms. magazine was particularly outspoken. In "The Equal Rights Amendment: What's in It for You?" published in 1972, Ann Scott mentions the turn-of-the-century "position of the American Federation of Labor that working conditions for women should be controlled by state protective laws, and for men by collective bargaining. . . . The AFL-CIO hasn't changed that position much over the years."[34] The same article also says, "ERA will not prevent discriminations by persons or by private industry. It will not, directly at least, change social relations. What it will do, over the long run and on a most basic level, is to prevent the government from determining the rights of women and men on the basis of sex. And that's a hell of a lot."[35]

There was even an avowedly classical liberal attitude toward the free market in some of the remarks of the pro-ERA forces. *Ms.* published an article by Elinor Langer in May of 1976 called "Why Big Business Is Trying to Defeat the ERA." In discussing the conservative campaign against ERA ratification, Langer writes, "A peculiar historical evolution has left 'conservatives' supporting protective units, the 'radicals,' in effect, advocating the free market. Classical economists would smile more sweetly on the supporters of the ERA than on its opponents."[36]

Enter Stop ERA

A conservative woman lawyer who had written a pro-Goldwater book in the 1964 campaign, *A Choice, Not an Echo,* decided to take up the cudgels against the ERA where Sam Ervin had left off. She began an Eagle Trust Fund; issued a monthly newsletter named after herself, *The Phyllis Schlafly Report;* and crossed the country debating, campaigning, and addressing legislators in uncommitted states. In the process, she got a national reputation as a force to be reckoned with.

In September 1974, she spoke out in her publication on the subject of "ERA and Homosexual 'Marriages,' " saying "What the homosexuals and lesbians have failed to achieve at the Federal, state and local levels, they are planning on accomplishing through the Equal Rights Amendment."[37]

In November 1976 she said, quite misleadingly, that "nobody knows for sure" what the meaning of the main section of the ERA will be, "because the decision-making power to interpret Section 1 will be in the hands of the U.S. Supreme Court. This is because Section 2 of ERA federalizes its enforcement."[38] First of all, *every* section of the Constitution and its amendments is open to interpretation by the Supreme Court, needing no enforcement clause. Secondly, the particular wording of Section 2 was taken from the Civil War Amendments, which had intended (unavailingly) to *diminish* the power of the Court, because Congress at the time felt that it had been Supreme Court decisions, especially the Dred Scott decision, that had brought on the Civil War. Schlafly then went on to claim that the amendments to the amendment that Sam Ervin introduced and that were voted down were the *entire* relevant legislative history of the ERA.

In December 1976, she asked, "Will ERA Force All Private Schools Coed?"[39] You guess the answer. By 1979 it was "How ERA Will Raise Insurance Rates."[40] And so on. Meanwhile, the Eagle Trust Fund's Eagle Forum was distributing catchy little pamphlets saying things like: "The Women's Lib Movement and the Federal bureaucrats have joined together in a plan that would drive wives and mothers out of the home and into the work force. The plan would provide financial incentives for women to abandon full-time care of their children, even when very young."[41]

Another pamphlet, this one attributed to Stop ERA (also headed by Schlafly) has a headline, "Don't Let ERA Give the Feds More Power," over a picture of an octopus whose tentacles are labeled *ERA, federal spending power, federal courts, OSHA, HEW, and Internal Revenue Service.*

And a very clever pamphlet lists "What ERA Will Not Do!" quite accurately—it won't give "equal pay for equal work," it won't help women get credit, it won't give better educational opportunities—right next to suppositions as to what it will do, including "may compel the states to set up taxpayer-financed child care centers for *all* children regardless of need" and "may give the Federal Government the power to force the admission of women to seminaries equally with men, and possibly force the churches to ordain women." And, of course, may legalize homosexual marriages.

Phyllis Schlafly even wrote a letter to the *Wall Street Journal* in which she asserted, in flat contradiction to the documentation of the Commission on the Status of Women and of Karen DeCrow's *Sexist Justice,* "I testified in more than 30 state legislative hearings, and the only state law cited by any ERA proponent as discriminatory to women was a very old, never-enforced law which said that wives cannot make homemade wine without their husband's consent."[42]

How did the supporters of ERA respond? They gradually abandoned the truth, too. Not in the same way as the Stop ERA forces, of course.

John Gardner, a founder of Common Cause, wrote a column supporting the ERA that just *juxtaposed* statements such as women can't get equal pay for equal work and "No industrialized country in the world has a smaller percentage of women doctors," etc., "than the United States" with the text of the ERA and a description of the fact that "Women now face a crazy quilt of archaic state laws and legal obstacles." He ended by saying, "I'm not talking about any crazy new rights—I'm talking about the oldest right in the world—fair play: the same chance a man has to exercise his God-given talents; a fair chance to get a job; equal pay for equal work; equality before the law; and the same chance as a man to enjoy the fruits of one's own efforts."[43] Anyone who thought this was meant to be a description of the results of passing the ERA just wasn't paying strict attention.

A Common Cause pamphlet aimed at women in Oklahoma also lumped together problems women faced "While our state legislators refuse to ratify the Equal Rights Amendment":

> inheritance laws penalize farm women,
> social security and pension laws ignore the career of the homemaker,
> adequate alimony and child support are difficult to obtain and even
>   more difficult to collect,
> *employers frequently pay women less money than men and promote
>   them less often,*
> *businesses continue to illegally deny women credit or make obtaining
>   it so difficult that women give up in frustration.*[44]

The last two items, of course, have nothing to do with the ERA; they could be held to be violations of the Civil Rights Act of 1964 and the Equal Credit Act. Later, the same pamphlet talked again of equal pay and of the many female-headed families that are in poverty. It profiled five Oklahoma women with problems in a way that assumed the ERA could help them with these problems—two of them were women with job discrimination claims who had not obtained relief from the Equal Employment Opportunity Commission!

After Congress extended the deadline for ratification, NOW began an ERA Yes campaign that featured statements about economics:

> The Equal Rights Amendment is much more than a symbol. It is a bread-and-butter issue. It means dollars and cents for women.
> Without the ERA, women will not have constitutional or economic equality in this century.
> Without the ERA, women will continue to earn only 59¢ for every dollar earned by men.[45]

What does this mean if not that the ERA will have a huge, unspecified impact on the economy? But this is agreeing with the conservative opposition—like King Lear, it will do such things, what they are yet, we know not. NOW sent out a fund-raising letter signed by Eleanor Smeal during this period, spelling out this new interpretation:

> The Equal Rights Amendment is in big trouble. Unless you and I take some extraordinary steps and take them now, we'll never live to see the concept of women's equality written into the basic law of the land.
>
> Unless we fight harder and in a more organized fashion than we ever have before, women will continue to be doomed to a second rate economic status of lower pay, unequal credit and inadequate job security.
>
> After all, that's what the ERA fight is *really* all about—making the lot of women *really* equal to the lot of men, especially when it comes to money. That's the critical litmus test of equality.

Two Views of Equality

Indeed it is a critical litmus test—because there are two absolutely contradictory views of legal equality floating around here. One is the view that was held by the supporters of protective labor legislation and was *repudiated* by the National Woman's Party and by 1970–72 ERA supporters. This is the view that it is the job of the legal system to redress all inequities by making up for them.

Union representative Myra Wolfgang told Senator Ervin's committee that the basis of government is "to give equality by its laws and rules and regulations" to those who would otherwise be unequal. She continued,

> Now, if one of the major and fundamental roles of government is this equalizing one, then the adoption of the so-called Equal Rights Amendment will negate this same equalizing function under the guise of broadening it. The Equal Rights Amendment will invalidate all the legislation, hundreds of pieces of it, which has been adopted over the last hundred years which were passed to permit a semblance of equality which has been denied women down through the ages.[46]

She was absolutely right. It was not only the legislation but the view that "one of the major and fundamental roles of government is this equalizing one" that was being challenged by the ERA.

In his seminal book, *The Constitution of Liberty*, F. A. Hayek, who considered that "The great aim of the struggle for liberty has been equality before the law,"[47] explains that equality before the law and egalitarianism are mutually antagonistic concepts. During the French Revolution, he says, "the basic principles of equality before the law were threatened by the new demands of the precursors of modern socialism, who demanded an *égalité de fait* instead of a mere *égalité de droit*."[48]

He argues,

> Equality of the general rules of law and conduct, however, is the only kind of equality conducive to liberty and the only equality which we can secure without destroying liberty. Not only has liberty nothing to do with any other sort of equality, but it is even bound to produce inequality in many respects. . . .
>
> It is neither because it assumes that people are in fact equal nor because it attempts to make them equal that the argument for liberty demands that government treat them equally. This argument not only recognizes that individuals are very different but in a great measure rests on that assumption. It insists that these individual differences provide no justification for government to treat them differently. And it objects to the differences in treatment by the state that would be necessary if persons who are in fact very different were to be assured equal positions in life.[49]

Hayek goes on to say: "From the fact that people are very different it follows that, if we treat them equally, the result must be inequality in their actual position, and that the only way to place them in an equal position would be to treat them differently."[50]

This last point was Myra Wolfgang's argument *against* the ERA and was blandly ignored by the NOW arguments that the ERA would make women economically equal to men. And it wasn't only NOW that noticed that the Stop ERA arguments seemed to indicate that voters *approved* of equal pay, equal credit, and job security—and just appropriated these equalizing attributes (already supposedly secured by various pieces of legislation) as aims of the ERA. In the extension period, as the battle heated up, article after article supported the ERA with such arguments.

Jane O'Reilly in "Support Your ERA. You Didn't Get Where You are Alone" (*Savvy*):

> How can we talk about gains, when women are still making 57 cents for every dollar men earn in the United States? When only 276 women serve on the corporate boards of the biggest 1,300 corporations? . . . Maybe that's the reason men tell us we don't need the ERA.
>
> Sure, it would be nice to be on the winning side. So let's make sure we are. Without equal rights, women will always be on the losing side.[51]

CHAPTER EIGHT

Contemporary Feminism

Today, any unity that support for the ERA brought among various parts of the feminist movement has evaporated. There still are a variety of feminist groups and differing individuals who think of themselves as feminist, some of them individualist in orientation, and some of them collectivist. As I have had occasion to mention before, you often wouldn't know that this variety exists from the media. From "political correctness" on campus to political activists mounting campaigns, it is generally collectivists who are most visible.

There is no one definition of feminism that people can generally agree on. In fact, it's not as easy as you might think to find specific definitions. Gloria Steinem was asked by Gail Sheehy in 1980, "Do you mind being a buzzword?" and answered, "Being a buzzword for half the human race is pretty diverse."[1] A letter to the *New York Times Magazine* in 1990 said, "Feminism is not a form of introspection. It is a social movement, aimed at changing the structures of society for both men and women, from the home and the workplace to the doctor's office and the courts." Two letters to the *Times* in 1988 responded to a previous letter (which held that feminism was "an attempt to foster masculine qualities within women and make women more like men") by saying, "Feminism is not a denial of femininity. It is an affirmation of humanity." And, "A woman is no less a woman, nor should she want to be, for doing what was once a man's job. We can do these jobs effectively as women. That is what the feminist movement is all about."

People who are *not* feminists may think feminism is monolithic, but more and more we see in the feminist press the idea that today there is no monolithic feminism—there are "feminisms," although people may not agree on how to describe them. But still, there are writers today who ascribe a uniformity of opinion to "feminists," whether or not they associate themselves with those opinions. Thus, Nicholas Davidson in *The Failure of Feminism* (1988) could write that, by the midseventies, "A unified point of view had emerged," which he summarizes as "the idea that men are collectively responsible for all the evils of history and for their perpetuation in the present."[2]

If Davidson exaggerates he is perhaps not entirely to be blamed: many radical feminists hope to promote the very identification of their particular point of view with feminism in general that he espouses. Alison M. Jaggar trenchantly summarizes the way Catharine MacKinnon did this in a review of MacKinnon's 1987 book, *Feminism Unmodified,* saying that MacKinnon believes "what is frequently called 'radical feminism' . . . to be the only true or genuine feminism because it alone speaks for all women," and that she lumps together all other feminisms as "liberal feminism," a way of helping to sanction the abuse of less privileged women.[3]

Is there still anything that the factions agree on? Yes, all feminists have an identification with, and a concern for, women in general. The British author of *The Sceptical Feminist,* Janet Radcliffe Richards, thinks the most general definition is

> that there are excellent reasons for thinking that *women suffer from systematic social injustice because of their sex.* . . . Feminism has come to be associated with particular theories about what kind of thing is wrong and whose fault it is; how it came about and what should be done to put matters right.[4]

Nancy Cott defines feminism today as having three components: opposition to sex hierarchy, the perception that women's condition is socially constructed rather than biologically determined, and "some level of identification with 'the group called women.' "

Above all, Cott says, feminism involves paradox.

> Feminism asks for sexual equality that includes sexual difference. It aims for individual freedoms by mobilizing sex solidarity. It posits that women recognize their unity while it stands for diversity among women. It requires gender consciousness for its basis yet calls for the elimination of prescribed gender roles. These are paradoxes rooted in the actual situation of women, who are the same as men in a species sense, but different from men in reproductive biology and the construction of gender. Men and women are alike as human beings, and yet categorically different from each other; their samenesses and differences derive from nature and culture, how inextricably entwined we can hardly know. . . . The ruling fiction of feminism, the conception "all women," is—like the ruling fiction "all men" in democratic theory—always observed in the breach.[5]

Not all feminists would agree with all of these points. Some feminists do not call very loudly for "diversity among women"; others are more interested in the group than in "individual freedoms." Cott's language reflects the strong hold that individualist classical liberal language and tradition still has in feminism today. But there are other aspects of the contemporary feminist movement, too.

"All feminists agree," wrote Barbara Sinclair Deckard in *The Women's Movement* in 1975,

> that women at present have lower status than men; that women are discriminated against socially, economically, and politically; and that this state of affairs is unjustified and must be changed. They differ in their analysis of the origins of women's inferior status, of why the lower status has persisted, and of what changes are necessary to end separatism.
>
> Within the women's movement, the three major ideological positions are those of the moderate or women's-rights feminists, the radical feminists, and the socialist feminists. Not all women active in the movement can be neatly placed into one of these categories, nor do all adherents of any one of these positions agree among themselves on all matters. These ideologies are still flexible and in the process of further development.[6]

Similarly, the authors of *Gender Justice* subdivided the left wing of feminism into other groups.

> Leftist feminism, to use a single encompassing phrase for several diverse positions, is centered on women's oppression, based variously on sex, or on women's marginal membership in a capitalist economy, or on some amalgam—some more or less "unhappy marriage"—of these two oppressions. . . . Leftist feminism, as we use the term, encompasses three main groups: radical feminists, Marxists, and socialist feminists. Each differs from liberal feminism in believing women are oppressed by men, or capitalism, or nature or all three, *because* they are women, not because of their individual traits or accidents of birth.[7]

Catharine Stimpson, like Nancy Cott, has a perception of feminism that is unified, not fragmented. She identifies three gifts, not three groups: "a moral vision of women, in all their diversity, and of social justice; political and cultural organizations (like battered women's shelters) that translate the vision into action; and political processes that enable men and women to re-experience and re-form themselves."[8]

Leah Fritz, who came out of the New Left and is critical of feminist factional wars, tried to distill the essence of feminism this way in 1979:

Fundamentally, feminists make a distinction between the reformism necessary to obtain "women's rights"—that is, equality under patriarchal law—
and the truly utopian aspiration of ending the primacy of man . . . (whether expressed by men or internalized by women) as well as his dominion
over this planet.[9]

But she later modified this implied identification of all feminism with "leftist
feminism" (as *Gender Justice* calls it). That identification, she says, only
worked in the early days, when the feminist movement was small and
parochial, before it spread into the population at large:

The feminists who came to the movement via Betty Friedan and Billie
Jean King are anything but knowledgeable about internecine leftist
squabbles. . . . And so a large part of the women's movement in the
United States has grown without reference to the left. . . . If radical
feminists in large cities help to provide fuel for widespread anger . . .
grassroots feminists determine their own course. The movement has grown
too big to be controlled by any self-appointed avant-garde.[10]

These grassroots feminists were not interested in ending "the primacy
of man." They were interested in finding out how far they could go, how
much they could change, what limiting assumptions they had accepted
without examination, and what they could do about it. They wanted lives
and relationships that were fulfilling. And a majority of them wanted
relationships with men. In *The Feminist Mystique,* Betty Friedan herself
had been at pains to explain that her ideas would save and rejuvenate
marriage and family:

There are no easy answers in America today: it is difficult, painful, and
takes perhaps a long time for each woman to find her own answer. First,
she must unequivocally say "no" to the housewife image. This does not
mean, of course, that she must divorce her husband, abandon her children,
give up her home. She does not have to choose between marriage and
career; that was the mistaken choice of the feminine mystique. In actual
fact, it is not as difficult as the feminine mystique implies, to combine
marriage and motherhood and even the kind of lifelong personal purpose
that once was called "career." It merely takes a new life plan—in terms
of one's whole life as a woman. . . .
    The only way for a woman, as for a man, to find herself, to know
herself as a person, is by creative work of her own. There is no other
way. But a job, any job, is not the answer—in fact it can be part of
the trap.[11]

It Started in the Sixties

The Feminine Mystique clearly touched a chord in many women when it was published in 1963, but the very point the book was making, that women had become isolated in their homes without meaningful lives, made it difficult for a social movement to begin. Liberal women were interested in lobbying Congress as social feminists had. The first issue taken up by the first contemporary women's organization, NOW, was to pressure the Equal Employment Opportunity Commission to ban sex-segregated want ads in newspapers. (It also picketed the *New York Times.*)

It was a tiny band of left-wing women that first rediscovered activist feminism in the 1960s. The French existentialist (and sometime apologist for communism) Simone de Beauvoir had tried in the early 1950s to write the definitive description of the inferior position of woman in her book, *The Second Sex,* but although the book influenced a number of women, it was not yet time for a general movement. About ten years later, however, the time was ripe for women in the "student rebellion" to reevaluate their condition, and since they were already organized in a movement, they used that organization to start women's caucuses and present resolutions and papers at movement meetings. This led to consciousness-raising sessions and ultimately the consciousness-raising movement.

But left-wing feminism has not disappeared. Let's look at what has been going on.

Marxist and Socialist Feminists

Marxist feminists are not a very large group and they have had a difficult row to hoe. They are committed to an analysis that implies that socialism would solve the problems of women, but communist regimes have clearly not done so. In 1981 the South End Press published *Women and Revolution: A Discussion of the Unhappy Marriage of Marxism and Feminism,* edited by Lydia Sargent, a book of thirteen essays, twelve of which discuss the thirteenth, which bears as its title the subtitle of the book. This essay, by Heidi Hartmann, says that Marxism had been too dominant in its relationship with feminism. It opens by saying, "The 'marriage' of marxism and feminism has been like the marriage of husband and wife depicted in English common law: marxism and feminism are one, and that one is marxism."[12]

But, she concludes, the two forms of analysis complete each other and should join in a "more progressive union." A number of the essays disagree in various ways with her analysis, although most seem to feel a continued alliance is necessary and possible.

Carol Ehrlich's essay, "The Unhappy Marriage of Marxism and Feminism: Can It Be Saved?" does not. In opposition to Hartmann, she calls for a replacement of Marxism by social anarchism, to encourage feminists to work for the breakdown of all power relationships in society. She begins: "One of the most vexing problems for marxist feminists has been to develop a feminist analysis within a context (marxism) that makes it difficult to have one," and she also points out that patriarchy still exists under "state socialism," and the question is why? It must be, she says, that "either marxist analyses of 'the woman question' are wrong, or they are incomplete."[13]

Radical Feminism

By far the most influential group of left-wing feminists have been the radical feminists, who decided that the "unhappy marriage" was not intellectually productive for them. When the first organizers of consciousness-raising groups —Marxist-influenced women who had become accustomed to activism in the New Left student movement—formulated their theories, they used the concept of oppression they had learned from Marxist theoreticians and applied it to the conclusion that all women of all classes were the victims of male oppression. These theoreticians were soon joined by other radical feminists who were not particularly interested in Marxist analysis but who also knew the value of creating media events like protests and sit-ins, and who found common cause in slogans or activities—some of which were really performance art. The Miss America Pageant was protested in 1968 by feminists who crowned a sheep as Miss America. Valerie Solanis wrote a manifesto for an organization she named SCUM, the Society for Cutting Up Men. A group of women adopted the acronym WITCH (Women's International Terrorist Conspiracy from Hell), dressed as witches, and invaded the New York Stock Exchange on Halloween in 1968. They distributed a leaflet that said in part, as quoted in Robin Morgan's anthology, *Sisterhood is Powerful,* "There is no joining WITCH. If you are a woman and dare to look within yourself, you are a WITCH. You make your own rules."[14] WITCH later hexed other institutions considered to be sexist, to the joy of the media.

Both the radicals and the Marxists called for a "feminist perspective" that would provide a complete and consistent analysis of society, placing male domination of women and male-inspired sex roles at the root of social problems, and such books began to come out in the early seventies. Kate Millett's *Sexual Politics* appeared in 1970; Andrea Dworkin's *Woman Hating,* in 1974. These books were angry. Kate Millett called feminism the hope that "a second wave of sexual revolution might at last accomplish its aim of freeing half the race from its immemorial subordination."[15] And Andrea Dworkin wrote in *Woman Hating,*

> We have begun to understand the extraordinary violence that has been done to us; how our minds are aborted in their development by sexist education; how our bodies are violated by oppressive grooming imperatives; how the police function against us in cases of rape and assault; how the media, schools, and churches conspire to deny us dignity and freedom; how the nuclear family and ritualized sexual behavior imprison us in roles and forms which are degrading to us. . . .
>
> The nature of women's oppression is unique; women are oppressed as women, regardless of class or race; some women have access to significant wealth, but that wealth does not signify power; women are to be found everywhere, but own or control no appreciable territory; women live with those who oppress them, sleep with them, have their children—we are tangled, hopelessly it seems, in the gut of the machinery and way of life which is ruinous to us.[16]

The repudiation of marriage was a hallmark for some of these early radical feminists. I remember coming across an account, in an underground feminist publication in the seventies, of a speech that had been made by a woman who today is quite a prominent and "moderate" mainstream feminist. She was apologizing to her audience for being married, but, she said, she wanted to explain that her marriage wasn't a violation of feminist principles because her husband was "an effeminate faggot."

One of my earliest recollections of a consciousness-raising group was when a woman who was to become one of my closest friends "confessed" to the other women she had just met that perhaps she didn't belong in women's liberation. She paused and looked down; clearly it was difficult for her to go on. "I *like* men," she said finally. This seemed so off the subject to the rest of us that we laughed.

But it turned out that she was a bit more sophisticated than we were. She knew about at least one radical group that was meeting in New York City. In 1969 a group that called itself simply the Feminists introduced a "quota system" for its members. Spelled out in capital letters, their "Membership Requirements and Benefits" described it this way:

WE HAVE A MEMBERSHIP QUOTA: THAT NO MORE THAN ONE THIRD OF OUR MEMBERSHIP CAN BE PARTICIPANTS IN EITHER A FORMAL (WITH LEGAL CONTRACT) OR IN-FORMAL (E.G. LIVING WITH A MAN) INSTANCE OF THE INSTITUTION OF MARRIAGE.[17]

This was not widely adopted in the women's movement, and as a matter of fact the concept was criticized by many feminists. In *Dreamers and Dealers,* Leah Fritz says it "fostered a distressing prejudice against women with heterosexual connections in the whole radical feminist movement for some time thereafter."[18] (Elsewhere in the same book, she says, "I once told a group of women who might be called 'feminist bigots' that to be utterly correct, one must be a 'lesbian prostitute on welfare who lives in a separatist community and has aborted several male embryos.' "[19]) Fritz herself is a (married) radical feminist who talks of marriage as oppression, but she draws a distinction between criticizing social institutions and presuming to judge the life choices of individual women.

Lesbian Feminism

The position of lesbians in the movement is perhaps worthy of attention. Kate Millett was confronted in a public forum shortly after *Sexual Politics* was published and asked to declare herself as a bisexual, which she did. This led to an attack on her and on "women's lib" at the end of 1970 in the pages of *Time.* The result was a show of solidarity in which straight women imitated the actions during World War II of the King of Denmark, who wore a star of David and encouraged all his subjects to do so when the Nazi conquerors required Danish Jews to wear them. A march was held on December 12, under the sponsorship of the New York chapter of NOW, at which all the participants wore lavender armbands as a stigma of lesbianism and distributed a leaflet saying "we all stand together as women."

Barbara Deckard in *The Women's Movement* says,

> At first lesbians in the movement hid their sexual orientation. They were afraid of being rejected by their straight sisters, who constituted the vast majority, and they were afraid of hurting the movement. In the early years, the taunt of lesbian had often been used against women liberationists. . . .
>
> In some groups and areas, a gradual change in attitude took place and lesbian demands were incorporated without bitter battles. In others, the issue proved extremely divisive.[20]

Rita Mae Brown had joined New York NOW in 1969 and resigned in 1970 to form a group called Radicalesbians, saying the women's movement was sexist and prejudiced against lesbians. By September 1971, the national organization of NOW passed a resolution saying "NOW acknowledges the oppression of lesbians as a legitimate concern of feminism," and the controversy seemed to be over. Today, there are many lesbian separatist organizations, as there are many feminist organizations with different agendas. As of 1992, there is no national lesbian umbrella organization. A National Lesbian Conference that took place in Atlanta in April 1991 hoped to form such a group, but did not. As reported in the June 1991 issue of the feminist national newspaper, *off our backs,* the conference, most of whose attenders were radicals, got into some organizational and scheduling difficulties through its emphasis on consensus and mediation rather than hierarchy. The report stated, "Some members of the steering committee and staff had refused to talk to reporters on an individual basis because they, as individuals, could not represent parity (50% lesbians of color, 20% disabled lesbians, 5% old lesbians)."[21]

There are a lot of ways in which feminists differ, but here the issue of personal lifestyle is at issue. And personal lifestyle or sexual interest in men is not a defining factor in feminism. There are radical feminists who are married as well as those who are single; there are Marxist feminists who are married as well as those who are single; there are, in both political groups, unmarried women who are sexually active heterosexuals and women who are sexually active lesbians; there are monogamous unmarried couples of both persuasions. Of *course* there are still feminists who are committed to the rhetoric of oppression and even sexual separatism, but they are part of the spectrum, not the defining color of the movement.

Nonpolitical Feminists

Feminist movements whose primary agenda is nonpolitical (at least in the narrow, activist sense) are alive and well. A 1980 *New York Times* article titled "Women's Groups: A Forecast for the 80's" interviewed "spokesmen" for a number of such groups. Among these groups were the National Committee on Household Employment, the Older Women's League Educational Fund, and Rural American Women (whose president and founder, Jane Threatt, was hoping to reach the thirty-two million rural women in the country, saying "As a country, we are going to have to turn to women who are self-sufficient, who have not turned to government or industry for support.") Another group, the National Congress of Neighborhood Women, stressed "a new concept of community." The *Times* quoted its executive director as saying, "The elderly, the handicapped, the disabled and children could be looked after in the community. . . . Instead of saying that poor working class women don't have skills, we should build on the skills they do have. Everyone doesn't have to be professional."[22]

A National Council for Research on Women was formed in New York in the fall of 1982 by twenty-eight women's scholarly centers to promote collaborative research projects, funded by the Carnegie Foundation.

A *New York Times* story by Tamar Jacoby on March 3, 1986, reports on a boom number of women's publications, some calling themselves feminist, others not. Jacoby reports that the 1986 edition of the Index/Directory of Women's Media listed "331 women's periodicals in the United States alone, as well as 81 women's presses and 48 women's bookstores." She quotes the editor of the directory as saying, "It's not just the numbers that are growing every year, but also the variety of the publications." Another member of the Women's Institute for Freedom of the Press, which publishes the directory, says that some of the publications are giving the word feminism new connotations. "Some may even be reluctant to use the word . . . but the driving force behind them all is concern for women's equality." Jacoby says, "Just when the women's movement seemed to be running into trouble, as the political fervor of the 1970's gave way to the pragmatism of the 1980's, a new generation of grass-roots women's magazines and newspapers has emerged around the country."[23]

In a Spring 1990 issue of the *Radcliffe News,* a column by Barbara Haber titled "The Decade in Review," summarized some facts and figures from the January 1990 *Clearinghouse on Women's Issues.*

> In 1970 no one even knew what a "battered women's shelter" was. Now there are at least 1,200 such centers or shelters in the US.
>
> In 1969 there was one Women's Studies program in San Diego. Today, there are at least 503 Women's Studies programs, serving about 250,000 students. Twenty-six of these programs offer a PhD in a subject that didn't exist 20 years ago.
>
> "Displaced Homemakers" were discovered in the early 70s. Now there are 700 displaced Homemaker groups and services in the US.[24]

Such feminists realize that feminism is not exclusively, perhaps not even primarily, concerned with political rights. Gerda Lerner, former president of the Organization of American Historians, said in 1981, "This feminist struggle for emancipation is much older than the struggle for women's rights and goes on after women's rights have been won."[25]

Not all feminists work in groups. Some feminists have a specific idea of what behaving as women entails, and wish to glorify what they see as the particular virtues of women. The novelist Nora Johnson wrote,

> Recently in a letter to *The Times* the feminist movement was described as promoting "the glorious perception that women can be valued for

our brains and not just our faces." I hope it's more than that. . . . Feminism is less an I.Q. contest than a system of values for which women are the symbol; strange, outlaw, this system listens to the heart, believes in intuition, is impatient with the rational and the logical, goes for love every time. It may even be a condition of the soul.[26]

And Madeleine L'Engle, who is both a novelist and a religious writer, put it similarly,

My role as a feminist is not to compete with men in their world—that's too easy and ultimately unproductive. My job is to live fully as a woman, enjoying the whole of myself and my place in the universe. . . . To live in an open and undetermined universe with courage and grace seems to me to epitomize feminine spirituality, and it is the way we are going to have to go if we are to survive as a human race.[27]

Two other movements that are so wide that they have no central organization are religious feminism and the feminist health movement.

Feminists within Organized Religions

When Elizabeth Cady Stanton spent years in the late nineteenth century compiling a *Woman's Bible,* which excerpted those parts of the Bible that she felt were particularly discriminatory to women, she did this as an opponent of organized religion. In our time, groups of feminists have arisen within religious communities—branches of Judaism, and Protestant denominations, as well as Catholicism—determined to assert their right to criticize and to change discriminatory practices, while adhering to and practicing their religion.

In modern times, religious ordination has been a male near-monopoly. The first woman to be ordained in the United States was Antoinette L. Brown, who became a minister of a Congregational church in 1853. (She later married Samuel Blackwell and became the sister-in-law of Lucy Stone and of Dr. Elizabeth Blackwell.) With the impact of feminism, the number of women seeking to be ordained has increased rapidly.

The Protestant nondenominational Harvard Divinity School had been accepting women since 1955, but, according to the *New York Times* in October 1986, it wasn't until the late 1970s that their numbers increased significantly. In 1971, the article said, 11 percent of the students were female; by 1981 the number was almost 50 percent. According to the same source, by the fall of 1986 a majority of the students in both the master of divinity and master of theology programs were women.[28] This does not reflect the number of women in the ministry, of course, but that has been increasing too.

An earlier *New York Times* report in 1983 said that "about half" of the Protestant denominations admitted women to the ministry, including the United Church of Christ, the United Methodist Church, the United Presbyterian Church, the American Lutheran Church, and, as the result of a controversial 1976 decision that split the church, the Episcopal Church.[29]

In that denomination, priests who are women may be excluded by a bishop from his diocese, and many still are. The Episcopal Church is part of the worldwide Anglican Communion, an organization of twenty-seven national churches all of whom were once connected to the Church of England. This Communion is itself deeply split over the ordination of women and is trying to find ways to include Anglican churches with differing views. In March of 1989, Bishop Barbara C. Harris was consecrated in the Boston diocese of the Episcopal Church and became the first woman bishop in any church in the Anglican Communion.

According to the 1986 *Times* article, Roman Catholics and Jews are both also seeing the rise of women in "religious leadership positions." Conservative, Reform, and Reconstructionist branches of Judaism had all accepted female rabbis; only Orthodox Jews had not. The article reports that the Jewish Theological Seminary, which trains Conservative rabbis, ordained its first woman in 1985 and a year later had thirty-nine women in its rabbinical program; as recently as 1983, there were none.[30]

Catholic feminists, of course, face special difficulties because of the hierarchical structure of Church authority and the attitude of the present Pope, but even they have made inroads. Women are being assigned to administrative and pastoral jobs in which they are able to do almost everything that a priest does, except consecrating the sacraments and hearing confession. Women chaplains in hospitals, for instance, can *administer* the sacrament as long as it has been consecrated by a priest. Women have consecrated the sacrament in masses not recognized by the Church. Altar girls, officially forbidden by Catholic doctrine, serve in a number of American Catholic Churches. A *New York Times*/CBS poll in November 1985, reported in the *Times,* "found that 80 percent of the Catholics in the United States believe that girls should be allowed to assist at the altar, while 52 percent said that women should be ordained as priests."[31]

A *New York Times* op-ed piece by controversial Catholic theologian Hans Kung called the position of women "the Number 1 problem for the Roman Catholic Church in the United States." He pointed out that women outnumber priests two to one "in the ministry of the Catholic Church in this country" and are a majority in divinity schools and seminaries, where they often teach. And, he says, women have learned to follow their consciences even against Papal teachings. "[Ninety-five] percent of young Catholic adults approve of artificial birth control, 89 percent approve of remarriage after divorce."

The Pope, he says, is trying to reverse these attitudes and to control American nuns, but Kung feels he is doomed to failure in any "war against women," because without women, "Catholicism in this country would have to close down much of its work."[32]

Like many other feminisms, religious feminism is a continuing commitment. Even those women who succeed in becoming rabbis or ministers or Episcopal priests—by 1987 there were approximately 8,000 of them nationwide, as reported in *Insight*[33]—have still the onus of getting positions and then of proving themselves to their congregations and the superiors who control the possibility of advancement for them. But the numbers still continue to increase.

The Feminist Health Movement

In 1969 a number of young women, dissatisfied with the health care they were receiving, formed a group to evaluate gynecologists in the Boston area. They soon realized that they had no criteria by which to evaluate, so they decided to establish standards by writing research papers and sharing them with each other. After a while they found that these papers had grown into a book, a book that demystified medicine and had information about female functioning that was just not available anywhere else in terms that the general reader could understand. The underlying message of the book was that women should take responsibility for participating in their own health care and should feel entitled to inform themselves and to ask questions. Since it was a group effort, not everyone agreed with every point in the original paper: such conflicts were resolved by including the disagreeing point of view.

There was a lot of interest in this book, and the group was besieged with requests for mimeographed copies. The group took it to an underground publisher, the New England Free Press, who agreed to print it if the group would pay the publishing costs; the press wouldn't finance it because it was "not political enough." Calling themselves the Boston Women's Health Book Collective, the group published the book, called first *Women and Their Bodies*. They renamed it *Our Bodies, Ourselves* for the second printing, and it sold between 200,000 and 250,000 copies without any advertising or publicity. This was the start of the feminist health movement, which became worldwide.

Because it was already a best seller, Simon and Schuster offered to republish it and offered the Collective an unusual contract with more control than authors ordinarily get. As of 1987, according to *Radcliffe News,* the book, which has gone through several revised editions, had sold 2.5 million copies.[34]

The Collective continued to meet weekly in each others homes and maintained a headquarters in which it established, with the royalties from the book, a women's health information center to answer mail and phone queries about health issues. Other books followed, as well as a Spanish edition of *Our Bodies, Ourselves.* A National Women's Health Network also ensued, with headquarters in Washington, and the Collective has inspired the establishment of health-care centers for women all over the country. Many of the people running these centers consider themselves to be socialist, but the message of questioning medical authority is as nonpolitical as it was when the New England Press thought it didn't want to finance the first printing of *Our Bodies, Ourselves.*

Summing it Up

In short, the feminist movement is wide and diverse. Even specifically socialist contributions to feminism have often been modified almost out of recognition by feminist concerns. Consciousness raising itself was originally touted as a "socialist" technique, but we have seen that it rapidly became something very different. Many of the multiple varieties of feminisms have been there from the beginning; many have developed more recently.

On the occasion of its fifteenth anniversary, *Ms.* asked a number of prominent feminists what each felt was the best and the worst of the women's movement. Erica Jong, author of *Fear of Flying* and other sexually explicit books, replied,

> . . . My own life would have been impossible without feminism. I've been a breadwinner, a single parent, I've supported a host of others. That was a way of living that was uncontemplated before feminism. What I object to is the dichotomy that was made—by some radical feminists— between being a sexually desirable woman and being ideologically correct. It was a hard-nosed politics that left out women who wanted to have babies. I've been criticized because my heroines slept with men, wore lace underwear, wanted to wear high heels. I expected to be attacked by male chauvinists, but I found it painful to be attacked by feminists.[35]

Today in the nineties, as has been the case for the last two decades, the majority of women who are self-identified feminists are non-Marxist, nonsocialist, nonradical, heterosexual women. Unfortunately, this is a well-kept secret, because they are not marching, not demonstrating, not protesting, and not talking to the media. Said Betty Friedan, in that same anniversary issue of *Ms.*,

> I see women reaching out, finding their own voice, and conceptualizing different values, in fields previously defined by men. They are demanding and creating new patterns of work and family life, intimacy, and power. Their new strengths and self-confidence, empowered by the Women's Movement, have taken them beyond simple demands for equality with men, to confront and transform the male model of success—"to have it all." Life is more joyous and responsible and *human.*
>
> What I'm upset about is sexual extremism—those who would make a fetish out of sexual politics. Although women have reason enough for anger, after centuries of repression and continually being put down, those who try to make a rigid ideology of Woman against Man throw the baby out with the bathwater. As it was wrong to define us exclusively by marriage, motherhood, and the home, those who *deny* these values dangerously distort the values of the movement.[36]

None of us can speak for "all women." Each of us can speak for herself, as a woman. Male feminists can speak for the justice of expanding individual choices. It's no wonder the media needs a hook in order to focus on this message: it may seem like vague stuff. But the women's movement, like the black movement, is inexorably making room for individual variations and individual points of view.

PART II

Policy Pros and Cons

PART I

Relief: Pros and Cons

CHAPTER NINE

Discrimination, Real and Imaginary

By now it should be clear that I am not going to say there isn't discrimination against women in our society; there is. Some of it is very individual: having to confound the negative expectations of male colleagues. Sometimes it takes the form of resentment or dislike of women in particular jobs or positions of authority. Sometimes, the form of unrealistic assumptions of difference. And sometimes, just the opposite—an assumption that what applies to men will apply to women, because, after all, they are a subset of men; of mankind. Some of these assumptions may be so general that it surprises everyone when they surface.

Consider the fact that women have been invisible when it comes to picking the subjects for scientific studies. Professor Carol Gilligan of Harvard began her work on gender differences in order to challenge the conclusions that Lawrence Kohlberg (long considered the dean of developmental psychologists) had reached about moral development. Gilligan was the first person to call attention to the fact that Kohlberg's developmental models were based on a twenty-year study of male subjects only—no females were included, although presumably the results of the study applied to them.[1]

The same assumption that Kohlberg made has been made in medical studies. There have been questions raised as to whether or not the effect of aspirin on *women's* heart attacks was the same as the effect in men. A Canadian study has indicated that it isn't, but, as of 1991, it has been seemingly too expensive to do a definitive study. In early 1991, Rep. Patricia Schroeder and the Congressional Women's Caucus made a formal request that women be included more often in government clinical studies. As recently as March 1991, a committee for the Institute of Medicine in the National Academy of Sciences asked the National Institutes of Health to include more women and minority members in its AIDS studies, because these had concentrated almost exclusively on middle-class white men.[2]

Are Women a Class?

Physiology is an area in which we ought to expect differences; behavior is much more complex. Some men are not yet used to seeing women in certain occupations, and they prejudge what women are going to do. This may be connected to a larger issue: women are often considered to be much more similar to each other than men are. That is, they are seen as members of a class rather than individuals, while men are assumed to be individuals who vary so much that their gender tells you little or nothing about them. In an address given in 1938, the British writer Dorothy L. Sayers referred to this phenomenon when she said, "A woman is just as much an ordinary human being as a man, with the same individual preferences, and with just as much right to the tastes and preferences of an individual. What is repugnant to every human being is to be reckoned always as a member of a class and not as an individual person."[3]

Almost fifteen years later, Simone de Beauvoir echoed the same thought in her famous introduction to *The Second Sex;* that man is the standard of the human being, whereas woman is defined by her physical and sexual characteristics. "A man would never get the notion of writing a book on the peculiar situation of the human male. . . . Thus humanity is male and man defines woman not in herself but as relative to him. She is not regarded as an autonomous being. . . . She is defined and differentiated with reference to man and not he with reference to her; she is the incidental, the inessential as opposed to the essential. He is the Subject, he is the Absolute—she is the Other."[4]

Part of the problem is that there are strong voices, some of them from feminists, telling us that women *are* such a class. The patriarchalists seem to look to the (perhaps mythical) good old days when the fact that women bear children implied that childbearing and child rearing are and should be woman's only division of the division of labor. Even if such a tradition has existed, it's hardly a tradition that, historically, American women have found familiar. From colonial days, from slavery days, from early factory days, from immigrant days, American women have worked side by side with men and often carried on for them after they died. They have ridden into the wilderness; they have helped operate the family trading post or the family store; they have taken over and run the business, the plantation, the ranch, even the statehouse or newspaper that they inherited.

But some feminists are making a similar "physiology is destiny" generalization about women. Because of their make-up, they say, women are uniquely qualified to understand emotions, to cultivate intuition, to bring a "feminist perspective" to any subject matter. They must not accept "male" values and compete with men in the world as it is.

Both views make it harder for the individualist feminist, whose aspirations of equal opportunity and equal responsibility have made great strides over the years.

If We're a Class, Look What the Law Can Do

The law, of course, is constantly creating classes of people. Any group affected by a specific category of law is a legal class. Children are a class, affected by age of consent laws, child labor laws, truancy laws, and many others. Employers are a class, affected by a multitude of economic laws and regulations. "Men" are *not* a legal class; but married women, and women in general, have been.

Private prejudice, although it may be unsettling, does not create the insuperable barrier that government action creates. It is the law itself that has created many of the problems of discrimination that women still face. First it was the common law, with its assumption that married women had no property or personal legal rights. Then it was so-called protective labor legislation, which legislated women out of the opportunity for many jobs and promotions, sanctioned by the Supreme Court in *Muller* v. *Oregon* as justified, even though "like legislation for men could not be sustained."[5]

There are more modern examples of governmentally created inequities. Let's take another look at what happened at the end of World War II that ultimately created the "feminine mystique" world. We know that in the wartime days of Rosie the Riveter, women had moved into every facet of the economy. They built ships, they worked on assembly lines, they took over every sort of work that had previously been considered to be a male preserve. And at the end of the war, suddenly, they left the work force in droves to retire to suburbia and have babies.

Popular wisdom has viewed this as a mysterious mass movement, based on a psychological desire to "nest," perhaps. But there was a more immediate reason. There was a law that required every employer who had employed a veteran before the war to give him back his job when the war ended. No one had any choice in the matter. A number of women who had found satisfaction in the opportunities and experiences of the working world were forcibly retired.

That's not the only effect that government actions were having in the postwar world. An article in *Technology Review* pointed out,

At the beginning of World War II, women earned about 45 percent of all bachelor's degrees and about 13 percent of all doctorates. In 1946, however, women's proportion of all degrees at all levels began to decline rapidly, with baccalaureates dropping to about 26 percent by 1950 and doctorates to about 9 percent.[6]

One might think that this phenomenon could be explained by the fact that, at the time, a lot of women were choosing to drop out of college and get married, but the article has another explanation.

> The phenomenon that fundamentally changed the proportion of men and women in higher education was the G.I. bill. Conceived by a nervous Congress as a palliative to almost certain unemployment and social unrest after World War II, the bill took no explicit notice of women. Nonetheless, it has probably affected women's educational and career opportunities more seriously than any other single event, not excluding the baby boom. Its impact continues today. In 1982, some 10 percent of all new male Ph.D.s still received primary support from this source.[7]

The article goes on to say that when more than 2.2 million veterans arrived to receive their free higher education, "they overwhelmed existing facilities," and many universities cut down on female enrollments to accommodate the influx. "Some accomplished this by setting higher admissions standards for women than for men, others by simply setting a quota. The University of Michigan, for example, reduced women's admissions by 30 percent in 1946."[8] It was also this period that saw the establishment of government agencies to support research: the National Science Foundation, the research programs of branches of the military, and the Atomic Energy Commission. With women students squeezed out, it was the veterans who got the funding. This in turn created the impression that women didn't care to go into the sciences, although, as the article goes on to say, "in 1982, 50,000 women held science and engineering Ph.D.'s, compared with fewer than 20,000 in the humanities. Today, about 4,500 women earn science and engineering Ph.D.s annually, while only 1,500 earn Ph.D.s in the humanities, and that fact speaks eloquently to the matter of women's abilities and preferences."[9]

A Useful Heresy

The classical liberal tradition from which American feminism arose in the nineteenth century was skeptical about government power and emphasized the importance of individual rights. The early feminist approach to the problem of discrimination suggested that it is governmentally enforced inequality that creates it, and that only a revival of the tradition of individual rights will solve it. This is not a popular approach today, but after analyzing the "help" that government is giving us, perhaps we will find this view a useful heresy.

Today, when we think of women's rights, one of the first things that may come to mind is affirmative action—that is, a requirement, usually a government requirement, that action be taken in favor of the members of some group which is seen to be disadvantaged. The hidden agenda in all affirmative action plans is the mistaken notion that, if there were no discrimination, all groups would be randomly distributed throughout every area of employment, school district, even residential neighborhood. Many of today's feminists have accepted the notion that such a random distribution of women, as well as of minority groups, in all areas of our society, is a desired goal that will be achieved only by government fiat, and this kind of equality by government fiat is what they are working for.

How Our Consciousness Was Raised

Historically, American women have become aware of their legal rights and disabilities as a consequence of the inclusion of educated women in movements to repair the legal disabilities of blacks. It happened in the abolitionist movement of the 1840s, when women first banded together to agitate to end slavery and became aware of how many laws enslaved *them.* And during the Civil Rights activism of the late 1950s and 1960s, women, once again, looked at discriminatory law and saw parallels between their legal position and that of southern blacks. Here too, they began to question social and legal assumptions that they had previously taken for granted, and another cycle of feminism was born. The impetus for change and the model of how that change should take place has been the movement to ensure civil rights for blacks.

Ending Segregation: The Army

Our society has tried very hard for years to make up for the mistakes of the past that were begun by the institution of slavery. It is almost forty years since the Supreme Court ended racial segregation in public schools in the landmark decision, *Brown* v. *Board of Education of Topeka, Kansas.*[10] Sixteen years before that, Harry Truman issued Executive Order No. 9981.

A lot of people have forgotten that one. That was the order by which President Truman ended racial segregation in the armed forces, on July 26, 1948. Before his action, blacks could not enlist in the Marines, blacks could enlist in the Navy only as cooks and stewards, and the Army restricted black personnel to a quota of 10 percent. Army units were segregated by race, although for three years there had been experimental assignments of black battalions and companies to white divisions. (It might be worth noting that the quota for women, restricting them to only 2 percent of the armed forces, was not ended for decades, until after the volunteer army was instituted in 1973.)

Nineteen-forty-eight was a time when all the southern states used the force of law to separate the races in public schools, public transportation, and privately owned "public accommodations" such as hotels, restaurants, and interstate buses and trains. The southern senators in Congress were not about to allow legislation to pass that would provide black soldiers with the experience of racial integration. They had refused to include an antidiscrimination provision in the Selective Service Act of 1948. So President Harry S. Truman desegregated the services himself, by an executive order that stated:

> It is hereby declared to be the policy of the President that there shall be equality of treatment and opportunity for all persons in the armed services without regard to race, color, religion or national origin. This policy shall be put into effect as rapidly as possible.[11]

And it was. By 1950 the 10 percent quota for Negroes had been dropped, all jobs and training courses were open to them, and they were no longer assigned to separate barracks and messes.

Ending Segregation: The Public Schools

The country's segregation laws were still in force, however, sanctioned by an 1896 Supreme Court decision, *Plessy* v. *Ferguson,* which upheld Louisiana's right to require that railroads provide "equal but separate accommodations for the white and colored races" and that "no person be permitted to occupy seats in coaches other than the ones assigned by race."[12] Homer Adolph Plessy looked white and, in fact, was seven-eighths white. But in a prearranged test of the law, he was asked to move to a "colored" car and sparked a Supreme Court case when he refused. The majority opinion in *Plessy,* the case that started it all, held that Louisiana's Jim Crow Car Act of 1890 wasn't discriminatory when it classified people according to race, because a state has the right to classify people as long as the classification is not "capricious, arbitrary, or unreasonable."

(Clearly this view is still around. As a matter of fact, the later-to-be Chief Justice William Rehnquist used the *Plessy* reasoning when he dissented in a 1973 case, *Frontiero* v. *Richardson,* and held that a federal law that automatically qualified the spouses of males in the armed forces for benefits, but required female personnel to prove that their spouses were dependent on them, didn't discriminate unfairly against servicewomen. It was "reasonable," said Rehnquist, because it saved bureaucratic paper-work.[13])

In the *Plessy* case, the majority said that classifying by race was permissible because the Fourteenth Amendment could not have intended to "abolish distinction based upon color or to enforce social, as distinct from political equality." The lone dissenter, Justice John Marshall Harlan, said that "separation of citizens on the basis of race, while they are on a public highway," *was* arbitrary, and it was also "a badge of servitude wholly inconsistent with the civil freedom and the equality of the law established by the Constitution." He went on to say, "Our constitution is color-blind, and neither knows nor tolerates classes among citizens." There were at the time "separate but equal" public school statutes not only in the South but in a total of thirty states, including much of the West, New York, Indiana, and Kansas.

Plessy v. *Ferguson* became the law of the land, and it was fifty-eight years before its constitutional sanction of racial segregation laws was ended, by *Brown* v. *Board of Education of Topeka, Kansas.*[14] This unanimous decision, written by the newly appointed Chief Justice Earl Warren when his predecessor died suddenly in office, relied heavily on an appendix to the NAACP brief that had been argued. Thirty distinguished American social scientists (chiefly psychologists and sociologists) contended that school segregation was psychologically harmful to both black and white children, but particularly to black ones, because it "generates a feeling of inferiority as to their status in the community that may affect their hearts and minds in a way unlikely ever to be undone." The Court, relying on these findings, overruled *Plessy* v. *Ferguson,* explicitly as it applied to public schools and implicitly with regard to other segregation laws.

Ending Segregation: The 1964 Civil Rights Act

A decade later, the Civil Rights Act of 1964 outlawed discrimination in all "public accommodations" that affect interstate commerce as well as in all public facilities. It prohibited voting registrars from applying different standards to white and black registrants; permitted the Attorney General to bring suit to desegregate state and local government facilities; banned discrimination "on grounds of race, color, or national origin" in both public and private programs that receive federal aid; and forbade discrimination "because of race, color, sex, religion, or national origin" by employers or labor unions in private business. This last section, Title VII, also created an Equal Employment Opportunity Commission to administer the title. Title VII also has the distinction of introducing the concept of sexual discrimination in employment—an amendment that was presented by a southerner in order to discredit the title, and, according to Betty Friedan in *It Changed My Life,* only adopted at the insistence of Congresswomen, who threatened a roll-call vote that would require their colleagues to go on the record as being "against women" if the amendment didn't pass.[15]

(It is worth noting in passing here, too, that the original Civil Rights Act of 1964 did not prohibit discrimination in *government* employment. It was not until 1972, the same year that the Equal Rights Amendment was passed by Congress, that amendments to the Civil Rights Act were passed that included government employment in their coverage. These amendments did not cover employment by the armed forces or in congressional offices.)

These three legal steps, the desegregation of the armed forces, the ending of school segregation (and by implication other laws mandating segregation), and the outlawing of official discrimination everywhere have together transformed our society. The specific marks of racism—doors labeled "white" and "colored"; laws against racial intermarriage; the herding of people into groups by color before they can travel, study, work, or play—have disappeared.

Quotas—Justice for the Group?

But what about that other mark of segregation that was ended in the Army by Executive Order No. 9981, the quota that restricted the percentage of blacks in the Army to their ratio in the population, at the time, 10 percent? That concept is being promoted again, this time by the very constituency that was outspoken against it—the organizations that speak in the name of people who are discriminated against. We have come full circle, it seems.

Before referring to "reverse discrimination" directly—that is, to the "set-aside" quota for a certain number of minorities or women in professional schools or occupations that minorities or women seem not be entering in sufficient numbers—let's look at an even more startling development. That is the limiting of black applicants (and perhaps female applicants) as a matter of public policy. Impossible, in this day and age, you say?

About the same time as the thirtieth anniversary of the *Brown* decision in 1984, a housing discrimination suit that had been brought five years before by several black families against a New York housing project built with New York State financial aid, Starrett City in Brooklyn, was finally settled. The plaintiffs were challenging a minority quota system that rented only 35 percent of Starrett City's 5,881 apartments to blacks and Hispanics, and they lost. The quota was upheld, even though it had resulted in a waiting list of 9,000 black families for the apartments designated for them, as against a white waiting list of 5,000 for almost three times as many apartments. The settlement was praised in a editorial in *New York Times* in the following words:

> In most of America, whites and minorities who go to school, work and even spend leisure time together still live in segregated neighborhoods. A housing development like Brooklyn's Starrett City is a precious rarity. The 46-building, publicly financed complex laudably sustains a commitment to racially integrated housing.
>
> Yet Starrett City maintains that commitment only by maintaining racial quotas. Sensibly, the proposed settlement of a lawsuit challenging this practice would retain a quota and stimulate efforts to expand housing opportunities mostly in other places.
>
> Regrettably but realistically, there is in integrated housing a "tipping point" at which whites begin to flee and leave a segregated community behind. To prevent such tipping, only 35 percent of Starrett City's 5,800 units are rented to minority families. But their demand is great and so this quota forces them onto a much longer waiting list than whites.
>
> Unfortunately, many of the families who brought the suit . . .have moved to other places, some out of town. But hundreds of others who will know the benefits of living in a stable, integrated community will be in their debt.[16]

In other words, if more black families were let in, white families might leave, and the complex could become all black, as a result of the choices of individual families. But, says the *Times,* we know that integration is socially desirable. Therefore, let the individual black families who brought the suit continue to suffer a clear disadvantage—because of a quota imposed by a publicly financed project on the basis of their race—in order to provide *other* black families with a "stable, integrated community."

Quotas—The Civil Rights Act

The quota for blacks in the pre-1948 U.S. Army was also defended as promoting "stability," desired by both blacks and whites. How did we get from there—the abandonment of legally mandated segregation and quotas—to here—legally mandated quotas—again?

It is definitely the case that quotas were at one point abandoned, in the 1964 Civil Rights Act. Title IV banned racial quotas in assignments to schools, and when the Civil Rights Bill was being debated, the idea of a quota on employment or even "any kind of preferential treatment to any individual or group" was specifically repudiated by the bill's floor manager, Senator Hubert Humphrey of Minnesota. He said to an opponent, "If the Senator can find in Title VII . . . any language which provides that an employer will have to hire on the basis of percentage or quota related to color . . . I will start eating the pages, one after another, because it is not in there."

What *is* in there is a barring of quotas, in the following words:

> Nothing contained in this title shall be interpreted to require any employer . . . to grant preferential treatment to any individual or group . . . on account of an imbalance which may exist with respect to the total number or percentage of persons of any race, color, religion, sex, or national origin employed by any employer.

The consensus for a while seemed to be that our Constitution is color-blind, as Justice Harlan said in his *Plessy* dissent. And many people assumed that when *Plessy* v. *Ferguson* was overruled, Harlan's dissent was affirmed. But there was a cloud on the horizon.

Quotas—The Schools Problem

The *Brown* decision had to be enforced by local officials who violently disagreed with it. An enforcement decision in 1955 directed local federal courts to oversee the public-school transition. School districts diverted tax money to segregated "private" schools for whites only. There was outright refusal to obey and even sporadic violence in eight states, and others delayed action. The governor of Arkansas called out the National Guard to prevent nine black children from attending a previously all-white school in Little Rock in 1957, and President Eisenhower federalized the same National Guard in order to escort the children to school past a jeering mob. Mississippi desegregated no school districts at all, until after the Civil Rights Act of 1964 allowed the withdrawal of federal aid-to-education funds.

In such a foot-dragging atmosphere, courts felt they had to decide how much integration was enough. In 1968 the Court started looking at statistical evidence in making such decisions.[17] In 1969 it announced that "the obligation of every school district is to terminate dual school systems at once and to operate now and hereafter only unitary school systems."[18] And in 1971, when a group of both white and black North Carolina parents charged that busing to achieve integration was unconstitutional because the *Brown* ruling required "color-blind" assignments, the Court disagreed and unanimously held that the existence of all-black schools "in a system that has been deliberately constructed and maintained to enforce racial segregation" created a presumption of discrimination. The courts, said the Court, might not only order busing, but, in seeming contradiction to section 2000c of Title IV of the Civil Rights Act of 1964, might also use racial quotas in desegregation decrees. This, it held, would comply with the spirit as well as the letter of the Fourteenth Amendment.[19]

Color-Blindness and Equal Protection

That was the beginning. But the concept of color-blindness still lingered in the minds of jurists. In a 1973 Washington State case, *DeFunis* v. *Odegaard,* Washington Chief Justice Frank Hale brought up Justice Harlan's famous dissent and asked (ironically, he thought) whether the Constitution may be color-conscious in order to be color-blind.[20] Marco DeFunis was the first white to charge that he was the victim of reverse discrimination, and he challenged the separate admissions policy for whites and minorities at the University of Washington Law School on that basis.

The case was ruled "moot" by a majority of five when it was appealed to the Supreme Court because a state court had ordered that he be admitted, so it was never heard in the highest court. In his dissent from the Court's ruling, Justice William O. Douglas reiterated the color-blind concept when he wrote, "The Equal Protection Clause commands the elimination of racial barriers, not their creation in order to satisfy our theory as to how society ought to be organized."

In 1976 the first black Supreme Court Justice, Thurgood Marshall, who had also been the victorious NAACP attorney in the *Brown* case, held in a case called *McDonald* v. *Santa Fe Transportation Co.* that section 1981 of the Civil Rights Act of 1866 and Title VII of the Civil Rights Act of 1964 both forbid employers to discriminate against whites to the same extent that they forbid them to discriminate against blacks.[21]

A Collision Course

But this view was on a collision course with quotas in the case of *Regents of the University of California* v. *Bakke* (1978), where it was decided that a *little* race could be taken into consideration in admissions policy in public higher education, although the Court was divided on the issue.[22] Four Justices held that a racial quota in admissions in a state medical school aided by federal funds was a clear violation of Title VI of the 1964 Civil Rights Act. "It seems clear that the proponents of Title VI assumed that the Constitution itself required a colorblind standard on the part of government," said this opinion. Four other justices, perhaps thinking of the busing quotas that they themselves had previously sanctioned, disagreed. They held that "our prior cases unequivocally show that a state government may adopt race-conscious programs if the purpose of such programs is to remove the disparate racial impact its actions might otherwise have and if there is reason to believe that the disparate impact is itself the product of past racial discrimination." These Justices also agreed, "No decision of this Court has ever adopted the proposition that the Constitution must be colorblind."

The swing vote who made a majority, Justice Lewis Powell, voted to strike down the quota, but based his reasoning on the Fourteenth Amendment, which nobody else did. There were six opinions in the case, all told. Justice Harry Blackmun defended the conclusion that the government may take race into account by saying, "In order to get beyond racism, we must first take account of race. There is no other way. And in order to treat some persons equally, we must treat them differently."

Then came the case of Brian Weber, excluded from an on-the-job training program in a private company, the Kaiser Aluminum Company, because he was white.[23] The program had been set up by the company and the United Steelworkers Union for minority workers, to qualify them for employment in order to *forestall* possible charges of discrimination by the Office of Federal Contract Compliance, the agency that enforced affirmative action guidelines for government contractors. Weber claimed that Title VII of the Civil Rights Act forbade such programs, as Justice Marshall had indicated in his 1976 opinion. In the *Weber* case, however, the majority decision, written by Justice William Brennan, said that the lower courts that had ruled for Weber had followed the letter but not the spirit of the law, which had been concerned with "the plight of the Negro in our economy."

One of the issues raised was whether a company was allowed to institute a "voluntary" racial training quota in a situation where it had not yet been found guilty of discrimination. In an angry dissent, Justice William Rehnquist denounced every racial quota as "a creator of castes, a two-edged sword that must demean one in order to prefer the other." He ended, "The Court has sown the wind. Later courts will face the impossible task of reaping the whirlwind."

So what is an employer to do? One expert, Alfred W. Blumrosen, says that these decisions mandate a double standard.

> Yet, the removal of "barriers" which favor white employees may, as in *Weber,* simultaneously appear to be preferences for minority employees. When that happens, the court must either treat minority or female claims differently than white or male claims or conclude that the statutes cannot improve the relative status of minorities or women. To implement the dominant legislative purpose identified in *Weber* the adverse effect concept of discrimination must be confined to groups whose status Congress sought to improve. White males cannot base their claims on that principle. Similarly, the proof process in individual direct discrimination cases has been structured to make it relatively simple for minorities or women to force employers to justify their actions because of the likelihood that such actions may be discriminatory. There is no such likelihood in the case of white males and therefore the proof requirements may be more stringent than in direct discrimination cases.[24]

This interpretation seems to put forward an analysis of the Civil Rights Act of 1964 that is in direct collision with the Equal Protection Clause of the Fourteenth Amendment.

How Did It Happen?

Since 1972, when AT&T was found to have discriminated against women, discrimination suits against companies have routinely used low work-force percentages of blacks or women to prove discrimination in employment. Supreme Court decisions that seemed to say that discrimination could not be proved entirely on the basis of a company's not reflecting in its employees the population statistics in the community were supposedly "corrected" by Congress in the 1991 Civil Rights Bill. There is an argument as to whether the bill mandates "quotas" or not.

Supporters of the 1964 Civil Rights Act agreed that it forbade quotas. Some Supreme Court Justices thought Harlan's dissent had become law when *Plessy* was overturned. But the resistance to desegregation left the Court groping for a way to find out if court orders were being complied with, and they seized on numerical standards as a way out of their dilemma. In a series of decisions they moved from forbidding the assignment of schools by race to mandating it in order to undo past segregation. We found ourselves with a contradiction. *Brown* said we should assign children to classrooms without regard to race, but subsequent decisions, supposedly to carry out its intentions, set up racial quotas and busing to achieve it. Why? Because the *Brown* decision didn't say that the problem was government herding by race—it said that not being in an integrated group produced feelings of inferiority in black children.

The same reasoning began to be applied to the workplace, beginning in 1971, when "affirmative action guidelines" for government contractors began to look at numerical standards there. Affirmative action's original meaning was that those firms and institutions receiving government contracts were required not only *not* to discriminate against blacks, women, and ethnic minorities but to make special efforts—to take affirmative action —to seek out and recruit qualified members of groups that had once been excluded or subject to disadvantageous treatment. This idea that government-funded projects should not only not discriminate but should make it clear that they do not discriminate has gradually become a policy of group rights that the government must enforce. The issue of reverse discrimination began to come up in the courts.

And a number of increasingly acrimonious split decisions found one group of Supreme Court Justices battling with another over whether the intention of the Civil Rights Act was to make the law color-blind or to improve the "plight of the Negro." Here, too, both sides had reason— Hubert Humphrey, the floor manager for the 1964 Civil Rights Bill, both denounced quotas and said that the measure should be judged by its spirit and not its letter, "for the letter killeth but the spirit giveth life."

And How It Applies to Women

So where does that leave American women? The Supreme Court has resisted attempts to treat race and gender on an equal footing, except when interpreting legislation in which Congress has said it must. Race is a "suspect category," while laws that deal with gender are not necessarily so. When it comes to sexual discrimination, the legal issue is whether or not laws that classify people according to gender are "inherently suspect" or "reasonable." No majority of the Court has been willing to agree that laws that are sexually discriminatory are as "inherently suspect" as it has ruled racial laws are, because of the Fourteenth Amendment.

Some preferential treatment of women and minorities in employment is now a must. But clearly, too much preferential treatment is not allowed. Can the totality of jobs for sleeping car porters (formerly called "Boy") or airline cabin attendants (formerly called "Stewardess") be reserved for blacks and women respectively? Clearly not. The safest course for an employer to take is to mirror the population in which his or her business exists, whether or not this means establishing quotas.

The sociological approach has won. The employer's motive is now of overriding concern, and if a court decides that the employer's motive is to reinforce a stereotype (such as that black men and all women serve white males) then the behavior can't be permitted, even if forbidding it leads to the denying of jobs to individual blacks and white women in the process.

And the motive is deduced from the figures. I heard recently of a dilemma faced by a business college in New York (whose record of affirmative action had recently been questioned), in trying to fill a vacancy in its history department. Four women candidates were up for the job: a woman from India who taught Indian history; a Hispanic who taught Spanish history; a white woman who taught Chinese history; and a white woman who taught Japanese history. The friend who told me this story said that since this was a business school, he and others in the department thought it would be exceedingly valuable for students to study Japanese history and culture. But at the first meeting to discuss candidates, the president of the college refused even to inquire further into the credentials of the professors of Chinese and Japanese history. The fact that they were women apparently was not enough to satisfy affirmative action—because they were both white.

So, affirmative action may be about to backfire on the white women who promoted it. As a policy, it was never intended to be particularly just to the individual, although some individuals managed to benefit from it. But what if white women now become part of the group subject to "reverse discrimination"?

A 1991 review of a book by a Philadelphia trial judge mentions another example of this sort of conflict between a white woman and a minority man.

> Judge Forer discusses the case of a young working-class woman with an outstanding high school and community service record who won a scholarship to nursing school. The scholarship was later taken away and given to a mediocre male student with disciplinary problems. The nursing school argued it had too many women. When the young woman sued, half a dozen civil rights organizations filed briefs in support of the school and the young man. No one supported her position.[25]

As at Starrett City, a preponderance of our "direct discrimination" category may be suspect. In 1987 the *New York Times* reported that trustees were worried because the University of North Carolina at Chapel Hill had enrolled a student body that was 59.2 percent female, under a blind admissions policy. One trustee was reported as saying, "Anytime you get over 50 percent, it's becoming more and more a girls' school," and the dean of admissions reported that the trustees had recommended that the admissions policy be changed.[26] The *trouble* seemed to be that "Of the candidates who apply here, the women present better credentials."[27]

And Don't Forget, Women Are Employers, Too

A great deal has been said and written elsewhere about the antilibertarian characteristics of affirmative action. Here, I'd like to point out that since affirmative action postulates that *groups* have rights to some sort of representation in various segments of the economy, as presently implemented in U.S. law it requires that the principle of equality before the law be subordinated to ideas of social benefit. It's the ERA/protective labor legislation fight all over again. No business or institution can be sure it is totally safe from the Byzantine requirements of affirmative action rulings (what would you bet would be a ruling on changing admissions policy in the Chapel Hill example?). At any given moment, a business may find it has to produce records, not only of the race and sex of all its employees, but of the race and sex of everyone who has been *considered* for employment or promotion, in order to defend itself from being found to be "discriminatory."

What makes all of these regulations and requirements even more bizarre is that they are under the umbrella of the Civil Rights Act of 1964, which expressly forbade the imposition of numerical quotas. So we found the Supreme Court faced with the argument, in the *Weber* case, that perhaps Kaiser had acted illegally in setting up a special training program for blacks *in the absence of a court finding that it had been discriminatory in the past,* which would then have mandated such a program. In other words, it's forbidden because it's not yet mandatory; but it must be one or the other.

If Not This, What?

So what should be done? We live in a society in which discrimination has operated for a long time. There is certainly reason to believe that the way the common law (and labor law) has treated women and the way that slavery and segregation laws have treated blacks have distorted our society both sociologically and economically. True equality before the law will stop further distortion, but will it correct presently remaining distortion? What can we do to improve our society in this respect?

First of all, it is important to recognize that much present-day affirmative action imposes a handicap on the very people it seeks to help. An article on professional schools at the time of the *Bakke* case quoted a young black lawyer as saying, "If you graduated from certain universities in certain years, your degree is suspect." Stephen L. Carter's book, *Reflections of an Affirmative Action Baby,* predicted the end in the near future of most racial preferences and detailed the personal costs that a beneficiary of such programs must bear—including, but not limited to, the requirement that such a person conform to the expectations of the leaders of the black community.[28]

A woman engineer I know says that affirmative action hiring practices in her field have led to a change in attitude toward her when she goes out on a job. Many years ago, she says, when her firm sent her into the field, the people she dealt with took the attitude that if a woman had that job, she must be *outstandingly* qualified to have been hired. Now, when she has much more experience, she finds she has to prove herself on each job, as her clients assume that she is not qualified, but has been given the job to satisfy affirmative action guidelines.

Anecdotes like these tell us that a lot of the problem of discrimination is a problem of attitude and expectation—areas in which government mandates have little direct effect. Worse than that, if the group is considered more important than the individual, then the individual will be sacrificed for supposed "group needs," as at Starrett City. But there are no group needs; that's a metaphor. Only individuals have needs.

The bottom line of the present policies for the employer is that for every category of employee, we must find that magic percentage that would ensure being *left alone* by regulatory agencies and would not lose *either* discrimination or reverse discrimination suits. And the bottom line for the well-qualified employee? Try to find a business small enough to look at your individual qualifications, without caring about what you mean to the government.

And what should the feminist do, as a feminist? Protest the creation of a world in which everything that's not required is forbidden. A world of free choice is an advantage for everybody—a conformist world is not, whether it is conformist by government mandate or by social pressure. The days when higher education was closed to individuals who were women, when myriad occupations were closed to individuals who were women are not that far in the past. Are we now to accept new rules that close off opportunities to individuals in other ways?

Feminists have always known that the opportunity to move back and forth between association with men and association only with other women is the best of all possible worlds. Educators have discovered that there are real advantages to all-girl schools and women's colleges, whether they think these differences attributable to nature or nurture. Deborah Tannen's best-selling book, *You Just Don't Understand,* familiarized a large audience with her detailed analysis of the differences in conversational styles of men and women, and of the fact that mixed groups adopt male styles.[29] Educators have known this for a long time; boys find it easier to speak in mixed classes than girls do. In 1986 Charol Shakeshaft reported that the research on gender and schooling kept coming up with two messages. "First, what is good for males is not necessarily good for females. Second, if a choice must be made, the education establishment will base policy and instruction on that which is good for males."[30]

In the 1970s, there was almost a rush to coeducation. Yale, Princeton, Dartmouth, and the service academies admitted women; Vassar and Skidmore admitted men. But by the eighties, this was being reconsidered by many women's colleges. They started emphasizing the advantages of their institutions; their graduates earn more money than graduates from coed schools; their faculties and administrators have a large percentage of high-powered women who can serve as role models. In 1987 the associate director of the Women's College Coalition said, "To go co-ed makes you one more small, non-name-brand liberal arts college. Theoretically, you get twice as many students, but you trade off your market niche."[31]

Women are not facing the forcible gender integration of these single-sex colleges at the moment, but black colleges are facing forcible racial integration. The black schools served by the United Negro College Fund are now required to take quotas of white students, although some black leaders (Bill Cosby has been particularly outspoken) feel that the best education for black students is precisely these black colleges, where they do not have to face the assumption that they got in through affirmative action. May we some day face a Bakke-in-reverse case, where a black student sues because of a set aside for a less qualified student who was white? And what will the courts say then?

Schemes to provide extra help and support for black inner-city students by establishing all-male black schools have also been attacked as segregationist and illegal. If they represent government herding by race and gender, of course they would be. But, if operated as "magnet schools" that no one is forced to attend or as private alternatives to the present inner-city education, such schools might provide a valid possible choice.

In the fall of 1991, inner-city girls' schools were proposed by a number of sources trying to help troubled girls. The president of the National Resource Center for Girls, a private organization that runs educational programs for a quarter of a million girls nationwide, says that inner-city boys get more attention, because "boys gone astray are considered dangerous and girls gone astray are considered blameworthy." An article in the *New*

York Times observes that "Many experts are torn between a belief that single-sex schools can help girls and a deeper commitment to coeducation on social grounds."[32]

Stand up for the existence of girls' schools and women's colleges and black schools and colleges—as long as they are creatures of choice, there are good reasons for their existence. Similarly, women have learned through experience the importance of consciousness raising and networks. Men are now following suit and discovering the reasons for the existence of men's groups. We do not need to be representatively distributed in every association we choose. If feminist separatists are legal, what about black separatists? Why not? And what about clubs? I think it's a good thing for clubs primarily devoted to business to decide to admit women—not on grounds of legal fairness, but on grounds of good sense. But it's also a good thing to have single-sex clubs.

When two women students at the University of Texas filed a grievance because they couldn't get into an all-male club on campus, the Longhorn Hellraisers, it was decided that the group violated federal law, which outlaws all such single-sex groups except sororities and fraternities. These are required by the Office of Civil Rights of the Federal Department of Education to have tax-exempt status, a membership that is primarily students, and to be a "social fraternity." "The office defines social fraternities as groups that do not base membership on academic pursuits or grades and that do not allow members to join other designated social fraternities."[33]

As a result of this complaint, twenty-nine all-men or all-women clubs had to admit the opposite sex to membership, including a group (the Orange Jackets) of women students who have been the official hostesses of the university since 1947. The president of the Hellraisers, however, said they would take steps to qualify as a "social fraternity" rather than admit women, saying, "Sometimes the guys just want to hang with the guys and sometimes the girls want to hang with the girls. . . . People need to understand that."

In a very interesting 1983 article in *McCall's*, Annie Gottlieb says that in the "prospect of a unisex world . . . men, mysteriously, have wilted." Men and women *do* have different needs, and men, she says, need "a clearly defined difference between the sexes."[34] She points to the research of Margaret Mead as discovering that there was a huge variation from culture to culture as to what men do and women do—as long as men have the "right, or ability, to practice some activity that women are not allowed to practice."[35] Gottlieb suggests three areas in which this need of men can be "filled in a way that is not at women's expense": fighting, following sports, and "gallantry." Most men need to feel that they could defend their loved ones if they had to, and in order to feel that they need some experience of not backing down from a fight. Since men are on average stronger and more active than women, team sports is an area they can identify with as "harmless celebrations of masculine capacities that helped our species to survive." And finally, says Gottlieb, "When a man opens a door for a woman, knowing full well that she can open the door by herself, he is not being chauvinistic or condescending. He is making a symbolic statement that his superior physical strength will be used to assist and protect, not harm."[36]

To which I would add, why shouldn't men be permitted to have clubs that only admit women at certain times? Women have ritual activities that *they* do with each other.

Feminists know that similarities among people can be an important bond—should we let our desire *not* to be excluded from the larger world of work and achievement turn into an insistence that people can't choose to be with their own group? Suppose a feminist company wants to hire only women—shouldn't it be able to do so? Should a battered women's center or a rape counselling service have to employ men in proportion to their representation in the population?

We shouldn't try to do it both ways. We can't use the power of the law to force our way into the bastions of male prerogative and then hope to have our own groups respected as a private choice. *Of course* the government shouldn't have required all the herding in the first place. But since government is power, power is all the bureaucrats know. Those feminists and libertarians who want to reduce government power know we have a double fight on our hands over every issue. First, to get the government to stop exerting influence in one direction, and second, to keep it from turning around and exerting it in the other.

Perhaps, like Sarah Grimké, in her nineteenth-century *Letters on the Equality of the Sexes and the Condition of Women,* we should say instead, "I ask no favors for my sex. . . . All I ask of our brethren is, that they will take their feet off our necks, and permit us to stand upright."[37]

CHAPTER TEN

My Body, Myself: The Right to Protection

There are some rights that need continuous feminist concern. When it comes to her own body and her own sexuality, woman has always been at a disadvantage. Of course, no one, man or woman, has a right to take any action he or she pleases that might violate the rights of others, but women have been particularly restricted. The fact that women produce children has historically led society to exert control over women's lives.

In this country, even after women had entered the workplace in a major way, their ability to use their talents to compete with men was limited by law. The Supreme Court decision *Muller* v. *Oregon,* which permitted so-called protective laws (which Richard Epstein has called the equivalent of Jim Crow laws for women) to be instituted in every state, prohibiting certain jobs to women and limiting the hours (including overtime hours) they could work, the weights they could lift, and the special conditions of employment that must apply to them—based its rationale on the fact that women bear children: "Woman's physical structure and the performance of the maternal functions place her at a disadvantage. . . . woman becomes an object of public interest and care in order to preserve the strength and vigor of the race."[1]

Of course, this "public interest and care" has not only controlled the economic activities of women, but as far back in history as we go it has controlled the sexual lives of women in various ways. It has also often failed to protect women adequately from sex-related violence: from being battered by the men in their lives or from sexual assault.

What kind of personal bodily control does the contemporary woman want? The watchword is *choice.* And choice is not, as it is sometimes used, a code word for abortion. Choice means the right to say "no"—or "yes"— under any circumstances she pleases and to have that right protected, not violated, by the legal system. Choice includes reproductive choice, but there's an antecedent right. Before deciding whether or not, and how, to bear a child, a woman has the right to choose or refuse a sexual partner and to be able to call on society for protection in that choice.

Protection from Violence

All people face the possibility of violence. Contemporary feminism, since its emergence in the late 1960s and early 1970s, has been very successful in calling attention to the special forms of violence women face. By the late 1970s, there was a revolution in the way rape was perceived (as a crime of violence, not as the result of sexual deprivation), and the crimes of incest and of wife beating were literally "discovered," as was the issue of sexual harassment. What about these special forms of violence?

Perhaps the most obvious is rape.

Since the law and custom of many societies holds that a married woman is literally the property of her husband, there is a long international history of the concept that when a married woman is raped, it is not her rights but her husband's rights that are violated. (Remember the war in Bangladesh, when an invading army raped thousands of women, and their husbands considered them to be damaged goods and wouldn't take them back?) As recently as 1982, an American husband sued his wife's lover for damages, arguing that the lover's "criminal conversation" with his wife was an invasion of his common law property right in the body and services of his wife. A three-judge court of appeals in the State of Washington turned him down, saying that the common law principle was "no longer legally viable." But it did get as far as a court of appeals.[2]

If a wife is a husband's property, it is not possible for him to violate his own rights, no matter what he does. The common law, which formed the basic law of all of the United States except Louisiana and reflected this property view of marriage, determined rape laws in a number of states, as late as 1985. As of that year, in Alabama, Arkansas, Kansas, Montana, South Dakota, Texas, Vermont, Washington, and West Virginia, a husband had total immunity from rape prosecution by his wife. In twenty-six other states, such prosecutions were allowed only if the couple was legally separated.

There is no record of an American man being tried for raping his wife in their home before a 1978 Oregon case, in which the husband was acquitted. The first rape conviction of a husband who was living with his wife didn't occur until 1984. A circuit court judge had held that William Rider couldn't be charged with raping his wife because there was an "interspousal exception" in the common law, but a Florida appeals court reversed that decision. Rider was convicted of punching his wife in the stomach, beating her on the head, and binding her hands with tape. He forced her into the bedroom, cut off her clothes with scissors, tied her arms and legs to the bedposts, raped her—and then took her to a hospital.[3]

A New York State law that protected a married man from prosecution for raping his wife unless they were legally separated was on the books until late 1984. Instead of repeating the common law exception, the statute, which defined rape as "sexual intercourse with a female by forcible compulsion," said that the victim of a rape committed by her husband was not legally considered to be a "female, in the meaning of the statute."[4]

As long ago as 1975, the F.B.I. said that a rape was committed every ten minutes in the United States. It was only in the 1970s that the laws saying a man could not be convicted of rape by the uncorroborated testimony of his victim were changed, and the incidence of reported rapes has been climbing fairly steadily ever since. As of 1991, the number of reported rapes was estimated at 100,000 a year, or one every *five* minutes, and not all rapes are reported.

By the end of the 1980s, rape had become a serious crime on college campuses. Harvard and Radcliffe students founded a student-run escort service in 1989, which provids a team of two escorts to anyone in the Harvard-Radcliffe community requesting it, between 10:00 P.M. and 4:00 A.M. every day of the week, to and from any place on campus.[5] Other colleges and universities have followed suit. By the fall of 1989 the University of Southern California and Brown University had both increased security in response to rapes on campus, and Syracuse University was planning to open a counseling center for rape victims. That November, the Women's Resource Center at the University of California at Irvine reported having received reports of 40 rapes and "40 other sexual assaults" that year, which prompted the university to install a system of specially marked security phones around campus.[6]

Either rape in general is increasing, or the publicity being given to the fact that rape is a crime of violence, not an extreme of frustrated affection, has increased the willingness of victims to come forward and testify against their attackers. Either way, it's certain that we don't have a rape-free society in the United States. Some people even blame feminists for increasing the level of rage among American males, and thus, if not exactly excusing, at least *explaining* the high levels of reported rape.

Feminists have probably increased the level of rape *reporting* in the United States; they have actively called attention to the inequities that have surrounded the prosecution of rape and done much to institute training courses for police personnel who deal with rape victims. They have also set up hot lines and counseling centers for victims.

Rape is an expression of hostility and a way for a person who feels powerless to assert power and control. It is not the only male-female sexual relationship based on power, although in others, violence may not be overt, or even identified. It is totally appropriate that sexual intercourse with children is considered to be a kind of rape; of particular interest to a feminist discussion is what being the target of this sort of power relationship with an adult male does to little girls. Years ago, Gloria Steinem said that incest was going to be the next feminist issue. At the time, this seemed like an exaggerated claim, but her prediction is coming true.

First, one proviso. Age of consent laws are often unrealistic, and people can be trapped in situations where in fact a young man and young woman do consent together but are technically in violation of the law. The relationship may be ill-advised, but that doesn't make it rape. Consider, for instance, the case of a fifteen-year-old girl who in 1986 was sent to juvenile detention by Connecticut Superior Court Judge Francis M. McDonald of Danbury, Connecticut, in an attempt to get her to testify against a school bus driver in a rape case.

The girl's parents filed a rape complaint against the driver, who admitted he had had sex with the girl on several occasions. She said she loved him and that he hadn't raped her. A group of women's rights activists came to her support, and she was released from detention and the charges against her lover were dropped. In some states, the admissions of intercourse would have been enough to convict him, because of her being under a technical age of consent.[7]

But there is no similar confusion in cases of incest and the abuse of very young girls. *Sexually Victimized Children,* by David Finkelhor, reported the results of a survey by questionnaire of "predominantly middle-class undergraduate sociology students" in which one out of five women reported that they had been sexually abused as children, as did one in eleven men. The book suggests that as many as 1 percent of all American women have been sexually victimized by fathers or stepfathers; most of the others fell victim to family friends.[8]

Allegations about this kind of abuse in day-care centers have been widely publicized, but even if some of them are true, that is not what is responsible for the bulk of the incidents of incest. The National Abortion Rights Action League (NARAL) had a handout, with an extensive late 1970s bibliography, called "The Facts About Rape and Incest" in which "Katherine McFarlane of the National Center for Child Abuse and Neglect estimates that there may be as many as 1,000 cases of incest per million a year—at least 100,000 cases. Other professionals consider a quarter of a million cases a conservative estimate. These estimates are supported by federal statistics of gonorrhea in children (contracted solely through sexual intercourse): 3,000 cases in children under nine, and 9,000 cases in children ten to fourteen."[9] (It's not really clear in reading this pamphlet whether these figures include boys or not.)

In a 1981 column in the *New York Times,* an expert on incest, Dr. Alexander G. Zaphiris, who has been working in the field since 1957, was quoted as saying that 90 percent of the sexually abused children in the country are victims of incest. He also said that, despite the common claim of the male authority figure who commits the incest that the relationship began in the child's adolescence, he "has never seen an incest victim who was not conditioned as an infant." This is done by sexually stimulating the child "as though this was normal affection." The article goes on to say that "Overt sex usually begins when the child is about 5 years old."[10]

A later study by Diana Russell of the prevalence in California of the sexual abuse of girls found that 16 percent of the randomly selected women she interviewed had been incestuously abused before the age of eighteen, and the author speculated that the increase in the number of families with stepfathers was directly related to an increase in incest; abuse by stepfathers occurred seven times as often as abuse by biological fathers.[11]

Incest is rightly called abuse. Many of the men involved rationalize it as "having the child learn the facts of life from someone she knows and trusts." It cannot be stressed too strongly that this *is* a rationalization, on somewhat the same level as calling bullfighting a "game." It isn't a game, or a loving lesson, for the victim. Incest may rarely be overtly violent, but that does not mean it is not traumatic. The work of Dr. Judith Lewis Herman of the Harvard Medical School has been finding similarities between the psychological traumas caused by incest and the traumatic stress disorders experienced by war veterans.[12]

What about sexual harassment? This is an issue that has raised some hackles among conservatives and has certainly been the subject of many jokes. (Of course, all women's complaints about how they are treated, from their attempts to get the vote, through their desire for education and nontraditional jobs, up to wife beating, have been the subject of jokes.)

Sexual harassment came on the scene as a public issue some time in the late seventies. There were some early failed attempts to bring cases to the courts; women who had left their jobs because of the advances of an employer were considered to have left for "personal" reasons. But in 1980, the EEOC issued guidelines, defining "unwelcome sexual advances, requests for sexual favors, and other verbal or physical conduct of a sexual nature" as harassment under two conditions. When they are a condition of employment or of receiving a benefit, a "quid pro quo"; or when they interfere with a worker's ability to do the job by creating a "hostile or abusive work environment" by sexual advances or personal comments. (An example of this last was reported to me by a friend of mine who worked in building construction. After she was hired, the foremen began showing stag movies where she had to stand in line to pick up her paycheck, in an attempt to embarrass her.)

Unions issued policy statements calling for the elimination of sexual harassment in the workplace. The AFL-CIO resolved in 1983 that this was an issue to be addressed through collective bargaining. But still, when the Supreme Court decided its first sexual harassment case, *Meritor Savings Bank* v. *Vinson,* on June 19, 1986, it was greeted with delight and some surprise by feminist lawyers. The *New York Times* quoted Catharine A. MacKinnon, then of Stanford University's Institute for Research on Women and Gender (best-known for her activities in the antipornography wars) as saying, "What the decision means is that we made this law up from the beginning, and now we've won."[13]

So what is sexual harassment? Is the crime made up, as well as the law? Well, the "crime" may be, but the offense is not. In the spring of 1984, I got into a written debate on the subject in the pages of *Inquiry* magazine. John Gordon, who taught at Connecticut College and was the author of *The Myth of the Monstrous Male and Other Feminist Fables,* was outraged by a Harvard University report that gave a long definition by enumeration of sexual harassment and then stated that one third of the women at Harvard responded in a survey that they had been harassed.[14]

He raised some valid points about not trivializing rape, and the folly of inviting the state "to come galumphing into an area where it has no business, no competence, and no possibility of competence, where it can do nothing but botch and wreck." But he concluded generally that what the Harvard women had experienced was "wooing" and that there was therefore no content to the concept of harassment, saying,

> The absurdities attendant on the current "sexual harassment" campaign are simply the latest sign that much of what passes for contemporary feminism amounts to a meretricious campaign to have it both ways: to advance the old standards of female privilege, of being especially protected from the world's rough and tumble, while enjoying all the hard-won benefits of being one of the guys.[14]

In answer to this, I pointed out that sexual harassment does exist and that what was missing from Gordon's definition were the twin concepts of taking place over time and taking place in a situation where repeated contact between people is essentially unchosen. I agreed that, absent the commission of a crime, it is not in general an area for state action, any more than bigotry is. But I disagreed that employer guidelines are equally inopportune. There *is* harassment, and if an employer will take it seriously, why shouldn't he say so? I went on to say,

> The word *harass* comes from a medieval French word meaning *to set a dog on.* The problem for the victim is one of escape, not revenge or punishment. Sexual harassment has only become an issue in recent years because until recently women assumed that when they were faced with it all they could do was leave—quit the job, drop the course, transfer to another college, even leave town—often at considerable cost to their livelihood or their future.
>
> As to Professor Gordon's contention that it is "mischievous" to find out how many women in an institution (such as Harvard) say they have experienced harassment, I must differ here, too. I view as slightly exaggerated the picture of hordes of men "scared into perpetual monkish silence," and hordes of women "sitting by the phone waiting for some tremulous swain to get up the necessary gumption." . . . A proper under-standing of just one word in the Harvard definition—cornering—should be enough to guide the bewildered to distinguish between harassment and, as Gordon puts it, "anything romantic."[15]

There was an interesting postscript to this exchange: I received a thank-you letter in response to my article from a woman who *had* been harassed at Harvard and had filled out the survey in question. She wrote,

> Let me add two points. In a free society, a private institution like Harvard University is free to set standards of conduct regarding sexual harassment, and to censure or even fire sexual harassers. Secondly, libertarians are against force *and fraud.* If I am hired with the understanding that my advancement will be based on the quality of my work, and I find that it is, instead, based on whether I will dispense sexual favors to my superiors, then they have committed a breach of contract, and, in a free society, I should be able to sue. Ditto for an educational institution that promises good grades *only* for good work.
>
> Unfortunately, I cannot sign my name. My harasser, seven years later, can still have a chilling effect on my career. So can the fact that "I believe" I was harassed, if it becomes generally known to my colleagues. You see, like John Gordon, many of them believe that such incidents only exist in the imaginations of prissy, hysterical women who should be avoided at all costs.

If any readers still think this may be the case, they should examine the allegations of some of the women who have charged sexual harassment by landlords. A New York welfare mother complained that she slept with the guard in a New York City welfare hotel because the latches on the door of her room were loose, she kept finding the windows mysteriously open, and he offered, if she slept with him, to protect her children. An Ohio court found a landlord guilty of violating the Federal Fair Housing Act when he evicted a tenant, her husband, and their son after she refused his sexual advances. And a court required that a Brooklyn tenant who wanted to remain anonymous be compensated by the landlord who molested her while making repairs in her apartment.

Now, libertarians may question whether the regulations that were used to punish the acts listed above are proper formulations of law in a market economy, but it is clear that unethical behavior is going on. None of these cases seem to involve "prissy" women, do they? From the standpoint of the feminist, it is as important to establish and publicize the concept of sexual harassment and encourage women to stand up against it as it is to report instances to whatever authorities exist. Often, the weapon of information can be as useful as legal reprisals. But in any case, I submit, sexual harassment is alive and well.

Another issue that has only been publicized and examined as a problem since the late seventies is wife beating. In 1977 the New Hampshire Commission on the Status of Women refused to approve shelters for battered wives because it concluded that the cause of wife beating was that "those women libbers irritated the hell out of their husbands," in the words of Commissioner Gloria Belzil of Nashua.[16] That was said in the same year that Roger Langley and Richard C. Levy wrote *Wife Beating: The Silent Crisis,* considered by many to be the first comprehensive book on the subject. It is filled with facts and figures, including a chapter on battered men and advice on what steps a battered woman had to take at the time to get the police to report her complaint (get them to be sure to respond to the call by saying "a man" instead of "my husband" has attacked you; take their names and badge numbers and insist that they file a report on the incident; write down everything they tell you about what legal recourse you have, because then they will be less apt to misinform you; insist that they take you to a hospital and try to get them to take pictures of your injuries—if not, arrange for pictures yourself at the hospital).[17]

A United Press International story, which also appeared in 1977, detailed a number of examples of wife abuse and quoted sociologist Dr. Murray Straus's testimony in Congress that "an estimated 3.8 per cent of all American men beat their wives in the past year."[18] There are a lot of other statistics that have been floating around since then; suffice it to say that wife beating is not an unusual phenomenon. Nor is it new.

The word "obey" in the traditional marriage vows has long been held to imply that husbands have the right to chastise those wives who *don't* obey. Sir William Blackstone recorded it in his *Commentaries on the Common Law* as a husband's right to "chastise his wife with a whip or rattan no bigger than his thumb, in order to enforce the salutary restraints of domestic discipline."[19] In 1871 an American court in Alabama finally held for the first time, in *Fulgham* v. *State,* that "The privilege, ancient though it may be, to beat her with a stick, to pull her hair, choke her, spit in her face or kick her about the floor or to inflict upon her other like indignities, is not now acknowledged by our law."[20]

According to Terry Davidson in *Conjugal Crime* (1978), a Pennsylvania state legislator introduced a bill in 1886 to make the punishment fit the crime and punish wife beating with corporal punishment. The bill read in part, "Be it enacted by the Senate and House of Pennsylvania . . . that whenever hereafter any male person shall willfully beat, bruise, or mutilate his wife, the court . . . shall direct the infliction of corporal punishment upon such offender, to be laid upon his bare back to the number of lashes not exceeding thirty, by means of a whip or lash of suitable proportions and strength for the purpose of this act." The rationale was that the family would be kept intact and the community spared the expense of supporting both the husband in prison and the wife and family through charity. But it didn't pass.[21]

In 1978 a number of laws were passed and agreements were made that required local police to change their procedures when called to a scene of domestic violence. The New York police agreed to arrest wife beaters, after being faced with a suit from twelve women (accompanied by affidavits from fifty-nine others) claiming that the police had refused to arrest their husbands even when presented with evidence that they had been beaten.[22] At about the same time, Massachusetts instituted a law that required policemen to read people complaining of domestic violence the following list of rights:

> You have the right to go to the district, probate or superior court and file a complaint requesting any of the following orders: An order restraining your attacker from abusing you; an order directing your attacker to leave your household; an order awarding you custody of a minor child; an order directing your attacker to pay support for you or any minor child in your custody . . . ; an order directing your attacker to pay you for losses suffered as a result of the abuse. . . .
>
> You have the right to go to district court and file a criminal complaint for threats, assault and battery, assault with a deadly weapon, assault with intent to kill or other related crimes. You may go to district court for an emergency on weekends or holidays.
>
> If you are in need of medical treatment, you have the right to demand

that the officer present drive you to the nearest hospital or otherwise assist you.

If you believe that police protection is needed for your physical safety, you have the right to demand that the officer present remain at the scene until you and your children leave or until your safety is otherwise assured.[23]

A December 1983 editorial in *USA Today* estimated that there were "six million American women trapped by domestic violence."[24] By that time there were 700 shelters for battered women across the country, 200 of them run by the YWCA, but the agencies running them reported that they couldn't handle 80 percent of women who needed help. And although the changed laws helped somewhat, it wasn't as radical a change as people might have hoped. In June 1986, Connecticut became only the seventh state to require arrest "in cases of probable domestic assault." A precipitating incident for the law was one in which a woman was partially paralyzed. The *New York Times* reported it on June 15, 1986.

In May of 1983, Tracey Thurman told the Torrington Police Department that her estranged husband had beaten her and was threatening to kill her. Mrs. Thurman later testified that she was told to come back in three weeks, when the officer handling domestic cases would return from vacation.

Two weeks later, she called again for help. When the police arrived 25 minutes later, the 21-year-old Mrs. Thurman lay critically wounded in her front yard. Her husband stood over her with a knife.[25]

In 1984 Mrs. Thurman sued the police department, and in June 1985 she won her suit. Hence, a new law.

In the August after this Connecticut law was passed, another dramatic case brought attention to Massachusetts.

In March of 1986, twenty-two-year-old Pamela Nigro Dunn had appeared before Judge Paul P. Heffernan in district court in Somerville, Massachusetts, to request a restraining order and police protection from her estranged husband, Paul J. Dunn, just as the 1978 Massachusetts law said she should. According to a *New York Times* account, the judge "told Mrs. Dunn, in open court with Mr. Dunn present, that she was wasting the court's time, that her fears of Mr. Dunn were unfounded and that she should act more like an adult."[26]

In August, Mrs. Dunn's dead body was found in a town dump, beaten, strangled, and shot. She had last been seen when Mr. Dunn abducted her a few days earlier when she was out walking with her mother. As a result of this case, Massachusetts started a program to train its district court judges to handle domestic violence cases, as it was reported that the 1978 law was too often ignored.[27]

Here is another area in which feminists have helped and can continue to help, by establishing centers for battered wives. This requires, first of all, a twenty-four-hour crisis line that battered wives can call. There is now a nationwide, toll-free, twenty-four-hour National Domestic Violence Hotline. The number is 1-800-333-SAFE.

But local hotlines are still valuable. The problem is that in the worst cases women are characteristically kept helpless, penniless, and as dependent as possible by their husbands. The employed woman without children can easily walk out if her husband hits her. But the woman with no job, no money, no friends, perhaps no family in the area, dependent on a man for her livelihood and that of her children, keeps hoping the situation will get better, and by the time she decides to call for help, it may have escalated to the point where her life is in danger or she realizes that her children as well as herself are threatened. She needs everything. In 1977, *Wife Beating: The Silent Crisis* reported,

> They are unemployed, and the only money they have is given to them by their husbands. It is not uncommon that there is precious little left over from the household allowance for the wife to use to help herself escape. A woman in Detroit relates it took her two years to save $1.75. When she got $5.00 from her grandmother at Christmas, she was able to buy bus tickets for herself and her daughter and flee her husband.[28]

So a battered-wife task force needs volunteers that will help, with carfare, with shelter, with legal and police advice, with encouragement. It needs a network of homes that can take in women with children on an emergency basis, for a maximum of three days. Then social service agencies, local clergy, and the crisis line should be in touch with a coordinator who can contact the available houses and take the woman seeking sanctuary to a place where she can stay, with her children.

Senator Joe Biden (Democrat from Delaware and chair of the Senate Judiciary Committee) held hearings on domestic violence in late 1990 and proposed the first federal legislation to deal with it, the Violence Against Women Act. The Act would triple federal financing of battered women's shelters, create federal penalties for abusers who cross state lines, and offer incentives to states for arrests.[29]

In some communities there are such shelters, community homes with a counselor, a nurse, and a couple of volunteers, plus facilities for cooking and bathing, and diapers, bottles, and toys for small children. But it is probably best if these are *not* government-run or government-supported.

The reason is that they have to be able to discriminate against men—especially violent husbands. To be useful, a shelter has to be well publicized, and this means that husbands who are determined to get their wives back, or those who simply want revenge, can go to a state-supported facility required to provide equal protection to both genders, openly or by pretending to be battered men, in order to reach the woman who is hiding. So there is a big legal question about the use of public funds to help battered women and their children.

All these details of rape, incest, and battering present a very unpleasant picture of what men are capable of, and some feminists have generalized that all men are basically angry at and exploitative of women, and men who commit such acts are just acting out what all men feel. That's not the message I wish to convey. Rather, my message is that there are always people who will commit crimes. If it is clear that the crime will go unpunished, it is more likely to be committed. The policeman or judge who asks the rape victim if she enjoyed it or asks the battered wife to give her husband one more chance—or the social worker who doesn't believe the child who brings herself to accuse her respectable and respected father—is making it more likely that such crimes will be repeated—often with the same victim.

When a crime, such as battering or incest, is committed under circumstances where there are also ties of affection, there may be conflicting emotions that are difficult to untangle. There is often a general assumption that the woman has "provoked" the assault, which may have some truth to it; there may be a pattern of communication leading to the violence that can be altered for the better. There are therapeutic specialists that are helping both perpetrator and victim in these circumstances, just as there are therapeutic programs that confront imprisoned rapists with victims of rape. There may be much hope in such programs.

But if a woman had a spirited altercation with a stranger she encountered on the street and he assaulted her, the police wouldn't ask, "What did you do to provoke him?" An upsetting verbal exchange is not considered sufficient provocation for a violent assault between strangers, and it is not sufficient if the man is a husband or live-in lover. It shouldn't be forgotten that the behavior was a violation of someone's rights, and it is the well-being of the victim that is and should be paramount. If the victim just wants protection, then protection is what she should get.

CHAPTER ELEVEN

My Body, Myself:
The Many Kinds of Choice

Choice means the right to decide not to have a child, but it also means, emphatically, the right of a woman to *have* a child if she is willing to take the responsibility of seeing that it is cared for. And choice also means the right to decide how and where she will have that child.

The lawyer protesting a court-ordered Caesarean section performed against a pregnant woman's wishes, the evangelical Christian home for unwed mothers, the in vitro fertilization clinic, the woman offering to be a surrogate mother—all are advancing reproductive choice.

There is a history, in Supreme Court cases, of family rights and a right to privacy that has been extended from the right of people to marry, have children, and educate them to the right of married couples to use contraceptives, to the right of unmarried couples to do the same, to a similar right for minors. But before getting into this area of "reproductive choice," let us consider some related areas that, to many people, do not seem as clearly to entail rights worthy of respect. Namely, prostitution and surrogate motherhood.

Prostitution

If it is appropriate that a woman be allowed to choose her sexual partner, and the time and the place, may she also choose, if he agrees, to be paid for the act? In January of 1978, a New York family court judge startled legal circles by dismissing prostitution charges against a minor girl, saying that prostitution laws discriminate against women. The fourteen-year-old defendant, whose name was not printed because of her age, was freed by Judge Margaret Taylor of the Manhattan Family Court. The judge said that the laws banning prostitution discriminate against women and are therefore invalid, and the act with which the girl was charged, whether paid for or not, would not have been a crime if committed by an adult and therefore was not a juvenile offense. She ruled, "However offensive it may be, recreational commercial sex threatens no harm to the public health, safety or welfare, and therefore may not be proscribed."[1]

The case was appealed, but it presaged a great deal of attention that has since been paid to the idea that prostitution is a victimless crime indulged in by two people, in which only one participant, the woman, is usually punished. Some European countries legally allow (and regulate) prostitution. France saw taxpayer revolts among prostitutes in the late seventies and early eighties, because although prostitution was nominally legal, fines for "soliciting" were ranging up to $700.00, and such fines became an important source of revenue for local police departments.

In 1979 a French prostitute sued the government for "pimping" when it assessed her for back taxes equaling $100,000, which it calculated by assuming that she had five customers a day in a 200-day working year—putting her in the 60 percent tax bracket. A Reuters dispatch reported:

> "Suddenly it seemed very clear," she said. "If the government says I'm a whore and then takes my money, that's pimping, and I don't even know a pimp who'd demand this much."
>
> The government can rule a woman to be a prostitute after she had paid fines for the offense and she is then subject to taxation.[2]

The first issue of a French prostitutes' newspaper, *Macadam,* complained in 1981 that punitive taxation was used by the government to hound women who had decided to retire. An article by Paul Webster in the *Press* commented, "One article is about Lisa, a 42-year-old woman who opened a hair-dressing salon with her savings but was forced to sell and go back on the streets because of a tax demand for about $100,000."[3]

In the United States today there's a similar split-personality attitude toward prostitution. The leading legalized brothel in Nevada was closed and seized by the IRS in 1990 and was actually operated for some months by that government agency before it was sold for back taxes. But while the federal government was running a brothel, prostitution was still illegal in most localities. Everyone knows that it exists, call girls are interviewed on national television talk shows, yet police on vice squads can still demand payoffs, and prostitutes are still routinely arrested and bailed out. This, while feeless "recreational sex," which Judge Margaret Taylor said in 1978 was not illegal even when "commercial," is now totally beyond the reach of the law in most localities, limited in scope only by people's concern about AIDS.

Prostitution has a long history of being the kind of personal service for money that society considers a crime. An almost identical activity, sexual surrogacy, is now a controversial, but recognized, aspect of the psychotherapeutic treatment of male sexual problems. Prostitutes say that they don't sell their bodies; they rent them. How can the law distinguish between the woman who takes money for the sexual use of her body because it is the only activity between herself and starvation, as was sometimes the case in postwar Europe; or because she is a healer trying to help a man solve what he perceives as a sexual inadequacy; or because she thinks it is great fun; or because she is self-destructively punishing herself? Or even because it means little to her but enables her to earn money to achieve her values: whether those values are tuition for professional training, a more self-indulgent lifestyle, private schooling for a talented child, or support for aged relatives? The answer is, the law can't distinguish, and shouldn't if it could.

Some women may indeed go into prostitution because they have been bullied or harmed or psychologically crippled by the circumstances of their lives, but these are not the reasons the profession is illegal. And some women perform the same acts for other reasons.

The answer again, it seems to me, is feminism. Some prostitutes are victims, and they may need rescue and help and protection. Feminist organizations are doing this, with outreach and group discussion and friendship, and this is exactly what it takes. But victims cannot be helped if they are also perceived as criminals, so feminist organizations should be working both to repeal the prostitution laws and to privately extend help (similar to that which they are now extending to battered wives) to those prostitutes who feel that in some sense they have not chosen the life, but have been pushed into it.

Surrogate Motherhood

Meanwhile, there is another way of renting one's body, as new as prostitution is old, that is now under fire. I am speaking of surrogate motherhood.

For a long time, men have been able to sell their sperm to sperm banks, to be used in artificial insemination. Sometime in the 1970s, in response, perhaps, to the growing discovery on the part of career women that postponing childbirth might mean incurring hitherto unexpected risks— of infertility or of bearing disabled children—young women started renting out their wombs. A well-off couple, who sincerely want children but have found they couldn't have them because of a fertility problem with the wife, arrange to pay a substantial sum plus childbirth expenses to a young woman willing to be inseminated with the man's sperm. Under other circumstances, some young women have even been willing to have a couple's fertilized egg implanted. Many of the women who have become surrogates bore children by contract as much because they enjoyed being pregnant as because of the money.

By the beginning of 1987, so many hundreds of such births had taken place that four bills to support the practice had been introduced in state legislatures, and one state, Louisiana, had introduced a bill to declare the contracts unenforceable.

Then came the case of Baby M. Mary Beth Whitehead signed a surrogacy contract through a Michigan lawyer who specializes in such contracts, Noel Keane. His contracts generally provided that the surrogate would be paid $10,000, Keane would be paid $10,000, and insurance, medical bills, and maternity clothes would cost the couple approximately another $5,000. The couple looking for a surrogate would interview prospects till they found someone they could relate to, preferably from their own locality. In the case of the child who became famous as Baby M, William and Elizabeth Stern (both doctors) became friendly with Mary Beth Whitehead and her husband and two children, taking the Whitehead children from New Jersey to New York for outings. The families lived near each other in New Jersey, and Mary Beth Whitehead and Elizabeth Stern often talked and visited together during the pregnancy.

Then the little girl was born, and Mary Beth Whitehead decided she couldn't give her up, refused to fulfill the contract, and fled from the law with the baby to Florida. After a trial complete with eleven mental health experts, the surrogacy contract was upheld by a New Jersey court in March 1987. Between March and December, seventy bills "seeking to ban, regulate or study surrogacy," according to the *New York Times,* were introduced in twenty-seven states and the District of Columbia.[4]

A controversy exploded. Some people suggested that women contracting to be surrogates should be strictly required to fulfill their contracts. Some suggested exactly the opposite: that such contracts be declared invalid. And a certain number of feminists decided that surrogacy exploits poor women and should therefore be banned. One solution that has been recommended is to allow the contracts, but give the "birth mother" the absolute right during a certain period to change her mind, as is now generally the case when prospective mothers contract before birth to give their children up for adoption.

Of course, there is a crucial difference between adoption and the surrogacy situation, which is a conflict between two genetic parents who have contracted about what will happen to the baby.

Marriage is a contract, but a wife who decided that she wanted her husband to have nothing to do with her child after it was born would not be upheld by the courts. *She* could decide never to see him again, but inherent in the marriage contract are certain rights that he would have, to see and be with his child. A burden of proof would be on the wife in such a situation to prove to a court *why* the father should be kept from his child, and she would have to prove serious moral delinquency for the court to support her.

It might seem inconsistent for the courts to reverse such a stand in a case where a man had never represented that he wanted the woman, but had only "married" the child. But, of course, it isn't completely inconsistent, because the basis of the contract was financial, and many people are distressed to see financial considerations and agreements (outside of the marriage contract) in areas that have to do with sex and reproduction. They are afraid of "baby selling," although they would not feel the same way about a conventionally married woman who wanted to give up custody of her child in return for a divorce settlement.

In San Bernardino County, California, in 1980, a sixteen-year-old boy sold his five-year-old cousin, Mary Agnes Cahail, to a convicted sex offender he had met casually. According to a newspaper account, the man, who had been married four times, "asked the boy if he knew of any young girls he could buy." The boy turned down $50 for his cousin, but finally agreed to deliver her for $230.00.[5]

This story plays into the hidden fear that people have about financial transactions over children. The emotional assumption is that a person who takes money for a child has no concern about anything that might subsequently happen to that child. And, further, that a person who *pays* money for a child wants to exploit it in some way.

Thus, an article in the *New York Times* about Baby M was titled "Taking the Money Out of Motherhood." A lower court had upheld the Baby M contract and authorized the child's adoption by Elizabeth Stern; the Supreme Court invalidated the contract and the adoption, calling the contract "illegal and perhaps criminal" and characterizing the transaction as "the sale of a child," forbidden by New Jersey law. Then it gave Mary Beth Whitehead visitation rights, but it left the child in the custody of the Sterns! Clearly, the court found the basic transaction was *good* for the child, but the offer of money had tainted it.[6]

In October 1990, a California Superior Court judge refused to rule that a woman who was a *complete* surrogate—that is, who had been implanted with a fertilized embryo from a woman who had a hysterectomy but still had ovaries—had a claim to the child that she had borne. The surrogate in the case had also signed a $10,000 contract, which the judge found to be valid. But a lower court had given the woman visitation rights, which the judge terminated, and he urged the California legislature to set guidelines. Disagreeing with the New Jersey Baby M court, he said, "I see no problem with someone getting paid for her pain and suffering. There is nothing wrong with getting paid for nine months of what I understand is a lot of misery and a lot of bad days. They are not selling a baby; they are selling pain and suffering."[7]

The March of Science

The new techniques of artificial insemination and in vitro fertilization on which surrogacy depends are raising a number of questions in themselves. The Roman Catholic Church finds them so unnatural that it has asked that all these techniques be legally banned. A ban on federal financing of fetal research, instituted in the 1970s in response to pressure from right-to-life groups, has been interpreted to include a ban on federal funding of the new reproductive techniques. But women who have not been able to have the children they want find that these techniques offer miraculous options—in late 1990, it was even announced that doctors had found a way for a woman to give birth to a baby after early menopause, by being implanted with a fertilized egg from a younger woman.

The paradox is that creation and destruction go hand in hand in many of these techniques. Some of them involve the possible destruction of fertilized embryos or fetuses in order to make it more likely for the desired pregnancy to take place. Fertility drugs often result in multiple pregnancies, for instance, that cannot all be carried to term at once. A woman who has had difficulty conceiving and then finds herself pregnant with several fetuses usually has to selectively abort all but two of them, in order to preserve those two. This is now so common there is a name for it; it is called "fetal reduction."

In human reproduction in general, half or more of all fertilized embryos fail to be implanted in the uterus and are lost. Because of this extravagance of nature, in vitro fertilization involves storing multiple fertilized embryos. This led to a bizarre divorce settlement in 1989, in which Mary Davis persuaded a Tennessee court to give her "custody" of seven frozen embryos fertilized by her husband, Junior Davis, because she said she wished to try to have a child by implanting them after the divorce. She called the embryos "children"; he called them "joint property" and tried to have her legally enjoined from making him a parent against his will. The judge said that "human life begins at conception" and gave Mary Davis "custody";

eight months later, Mary Davis, now remarried, decided to donate the "children" to a fertility clinic.[8]

Scientific advances have created other dilemmas, too. The medical use of fetal tissue has turned out to be crucial for the treatment of Parkinson's disease and other nerve disorders, primarily because it is not subject to rejection as other tissue is. The fetal tissue used in early experiments in this technique has come from aborted fetuses, but as early as 1987, the *New York Times* reported on its front page that a company was planning to market *cells* grown from fetal tissue, which is fairly far removed from the issue of abortion.[9] But the antiabortionists have raised the possibility that women might become pregnant in order to abort and have fetal tissue available, either for a loved family member or for sale, and in 1988 they succeeded in getting the Reagan administration to refuse federal funds for fetal tissue transplant research, a ban that the Bush administration has continued.

The possibility of transplanting organs and other body parts has become the subject of a number of best-selling medical novels postulating venal doctors harvesting organs from unsuspecting patients. The fact that fetal tissue is not rejected the way other tissue is makes it valuable for brain transplants in cases not only of Parkinson's, but also for diabetes and perhaps Alzheimer's, but the fictional supposition here is that abortion will be at least encouraged, if not underwritten, by unscrupulous doctors. In organ transplants, such as giving one's eyes to the eye bank or donating other body parts for transplant in one's will, a distinction is made between the medical use of body parts and how they are obtained—a person could not profit from the body parts of someone he murdered any more than any criminal may profit in anyway from a crime, but this doesn't mean that a will donating body parts to science wouldn't be honored if the person had met with unrelated foul play.

Similarly, it is understandable that the law may decide to look askance on the use of fetal tissue for family members who need it, but that doesn't mean that the tissue from a legal abortion should not subsequently be used to save a life. An interesting case occurred in early 1991, which illustrates the complexity of the ethical issues that may be involved. For the first time, a fetus-to-fetus tissue transplant was tried in the United States, in an operation carried out to save an unborn child from a genetic disease. The parents of the unborn child, Guy and Terri Walden of Houston, were staunch opponents of abortion (he is a minister), but they had already lost two children to a rare disease that causes retardation, crippling, and ultimately death. Their first child died at the age of eight; the second child was diagnosed while a fetus and doctors urged an abortion, which the parents refused. That child also died. When the third fetus was shown to have the same defect, the Waldens decided to go along with a tissue transplant. The Waldens said they ascertained that the abortion providing the tissue had been done to save the woman's life, and a child was subsequently born to them who is in seeming good health.

The Waldens testified before a Congressional subcommittee considering medical funding on April 15, 1991, recounting their experience, supporting the treatment, and asking for an end to the ban on research funding.

The *New York Times* quoted Mr. Walden as saying, "We accept tissue donation from people murdered in holdups. Does that increase the number of murders?"[10]

On November 21, 1991, the Reverend Guy Walden announced to a *Times* reporter that the treatment had been "miraculous," as he was preparing to testify before Congress again in favor of the restoring of federal funds. The treatment's success, he felt, "was a message from God that fetal tissue research should go forward." He also said, "I don't believe in abortion, but to let the tissue from these babies rot in the grave or be thrown in the trash—we are just letting more children die who might be saved."[11]

The increasing value that some potential parents are putting on the possibility of having children is reflected in the growth of the field of prenatal fetal surgery. It used to be that many antiabortionists wanted to discourage or even outlaw amniocentesis for pregnant women—genetic screening of the amniotic fluid, which surrounds the fetus, to detect abnormalities in the fetus—because so many women chose abortion if they found they were carrying a severely deformed fetus. Amniocentesis will not yield results until about the fourteenth week of pregnancy and is usually done between the fourteenth to sixteenth weeks; the results then take at least three to four weeks to determine, so if an abortion is to be performed it is a late one. Pregnancy takes forty weeks: the Supreme Court in its *Roe* v. *Wade*[12] decision divided it into three trimesters of roughly three months each, with abortion fairly unrestricted in the first trimester, regulated in the second, and permitted after viability (which the Court said was usually placed "at about seven months (28 weeks) but may occur earlier, even at 24 weeks") with severe state restrictions, including the possibility that it may be forbidden except to save the life or health of the woman. The Court considered in 1973 that the fetus was viable outside the womb at the beginning of the third trimester; medical science now can save some fetuses outside the womb as early as twenty-three weeks.

More than 90 percent of all U.S. abortions are performed in the first twelve weeks. About 10 percent of all second trimester abortions are performed because amniocentesis—recommended as a routine precaution for women over the age of thirty-five—has discovered severe defects in the fetus. But the choice of abortion after such a discovery is no longer as uniform as it used to be. Rather, there is an increasing possibility that surgeons can operate on the fetus within the womb to correct a variety of disorders, and such operations are becoming more and more common and more and more successful.

When it comes to having children, choice has widened. Science is creating miracles. It can help the woman who thought she couldn't bear a child to bear one, even after menopause has set in; it can operate to save the fetus that would previously have been lost or deformed; it can carry surrogate motherhood to the extreme of nurturing a couple's genetic child in a host mother. It is even possible to test the unfertilized ovum for genetic problems, so that mothers with a family history of genetically transmitted defect can theoretically avoid the trauma of aborting a genetically damaged fetus by selecting eggs that are free from the defect, to be used for in vitro fertilization.

Abortion—A Thorny Topic

The other side of this choice has also widened in the last twenty years. Abortion is legal and available and safe, not only in the United States but in a number of countries all over the world. And here, too, technology is changing the landscape. Already the French "abortion pill," RU 486, can induce an abortion in the privacy of the home up to twelve days after the first missed menstrual period with a combined pill and injection or suppository, even though the procedure is supposed to be done only under a doctor's supervision. It is safer and less expensive than a surgical abortion. If, as is now suggested, it is introduced in the United States, women could visit a doctor's office and then go home, without the need to cross picket lines around an abortion clinic.

Abortion by pill is at least theoretically a procedure that a woman could perform on herself. The Upjohn Company has developed a suppository that induces abortion after the first twelve weeks, a procedure that could also be self-administered. And the feminist health movement began in the 1970s to teach women the principles of menstrual extraction, performed on each other to avoid the inconvenience of a full menstrual period but also able to effect a relatively safe early abortion. After the Supreme Court *Webster* decision in 1989 raised the specter of increased state regulation of abortion, some chapters of NOW began holding classes in the technique, just in case.

All of this means that the indisputable fact that a woman has control over her own body and that no one knows as much about whether or not she is pregnant as she does has been aided by technology. Today a woman can determine that she is pregnant by buying a kit; for less than $100 she can then buy another kit to extract her menses and do so, with a little help from her friends. Technically, she doesn't need to see a doctor during the entire procedure. The genie is not going to go back into the bottle; abortions will be harder and harder to police, no matter what the law says. Of course, if the law throws up roadblocks, abortion will be easier for some women than for others—not because of the cost, which can be minimal, but because not all women are self-assertive enough to take such responsibility for their own lives. Some women may be less likely to *think* of self-help abortion, or to discover how to effect it.

And there is a move to recriminalize abortion. After the 1989 case, *Webster* v. *Reproductive Health Services,* extremely restrictive laws banning all abortions except to save the life of the woman were introduced in Utah, Alabama, Minnesota, Idaho, and Louisiana, and they actually passed in Idaho and Louisiana before being vetoed by the governors of those states. A referendum in the 1991 election in the state of Washington, to permit abortion in the state even if *Roe* v. *Wade* were overturned, passed, but very narrowly.

People are troubled by abortion. Doctors don't want to specialize in it, but the trend toward specialization is pushing some of them in that direction. The majority of abortions are done in clinics that do nothing else; the doctors who try to combine gynecology, obstetrics, *and* abortion face picketing and boycotts from antiabortionists until they give up either abortion or the rest of their practice. Their abortion clients will cross the picket line; their other patients feel less urgent about it.

Polls show that people respond differently to questions about preserving the fetus and questions about a woman's right to control her own body, although in both instances a majority of Americans think that abortion should be legal. Many of them, however, question the validity of some reasons that might motivate an abortion.

No one really expected that there would be *so many* abortions—over a million a year. The secret that many women who support legal choice, like myself, don't want to discuss is that, when you are pregnant with a wanted pregnancy, you feel very early that there is a person inside of you. Long before there is any possibility of brain survival should a fetus be expelled, a woman may pick out a name, toys, furniture; she may even start conversations with the unborn. This is the reason a miscarriage can be so traumatic an end to a wanted pregnancy, even though society does not expect a fetus to be mourned as if it were an infant who was lost. To the bereaved woman, it seems indeed to be a person who was lost.

But, it wasn't. A pregnant woman may *imagine* that a fetus responded to her, but it could not have; she may have talked to it, but it did not answer. She has projected her expectations onto a bundle of sensations that she might not even have noticed if she hadn't wanted to be pregnant. As a matter of fact, when a woman doesn't want or expect to be pregnant, she may not even identify when a fetus is developed enough to have moved inside of her—clinical records are full of reports of women who were genuinely shocked to find that they were in an advanced stage of pregnancy.

Nature is profligate in the manufacturing of offspring. Women produce eggs by the thousands; men produce sperm by the millions. No one yet considers that a human life is involved. When an egg is fertilized, it is not yet able to grow unless it implants itself in the placenta—in nature or in the laboratory, at least half of such fertilized ova do not take, given the chance. Once it implants, it is called a "pre-embryo," for approximately two weeks. Its cells are not differentiated; it can even divide into twins and then recombine at this stage.

According to a *New York Times* article in 1991, two important scholarly articles by Roman Catholic ethicists (Rev. Richard A. McCormick in the first issue of the *Kennedy Institute of Ethics Journal* and Thomas A. Shannon and Rev. Allan B. Wolter in *Theological Studies*) "argue that the pre-embryo is not at all the kind of distinct individual that church teaching supposes." The *New York Times* quotes the *Theological Studies* article as saying "the pre-embryo lacks the 'determinate and irreversible individuality' that is 'a necessary, if not sufficient condition for it to be a human person.' " It also quotes Father McCormick as saying that the pre-embryo does not have "developmental individuality." There is now a movement advocating the concept of "brain birth" to mark "the beginning of personhood"; Dr. Shannon is quoted as accepting it, "But he notes that different proponents of 'brain birth' have chosen points in the development of the nervous system ranging between 8 and 28 weeks of pregnancy."[13]

In other words, there is a lot of scientific and even theological controversy over just what we are talking about. In *Webster* v. *Reproductive Health Services,* the Eighth Circuit Court of Appeals had declared the preamble to a 1986 Missouri law unconstitutional because it says that life begins at the time of conception, which it defined as "the fertilization of the ovum of a female by the sperm of a male." The preamble went on to say that therefore Missouri must provide the unborn with "all the rights, privileges and immunities available to other persons, citizens and residents of this state." Justice John Paul Stevens wrote a separate opinion dissenting in part, saying that the Supreme Court should have upheld the Appeals Court and declared this preamble unconstitutional, as adopting a particular religious view. Instead of doing this, the majority opinion called the preamble a "value judgment" that the legislature had a right to make.

Everyone knows that there is a continuum from sperm and ovum to fertilization to fetus to birth, but that is where the agreement ends. Many of those who consider the pre-embryo to be in some sense a human being want to outlaw not only in vitro fertilization but certain contraceptive devices that interfere with implantation, such as the IUD and some forms of the pill. Those who have quite a different and more empirical sense of when human life begins may have no moral difficulty even with the destruction of a severely deformed late fetus, particularly one that could not live for any length of time after delivery. But others can't accept it. Some medical facilities with religious affiliations, for instance, have insisted that a fetus that has developed without forming a brain must still be brought to term, even though brain birth will never occur and postpartum heartbeats will only last for, at most, a few hours.

If medical technology can create miracles, it can also create monsters today. It can keep fertilized embryos frozen indefinitely; it can keep fetuses without brain development that will never develop into human beings in a state of animation, at least for a time; and, at the other end of life, it can keep brain-dead bodies that are no longer human beings in a similar state of animation. These Frankenstein possibilities of medical science cannot and should not be determinants of our definition of rights.

The main philosophical argument about abortion is over whether a potential human being can be said to have rights, in the sense that a human being has—and the axiom from which one starts determines the outcome of the argument: one side says it's a potential *human being,* and the other says it's a *potential* human being. Since the differences are axiomatic, and incapable of proof, the two sides will never agree.

I do not consider that abortion is murder, and I contend that I have a legal right *not* to consider that abortion is murder. There can be a difficult moral question for anyone faced with the decision of abortion—there should not be a difficult legal question.

It was established in fourteenth-century England that a woman has a common-law right to terminate a pregnancy before "quickening," by judges who were themselves Catholic. This common-law right was assumed by U.S. courts until it began to be preempted by legislation, well into the nineteenth century. In the 1820s, some prohibitions of *methods* of abortion considered life-threatening to the woman were passed, but the first enforceable U.S. law against more than one method of abortion went into effect in New York State in 1830, according to historian James Mohr, and it was intended to protect pregnant women, not fetuses.[14] The New Jersey Supreme Court said in 1858, of a New Jersey statute modeled on this New York law, "The design of the statute was not to prevent the procuring of abortions, so much as to guard the health and life of the mother against the consequences of such attempts."[15]

In other words, due to the fact that in the nineteenth century an abortion was more likely to be fatal to a woman than delivering a child, antiabortion laws, like later protective labor legislation for women, were an exercise of the state's power to protect women from making decisions that might be unsafe, in order to preserve the future of the race.

But the state no longer has that excuse. Abortion is now *safer* for the woman than natural childbirth. After abortion was legalized in the United States in 1973, the death rate from abortions, which had been 4 per 100,000 in 1972, dropped to 0.5 per 100,000 in 1985, making abortion *seven times* safer than natural childbirth.[16]

Controlling Women's Bodies

The law has never, until the current rash of proposed "human life amendments" and statements like the 1986 Missouri preamble, held that the unborn fetus is fully a person. It has made a distinction between quickening and nonquickening, and later between viable and previable fetuses. When the 1973 *Roe* v. *Wade* decision defined this period as starting from twenty-four to twenty-eight weeks of gestation, it went on to say, "If the State is interested in protecting fetal life after viability it may go so far as to proscribe abortion during this period except when it is necessary to preserve the life or the health of the mother." Notice that *still* the fetus is not legally considered to be fully a person; one may not legally kill an aged parent or a contagious guest in order to preserve one's life or health. It was to overturn this definition that amendments to the Constitution were introduced but never passed—the 1981 amendment introduced by Senator Jesse Helms read: "The paramount right to life is vested in each human being from the moment of fertilization without regard to age, health, or condition of dependency."[17]

There was then a move in Congress, which didn't get very far, simply to pass a law saying that fetuses were persons as defined in the Fourteenth Amendment—unfortunately, the relevant Fourteenth Amendment language is: "All persons *born* or naturalized in the United States, and subject to the jurisdiction thereof, are citizens of the United States and of the State wherein they reside." (Emphasis added)

Unfortunately, too, before it is born the fetus is within someone's body and gets all its sustenance from that body. If a woman doesn't have the basic legal right to decide what operations and treatment may be done to her own body, as well as what risks she may take, this is a serious diminution of her legal rights. More than that, one of the most important principles of Anglo-Saxon law and legal procedure is to give the benefit of the doubt to any accused (even in those cases where everyone "knows" the existence of guilt) by assuming his or her innocence and requiring definite proof of guilt. If destroying a fetus were legally murder, we would have a legal situation in which the presumption of innocence would be replaced by a presumption of guilt. An investigation, or sometimes an inquest, is legally required in the case of every death that doesn't have a doctor's certificate.

There used to be such presumption-of-guilt laws. Sir Walter Scott's novel, *The Heart of Midlothian,* is a fictionalized account of an actual case: the ordeal of a woman who ran afoul of a Scottish law that required a murder charge against any woman who *had* been pregnant and was so no longer, if she couldn't produce either a baby or witnesses that she had been preparing a layette for the birth. The heroine of the book is the victim's sister, who refuses to lie in order to save her innocent sister's life, but then *walks* from Edinburgh to London to persuade the English Queen Anne to issue a pardon.

If the fetus is ruled to be a human being, then every time a pregnant woman miscarried (which happens spontaneously in up to 25 percent of all pregnancies), she could be faced with an inquest and would be liable to manslaughter charges if a child were born dead. How do you prove that a miscarriage or stillbirth was *not* the result of an illegal or negligent act? On the other hand, how does a prosecutor prove that a fetus was alive at the exact moment of miscarriage?

It cannot be done within the confines of Anglo-Saxon jurisprudence, with its safeguards for the rights of the accused. This area could only be controlled by the state by extending the power of administrative agencies to forbid or condemn certain actions without trial or proof. It was the impossibility of proving that an aborted fetus had been alive at the moment an abortionist intervened that led to the common-law right in the first place.

The law has to deal with facts, and the fact here is that the pregnant woman *does* have rights, which the state may not properly abridge. Governments know they cannot meaningfully take away a person's right to suicide, since laws against suicide can only be enforced when they are not successfully broken. A person may be wrong, even immoral, in exercising this right, but the right is inherent in the nature of human life. Professor William B. Irvine in a 1991 article in the *Freeman* points out that if you have a right to something, you also have a right to dispose of it in any way that doesn't "expose others to risk":

. . . if the state declares that our right to life cannot be relinquished— if, that is, it declares that we cannot decide when and how we end our lives—it has not only deprived us of an important element of self-determination, but it has to some extent transformed our right to life into a duty to live—or, in the case of brain-dead people, into a duty to go on breathing. . . . It is, by the way, important to keep in mind that those who argue that we have a right to die are not arguing that sick people should be put to death against their will (they are not, that is, arguing that we have a duty to die); rather, they are arguing that terminally ill patients who are sound of mind should be allowed to die, if they choose to do so.[18]

Similarly, libertarians do not hold that a right to bear a child is a duty to do so; the state shouldn't demand that a woman incubate a fetus because of the fetus's rights, any more than it should demand that she provide her child with a kidney because that child will die without it.

The fact that in these cases a life-and-death decision may be involved doesn't by itself give the state the right to act. Even if one held that the fetus was a person, we may not legally enslave or invade the body of one person to preserve the life of another, after both are born. The individuals have equal rights. This is not possible in the case of a pregnant woman and a fetus. The rights of one of them *must,* by the nature of pregnancy, be held to be superior. Either the woman is unhampered in her right to make decisions about what happens to her body and what risks she takes with it, which gives her the right to potentially endanger the existence of the fetus; or the fact of the fetus preempts that right and can require her to acquiesce to procedures that she feels are against her best interests in order to preserve the fetus. The Catholic Church for a long time required a woman's husband and her doctor to choose the life of the fetus over hers, if a medical choice had to be made. As we will see later in this chapter, so do some contemporary courts.

In April 1989, the legislature of New Hampshire passed a law that said, "The state shall not compel any woman to complete or to terminate a pregnancy." (The New Hampshire governor later vetoed it.) This language, taken from a briefing handbook prepared by the Women's Rights Litigation Clinic of Rutgers University, was acceptable to supporters of choice as well as to conservatives who didn't want government interference but were personally opposed to abortion, because it didn't claim that abortion was moral or a right; it merely kept the state out of it. Many legislators didn't want to take sides between "pro-abortionists" and "pro-lifers."[19]

This language has another important implication. It spells out both halves of the reproductive choice decision. One of the main problems with "legalizing" abortion is that situations arise where abortions may seem to be mandated—and not just by recognizably totalitarian governments with known population problems. In 1984 a woman who had been forbidden by a Florida court to bear children as a condition of parole was sent to jail after she gave birth to a second child.[20] In 1989 seven women who had worked as guards for the New York City Correction Department charged that they were told to have abortions or resign when they became pregnant.[21] Women on welfare have been told to have abortions as a condition of receiving benefits. There are people in the environmental and secular humanist movements who believe in a "right" to abortion with no corresponding right to decide to have a child.

This seems to be a matter of "who pays the piper calls the tune." To the extent that "society" is considered to be morally responsible for subsidizing the birth and prenatal care of poor children and their mothers, it is only a step to legally trying to control future fertility in families causing problems for society. In a 1927 case, *Buck* v. *Bell,*[22] Justice Oliver Wendell Holmes authorized the state-required sterilization of a feeble-minded woman in an institution with the famous words, "Three generations of imbeciles are enough." Today it is child-abusers whose fertility may be legally interrupted or terminated; judges are getting on that bandwagon. In 1988 there was an uproar when a judge told such a woman to be sterilized or face a long prison term.[23] There have been cases in the past of sentencing women to use birth control, but technology now allows compliance with the sentence to be checked, and in November 1990 another judge sentenced a seventeen-year-old girl to ten years of implanted birth control after a jail sentence, as a condition of parole to be checked by the parole officer.[24]

If a woman treats children criminally, she should be punished, but not by being maimed or having mandated operations. And in the case of abortion, it's even more true that the only proper solution is for the state to stay out of the picture and neither forbid abortions nor mandate them.

In principle, once you decide that rights that the government may not invade are involved, you can't take it back. Either the fetus has legal rights that supersede the rights of the woman, or it does not. It can't be that some fetuses have rights and some don't. And if the fetus has rights, since a woman can be impregnated against her will, all women are the potential property of the state, which can utterly control their lives and working conditions and personal habits, under the guise of protecting the unborn—or perhaps even of protecting the *potentially* existing unborn.

In the May 1979 issue of *Ms.* magazine, Rhonda Copelon, a staff lawyer with the Center for Constitutional Rights, predicted some of the dire consequences that passage of a "human life amendment" might entail, including: "A pregnant woman's eating, drinking, smoking, and sleeping habits might become subject to the criminal law because of their potential threat to the fetus."[25] What seemed way out in 1979 may be on the way to becoming routine in 1991.

Although under common law as well as constitutional law the fetus was never a person, some states have decided that under some circumstances a viable fetus may be considered a person for purposes of bringing action under a wrongful death law.[26] A fetal-rights movement, similar to but not necessarily identical with the so-called right-to-life movement, is busy supporting such legislation as well as taking other legal actions to force women to take actions during pregnancy that they might otherwise not take.

In an article in the *Wall Street Journal* on April 12, 1985, Dr. Margery W. Shaw, described as "a physician and lawyer who teaches genetics and health law at the University of Texas at Houston," was quoted as calling for obligatory genetic testing if family history shows a risk of hereditary disease. It was not clear from the article whether she foresaw that an abortion might be mandated in the case of defect, or whether perhaps fetal surgery might be legally required, whether or not the woman wanted to permit it. But Dr. Shaw did call for "civil or criminal charges" against women who "negligently or purposefully bring defective fetuses to term." And she included a wide range of activities as "negligent fetal abuse," including "improper nutrition or working with dangerous chemicals."[27]

This might seem like something out of science fiction if there hadn't already been a number of bizarre legal cases giving the well-being of fetuses the right to determine women's behavior. In 1981 the Georgia Supreme Court ordered a Caesarean section done on a pregnant woman against her wishes, after doctors had testified that without the operation both the woman's and the fetus's health would be endangered. In that case, the woman refused and went home to deliver, and the doctors turned out to be wrong—there were no complications for either mother or child. But by 1988, fifteen cases asking for court-ordered operations on unwilling women for the medical benefit of fetuses had been filed in local and state courts, and only one was not granted.[28] Contrast this with the refusal of courts to order operations on suspected criminals in order to recover bullets that might be evidence of crime—in such a case, an operation is considered to violate the Fourth Amendment "right of the people to be secure in their persons."

One dramatic case involved a pregnant woman dying of cancer who decided (with the agreement of her husband, family, and doctors) that her own care and comfort should take precedence over the care of the fetus. She agreed to life-prolonging treatment to give the fetus a chance to develop enough to be born, but would not agree to a Caesarean. When she was twenty-six weeks pregnant, the hospital's lawyers obtained a court order requiring her to submit to a Caesarean section in the interest of the fetus, because experts testified it would have a 50 to 60 percent chance of survival. The fetus died two hours after the operation, and the woman died within two days.[29]

The woman's lawyer, Lynn M. Paltrow, staff counsel of the American Civil Liberties Union's Reproductive Freedom Project, asked, "Are we to act as though the mother is not there saying no? That it's her body that must be invaded by surgery? That it is she who is going to be taking all the risks incumbent in surgery and medical treatment?"[30] Apparently, that is just how we are to act. It has already been decided by courts that a woman cannot be forced to take a blood transfusion for her own well-being, but can be for the sake of the fetus. In 1987 a four-month-pregnant woman prisoner who became comatose after trying to hang herself was required to continue her pregnancy while unconscious, over her mother's petition, even though the woman had an undoubted right to have an abortion on her own request. The court went so far as to appoint a guardian for the fetus.[31]

In the well-publicized case of Nancy Klein on Long Island in 1989, abortion opponents fought legally to keep Martin Klein from assuming legal guardianship over his wife (who was also comatose and eighteen weeks pregnant) in order to authorize an abortion, which doctors hoped would improve her condition. After fighting in three New York State courts, Mr. Klein finally prevailed and the abortion was performed—ultimately the doctors' predictions came true and Nancy Klein recovered from her coma. But, of course, doctors can be mistaken, and the issue was and should be whether Martin Klein or antiabortion strangers who petitioned for guardianship should decide what medical treatment his wife would have wanted.[32]

In a more hopeful case, this one in December 1990, Denise Lefebvre, a South Florida woman suffering from manic depression who had been hospitalized in a mental institution, was ordered by a court to have an abortion that she didn't want. With the backing of both pro-choice and antiabortion groups, she was able to successfully refuse both to have the abortion and to take prescribed drugs that she feared might harm the unborn child. A court declared her incompetent and appointed a guardian for her, but the guardian, Kathleen Phillips, honored her wishes and helped Ms. Lefebvre to have the baby.[33]

But the trend seems to be toward asserting that the unborn has rights to somehow control actions of the pregnant woman that might put its

health in jeopardy. Research has been discovering more and more circumstances under which a fetus may be harmed by the behavior of the
woman carrying it, but there are still many circumstances that may or
may not be harmful. For instance, as many as 3 percent of all babies
are born with severe birth defects; some may be caused by medications
taken during pregnancy. In 1980 the Food and Drug Administration announced that coffee, tea, and other caffeine-containing products might
possibly cause birth defects, although they never got to the point of requiring
warning labels on such products.[34] Cigarettes do require warning labels,
as do containers of alcoholic beverages, and in some states bars are required
to post signs detailing these warnings. In a few jurisdictions, prosecutors
have tried to indict pregnant women for child abuse for transmitting alcohol
to a fetus, but since it is only a misdemeanor to give alcohol to a minor,
this has not been a widely sought solution.

The punishment for violating drug laws, however, is another matter.
In the midseventies, courts for the first time permitted charges of child
abuse to be brought against women who took illegal drugs during pregnancy
and allowed the removal of children born from such mothers, on such
grounds. In 1988, for the first time, a woman who gave birth to a child
addicted to cocaine was charged in Florida with *both* child abuse and drug
delivery to the unborn, because, according to the *New York Times,* "Conviction of child abuse generally carries a sentence of no more than 60 days.
The drug charge carries a maximum sentence of 30 years."[35] In 1989 another
Florida woman, Jennifer Johnson, was the first woman to actually be convicted on a drug-delivery charge involving a baby, and she was sentenced
to a year in a drug treatment program and fourteen years on probation.[36]
A Michigan prosecutor tried to avoid the debate over when a fetus becomes
a person by charging Kimberly Hardy with delivering crack to her son
through the umbilical cord in the few seconds between the time when the
child was born and the umbilical cord was cut. The charge of delivering
drugs of less than fifty grams in Michigan carries a minimum jail sentence
of one year and a maximum of twenty years.[37] In April 1991, a unanimous
Michigan Court of Appeals rejected the state's argument in this case.[38]

Between 1987 and the spring of 1991, according to a 1991 *New York
Times* story, about sixty criminal cases had been "set in motion in 19
states and the District of Columbia against women for abusing drugs during
pregnancy. The charges include criminal child abuse, assault with a deadly
weapon and manslaughter."[39] You have to remember that the Supreme
Court has ruled in several cases that *being addicted to drugs* may not
be forbidden by criminal law. But now, apparently, because of the enormous
concern about babies who show signs of drug abuse or drug damage when
they are born, if one is a pregnant woman, one does not have that same

legal protection.

And although it has been easier for prosecutors to form cases around the issue of illegal drugs, there have also been moves in the direction of prosecuting other actions that turned out to endanger the unborn, perhaps the action of not obeying doctor's orders. A dramatic 1986 case was that of Pamela Rae Stewart Monson, a California woman who was afflicted with a condition called placenta previa, in which the placenta can easily separate from the uterine wall, thus ceasing to nourish the fetus. Mrs. Monson was warned by her doctor not to have sexual intercourse or take medications during her pregnancy and to go to a hospital immediately should bleeding start. Apparently she took both barbiturates and amphetamines in her ninth month and bled for six hours before she got to a hospital, where she was delivered of a brain-dead son.

She was charged by authorities with criminal conduct of her pregnancy, although the charges were later dropped. This is perhaps the most extreme example of the move to charge women who do something during pregnancy that turns out to have endangered the fetus.[40]

A discussion with people who had views on both side of the issue of "Punishing Pregnant Addicts" was printed as a forum in the *New York Times* on September 10, 1989. It illustrates quite well the fact that, in the case of pregnancy, the rights of the woman and the fetus cannot be equal. Dr. Jan Bays, who was then the Director of Child Abuse Programs at Emanuel Hospital in Portland, Oregon, went so far as to consider curtailing the right to *be* pregnant and seemed to be considering legally enforced sterilization. He was quoted as saying:

> Eventually society will get fed up with the huge burden of drug-affected babies. We can't say forever that people have unlimited rights to have a child. We license people to cut hair but we don't have to have any kind of training to have a child. What's more important—a bad haircut or a permanently damaged child?[41]

To which George J. Annas, Professor of Health Law at Boston University School of Medicine responded:

> I agree the unborn need protection but that takes hard work to make pregnancy a healthy condition for all women, including the poor, and to prevent pregnancy for those who use drugs but don't want children. That must be through prenatal care for everyone and available birth control, not through sterilization. There is no question women have the constitutional right to become pregnant and give birth. Are we willing to sterilize everyone who has a disease that can be passed to a fetus?[42]

A staff attorney on the ACLU Women's Rights Project in New York, Kary L. Moss, said:

> These cases for the first time force a pregnant woman to act in the service of another, the fetus. If you see a child in a burning building, you are not required to risk your life to save the child. These cases ask a woman to sacrifice her right to privacy and open herself to policing during pregnancy. All of a sudden the behavior of pregnant women is open to state controls to which no one else is subject.
>
> Will women next be arrested if they smoke or engage in sex against their doctor's orders? Where do we draw the line and who will do the monitoring?
>
> These drug statutes were not intended to apply to fetuses and prenatal behavior and it was not considered a crime to take drugs during pregnancy when these women did that. They could not have known they were committing a crime.
>
> Parents often exhibit bad judgment and drug use is bad judgment. But never before has that been grounds to take a child away or put someone in jail.[43]

It should be pointed out that, although not all pregnant drug users are poor, perhaps a majority of them—certainly a majority of the women brought to court—are. And the way in which many such women are trying to escape their dilemma is to avoid going for prenatal care, both because disobeying doctor's orders can be used as evidence against them, and because the public medical facilities available to them turn them in for drug use. (Prenatal care can alert a woman to potential problems for both herself and the fetus.) At the same time, government programs designed to help drug users either do not admit pregnant women or have only a handful of places for them. The state of Massachusetts, for instance, was at one point sending pregnant women who had been required by a court to go for drug rehabilitation into a women's prison that excluded them from rehabilitation programs, because the prison programs were only open to convicted felons! In the summer of 1990, an article in the *Radcliffe News* reported that "of 78 drug treatment programs listed in New York state, 54 percent would not treat pregnant women, 67 percent excluded Medicaid clients, and 87 percent denied services to pregnant women on Medicaid who were also addicted to crack."[44]

By depriving pregnant women of rights and punishing them for not availing themselves of nonexistent treatment, Big Brother certainly doesn't act like a sister.

Jobs versus Motherhood—Again

If all of a pregnant woman's actions are to be scrutinized because of possible impact on the fetus, what about the kind of work she does? A number of firms tried to deal with the question of hazardous working conditions by restricting certain work to men, or to women who could not bear children. This policy spread rapidly during the eighties in the semiconductor, rubber, and automotive industries. The American Telephone and Telegraph Company took so seriously a university study that found a higher incidence of miscarriages in women working in rooms where computer chips were manufactured that in 1987 it transferred all pregnant women who had held such jobs to work elsewhere.[45]

American Cyanamid as early as 1978 had told woman workers in their Willow Island, West Virginia, plant that they might lose their union-wage-scale jobs unless they were over fifty or could prove that they were infertile, and five women chose to be sterilized as a result. The ACLU encouraged them to sue, and in 1983 American Cyanamid settled with them out of court.[46]

Back in the 1920s, it was clear to the journalist, sociologist, and lawyer Crystal Eastman that restricting women's jobs was an easy way out, because men are affected by (and transmit to the unborn) the same poisons in the workplace that women are, but often want the jobs anyway. She is quoted in a 1978 Oxford University Press book, *Crystal Eastman on Women and Revolution,* as saying,

> The exclusion of women from the painting trade in England and in America, rests on a theory that lead poisoning frequently causes mis-carriage. . . .
>
> But—the poisoning, in bringing about miscarriages, very often goes through the male as well as the female. For example, there is one set of figures affecting workers in lead mines, where the wives have never worked in the mines . . . and 40 percent of a given block of pregnancies miscarried.[47]

Crystal Eastman was speaking about *laws* that excluded women from certain jobs, but the Supreme Court case that scotched such policies on March 20, 1991, *Automobile Workers* v. *Johnson Controls,* did not involve a law. Although, through an interesting coincidence, it was concerned with the same poisonous substance—lead. Something like seventy years after Crystal Eastman was writing about the painting trade, women were being barred from making automobile batteries unless they showed proof of sterility, to protect them from lead exposure. It seems unusual, to say the least, that, generations later, the issue should be arising as if it were brand new—and that the same solution, using men in place of fertile women, should have been hit upon. This time, however, the companies had a concern that the Court seemed not to address completely—liability in lawsuits alleging responsibility for prenatal injuries.

All nine Justices agreed that the 1964 Civil Rights Act was violated by the company policy, but they differed over whether narrower policies would be permissible. Justice White said employers should be able to take potential liability into account, but Justice Blackmun, who wrote the majority opinion, said that legal liability "seems remote at best." The *New York Times* report on the decision said that Blackmun suggested "that compliance with Federal civil rights law would shelter employers from damage suits."[48] But who knows?

If the Court pays attention to arguments that women should take the responsibility of deciding for themselves what level of risk they are willing to undergo, it seems only fair that companies should be able to make similar decisions. There's a pretty close parallel. Blackmun's opinion said,

> Decisions about the welfare of future children must be left to the parents who conceive, bear, support and raise them rather than to the employers who hire those parents. Women as capable of doing their jobs as their male counterparts may not be forced to choose between having a child and having a job.[49]

Future lawsuits seem to be of exactly the same degree of speculation as future children, and since it is "the employers who hire those parents" who have to *bear* the inconvenience, *support* the defendants, and *raise* the money to pay for the future lawsuits, don't they also have a right to contingency plans?

That having been said, it should also be noticed that there is a long history of trying to keep women out of the work force on the *Muller v. Oregon* "cradle of the race" theory. This is especially true in economic hard times. During the 1929 Great Depression, for instance, according to Robert W. Smuts in *Women and Work in America,* "Many state and local governments revived old bans on the employment of married women in teaching and other public jobs, and several state legislatures considered bills to prohibit the employment of wives in private industry."[50]

It used to be done by passing a law; today it is being done by industry-instituted fetal-protection policies in unionized, well-paying jobs. And as the fetal-rights movement gains momentum, it would not be surprising to see more and more occupations considered dangerous for women who might become pregnant. If women are to be held criminally responsible for actions causing fetal damage, can companies be far behind? What will companies be able to do about such prospects, if discrimination law keeps them from instituting on a company level some of the policies that used to be mandated by state law, including that old standby of protective labor legislation, a ban on "occasional heavy lifting"?

From a libertarian point of view, judging these policies is a complex issue. They are clear violations of civil rights laws and of the 1978 Pregnancy Discrimination Act, which is why the Supreme Court said they were invalid. But from a libertarian perspective, stringent requirements against private "discrimination" (such as those that have led to the ruling that black colleges must admit a quota of white students, and that might in the future require women's colleges to take male students) are not in the best interest of the groups that the Civil Rights Acts were intended to protect.

The libertarian and classical liberal solution is to cut down on government entities through privatization, to have strong antidiscrimination rules for all government entities, and to allow private institutions to do what they wish, even when their policies are clearly short-sighted or even bigoted.

It was the Automobile Workers Union that brought the *Johnson* case to court, and it may very well be that, in the large industries that have welcomed such protective policies, a next step will be union negotiation that will improve the workplace for men and women alike. The newspaper descriptions of conditions in the Johnson Controls plants recount stories of both men and women furloughed from work because of unacceptably high lead levels in the bloodstream. In a Johnson Controls factory in Burlington, Vermont, respirators had been provided for about seventy-five workers who had high levels of lead concentration in their blood.[57] Workplace safety certainly is an appropriate union concern, and union safety monitors should be able to do a better job than random government inspectors or government regulation.

What More Freedom Might Entail

This business of choice is obviously very complex. One of the things that it is about is options. And to the credit of those opposing abortion, they have been willing to do more than just try to punish those women who want to act in a way they think is wrong. As Betsy Powell, the 1989 president-elect of the San Jose Right to Life chapter, put it, "We had to put our money where our mouths were." They founded Heritage Home in 1985, an evangelical Protestant residence home for unwed mothers, which is an instance of what the *New York Times* has called "a network of alternative services for pregnant women contemplating abortion."[52] The services offered can include baby clothes, legal help, job counseling, and even day-care centers, and some of the services continue to help for a long time after birth. There are a number of homes, including seven centers in the U.S. and Canada all called "Mom's House," that provide residences for single mothers and their children. Mary Cunningham Agee, formerly with the Bendix Corporation, started the Nurturing Network, a group with no declared ties to the antiabortion movement, in 1985. It provides single pregnant women with "counseling, housing, employment and educational opportunities."[53] It is based in Boise, Idaho, and includes 4,500 volunteers and 400 employers willing to provide jobs.

This movement started with maternity homes. In 1965 there were 200 maternity homes in the United States with room for 6,200 women; this dropped to 99 homes by 1980, but by 1989 there were 140, most of them run by religious organizations.

Over the years, the services provided by such homes has expanded. Heritage Home helps women consider adoption and look for congenial adoptive parents; it finds jobs for women who plan to keep their children; it refers drug users to counseling; it baby-sits the children of former residents. There is also a large network of crisis pregnancy centers (some of which have been criticized for deceptive advertising, but most of which are direct about their point of view) that urge pregnant women to have babies and offer free maternity clothes and layettes. Literally hundreds of organizations are devoted, not just to persuading women not to abort, but to helping women get the education and jobs they need in order to function as mothers.[54]

The whole area of procreation has been distorted by government action. People running maternity homes report that the women most determined to keep their babies are almost uniformly the women least qualified to care for them properly—least qualified personally and emotionally, but economically, they can apply for welfare. And so they do, and keep their babies.

Government sponsored sex education has been another factor. First of all, the public schools have to be politically responsive to community attitudes, and community attitudes make contraceptive information an explosive issue. Secondly, some of the material used to teach sex education is a disaster from a feminist point of view. In the late 1970s, I was part of a women's group in Berkshire County, Massachusetts, that was asked to view—and endorse—a sex-education film made to be shown in public school classes. It was certainly not feminist! It included idyllic photographs of intimate sex play filmed through cheesecloth and realistic, frank group discussions among students, with an "expert" moderating. But, as was clear from observation then and has been the subject of sociological studies since, girls do not speak up in mixed groups as readily as boys do. So the group discussions spent a disproportionate amount of time on boys who were describing their urgent desire for sex, with the moderator telling them that this was natural, healthy, and nothing to be ashamed of. So far so good. But since no girl spoke up to say she didn't *want* intimacy with a boy who had asked her, to be told *that* was natural, the inescapable impression left by the film was that boys had healthy desires that shouldn't be refused. I think it's possible that a lot of pregnancies resulted from the showing of that film.

Today teachers of sex education are supposedly teaching "abstinence" as well as giving information on contraception. But what does that mean? If abstinence means appeals directed at boys not to initiate intercourse, or unisex appeals to "wait until you're older," it doesn't address the problem of pressure that girls may face.

In the August 1987 issue of *Ms.*, Ellen Willis summed up an article called "Teen Lust" by saying,

> While conservatives make speeches about chastity, and liberals call for pragmatism . . . a feminist approach to the issue of teenage sex would assume that girls ought to have the power to define their needs for sexual pleasure, emotional satisfaction, and (in the age of AIDS) safety—and to resist male pressure for sex on any terms that violate those needs. In short, we need not only contraceptives and sex education in our schools, but feminist consciousness-raising—and a feminist movement.[55]

I agree with the spirit of this passage, if not with the implication that the public schools could, or would, be the source of such feminism. I think feminists should do it themselves. Why doesn't NARAL set up a division to give specific sex and contraceptive information, as well as assertiveness training, to girls? As for the amorphous rest of what people call sex education, the part that has to do with conduct and values, I don't think it belongs in the schools—or the streets. Often not in the family. That aspect of sex education belongs in art. Art is what reflects our values and helps form our values. That was what was so chilling about this sex-education film—it was effective precisely *because* it was a dramatic film.

(Of course contraceptives should be available, especially to girls, who need to be able to take steps themselves to prevent pregnancy and not to rely completely on the responsible behavior of their partners. The Supreme Court has extended the right to buy contraceptives to minors. But there's a difference between availability and official provision. Perhaps we make a mistake in assuming that most teenagers have to get their information and their contraceptives and their values all in the same place, the schools. We don't make a similar assumption about adults.)

What has happened to romance among today's youth? Sex is presented as a "realistic need" having little to do with commitment or family or future. And it seems to be the most unfortunate who are buying that message. It seems possible that for many girls, particularly girls in troubled families and troubled neighborhoods, the idea of romance with a baby has replaced the idea of romance with a boy. A relationship with a baby can realistically be projected as permanent. So you have the phenomenon of the girl with nothing, wanting a baby to share that nothing with her, and having that burning desire underwritten by government bureaucrats. This is a road that often leads to crack babies and to child abuse—the unintended consequences of interlocking government programs.

Whatever is going on seems to lead to younger and younger pregnancy. Kathryn E. McGoldrick, M.D., editor-in-chief of the *Journal of the American Medical Women's Association* and a professor at Harvard Medical School, says that "in the United States the actual number of pregnant teens is increasing. And although the overall rate of teenage pregnancy is decreasing, in one very ominous age group—10 to 14-year-olds—it continues to rise."[56]

We never used to think of ten, eleven, and twelve as teen years, but for purposes of motherhood, apparently they are. Remember the incident in Chicago in 1982 that got some media attention, when Joseph Scheidler, executive director of the Pro-Life Action League, tried to stop an abortion scheduled for an eleven-year-old girl? He hired a private detective to find the mother and pregnant daughter, went to their apartment, and telephoned from their next-door neighbor's when the mother wouldn't let him in, asking to talk to the daughter alone. The mother refused.[57] Imagine someone asking to see an eleven-year-old to talk her out of having her tonsils out, and you can see the preposterousness of this idea.

How does a ten-year-old get pregnant? Did she know the facts of life? How old was the boy who impregnated her, or was it a man? Did she have sex because she wanted to?

The Alan Guttmacher Institute did a study in the mid-1980s comparing teenage contraceptive use in five European countries and the United States. It found that in all the European countries, parents were more concerned about unwanted pregnancies than with sexual activity in their children; in the United States, the big concern was a condemnation of teenage sexual activity rather than its possible consequences. In an article in the *New York Times Magazine,* a science and health reporter quotes the chief of research for the Alan Guttmacher Institute as saying the result of American parents putting such stress on the moral issue was "that for teen-agers it came to seem acceptable to have sex only without planning. 'It is not so much the spontaneous sex that seems sinful to the young women, but the premeditation.' . . . Young women in America have double the number of unplanned pregnancies."[58]

Feminists shouldn't take the wrong way out—more social programs, an extended role for the public schools, all the trappings of the extended welfare state that tries to do something (generally not too well) about the *results* of social problems. After all, one thing teenagers who want babies need is more confidence that there is something else to do with their lives, and that literally manufacturing a human being by having a baby is not the best road to permanent close relationships. We need more individuality and more community, not more bureaucracy.

There are some things we can do about results, of course. The private programs to help young pregnant women to get on their feet and start realistic lives are a good start. (It would be nice to have programs for young women to help them get training, jobs, and support *before* they got pregnant.) But there is plenty of room for more. Could we find an ingenious computer-matching solution to the lack of coordination between the almost 500,000 teenagers giving birth each year and the large number of people seeking vainly to adopt? The present centers helping to provide alternatives to abortion say they cannot serve all of the women that they might reach. With total freedom of choice, we may get more. Expanding options, that's the way we should be thinking.

These different kinds of personal bodily choice may be the most important feminist issues of the nineties. They are certainly issues that can galvanize women into the feminist camp. When the Supreme Court began to narrow its interpretation of *Roe* v. *Wade* in its 1989 decision, *Webster* v. *Reproductive Health Services,* both NARAL and NOW gained about 50,000 new members each. If the Court goes even further, as seems more and more likely, we may see a fully revived individualist feminist movement before the turn of another century.

CHAPTER TWELVE

The Temptation of Political Expediency: Antipornography

When antiabortionists joined with pro-choice groups to support the choice of a woman in a mental institution who wanted to have her child rather than submit to an abortion, women considered "left" and women considered "right" found common cause. And this has happened on other occasions. In May 1990, Kate Michelman, executive director of NARAL, applauded the work of most crisis pregnancy centers, saying "It is very important to have programs and services that do in fact insure that women facing a crisis pregnancy have real options. If they are serving women without any ideological coercion, that is nothing but good."[1]

A lot of high-powered women in the United States are actively trying to win support for policies they think will benefit women. This is nothing new. Since the beginning of the woman-movement activism of the nineteenth century, women have formed organizations of all sorts to change society, from suffrage associations to the dissemination of birth control. The indispensable raw material is motivated troops.

When Wilma Scott Heide led a contingent of feminists to disrupt a meeting of a subcommittee of the Senate Judiciary Committee to demand immediate consideration of the Equal Rights Amendment, she unleashed an issue on the political scene that united many feminist women of many different points of view.

It also polarized women. After the ERA went to the states for ratification, Phyllis Schlafly and other conservative women found that an *anti-*ERA movement was the catalyst that could unite *them,* despite their differences.

For ten years, women on both sides lobbied politicians in state after state; they marched in the streets; they wrote books and articles and pamphlets and newsletters. Finally, on June 30, 1982, the battle was over. Even after an extension of time, the ERA expired, having gained only thirty-five of the thirty-eight states needed to make it part of the Constitution.

But there were all these women out there, who had honed their political and communication skills for ten years and had become adept. By the end of the fight, according to an article in the *Wall Street Journal,* NOW claimed "to be bringing in more money a month than the Democratic National Committee," and much of the money came from people who had never before made a political contribution.[2] Something similar was true of the anti-ERA forces. And on both sides of the issue, activists had made new, invaluable contacts, with foes and allies alike.

"For the first time," wrote Joann Lublin of the *Wall Street Journal,* "there appears to be a measurable women's vote. . . . The women who have created this 'gender gap' represent 'a great new constituency to look to,' argues Betsy Griffiths, a Republican feminist activist."[3]

The question was, how could this energy be harnessed to make some sort of political difference? ERA supporters were quick to try to keep the alliance they had forged intact, staying in touch with unions and civil rights organizations they had worked with, targeting other issues that might be less controversial—shelters for battered women, job counseling for widows and divorcees who had to enter the work force, perhaps day care. They were looking for issues to bring people together and to conserve the money, resources, and enthusiasm that the ERA fight had produced. They were looking for coalition politics—alliances with people already in politics who generally had other goals, but who might have an agenda that overlapped on some issue with the feminist agenda.

Equal Rights and the Right to Choose

Betty Friedan identified in her 1977 book, *It Changed My Life,* the issues that ultimately appeal to women all over the world: equality before the law and reproductive control. In communist countries and countries dominated by religious leaders, these rights are eroded in various ways; if women have no legal equality and no control over when and if they have children, then the state has seriously invaded their rights. This concern with individual rights as they uniquely apply to women should be, to my mind, the heart of feminist political activism, and many feminists who do not label themselves "individualists" agree with me. (Joann Lublin quotes Eleanor Smeal, then president of NOW: "What issues should determine feminists' support for a contender? The ERA and abortion rights at a minimum."[4])

But if one is trying to reach out to nonfeminist (or even to antifeminist) activist women, these can be divisive issues. These are issues that attribute independence to women as a natural right, and, unfortunately, people who deplore feminism view a stress on independence as negating the importance of relationships, particularly the marriage relationship. (Of course, as marriage has legally been defined in the past, they may be right. Historically, marriage, in different ways, in different countries, has been a main source of the denial of legal rights to women.) So, if the goal is to reach activist women who are very traditional, emphasizing rights might be counterproductive.

To reach them, you have to have a political goal that avoids divisiveness, one that can send a message speaking particularly to women without bringing up issues that are too troublesome. And when all the other feminist social movements were happening in the late 1970s, some feminists took up an issue that seemed to have the potential for unifying women on the left and the right. It was action against pornography.

Pornography Wars: The Beginning

Susan Brownmiller may have started it all in 1975 with the publication of *Against Our Will: Men, Women and Rape,* in which she called pornography "the undiluted essence of anti-female propaganda," which "promotes a climate in which acts of sexual hostility directed against women are not only tolerated but ideologically encouraged."[5] This formulation hit a responsive chord in many women.

One of the first organizations targeting this issue was WAVAW—Women Against Violence Against Women. In 1976 Warner Communications erected a billboard on Sunset Strip in Los Angeles to advertise their new Rolling Stones album. The billboard showed a woman who was bound, battered, and bruised, with the caption, "I'm Black and Blue from the Rolling Stones and I Love It." An ad hoc group of feminists that was to become WAVAW staged a demonstration and, as the 1979 WAVAW coordinator, Joan Howarth, later said, "We invited the Rolling Stones to join us in a press conference in front of the billboard or get the billboard down. They took it down."[6]

This began a two-and-a-half-year campaign against violent record album covers by WAVAW, especially targeting those produced by the Warner Communications (WCI) record group. WAVAW spokeswomen called WCI "a major offender in the recording industry." WAVAW tried to "raise the consciousness" of the industry about how offensive they found the covers and called for a boycott against Warner, Atlantic, and Elektra/Asylum Records.

And WAVAW won. In November 1979 the president of WCI, David H. Horowitz, issued a joint statement with WAVAW in which he said, "The WCI (Warner Communications, Inc.) record group opposes the depiction of violence, against women or men, on album covers and in related promotional material."

And Joan Howarth of WAVAW said,

> WAVAW, which has been advocating a boycott of WCI's record subsidiaries . . . now happily calls an end to that boycott.
>
> By publicizing this policy, WCI is acknowledging that the commercial use of visual and other images that trivialize women victims is irresponsible in light of the epidemic proportions of real-life violence against women.[7]

In December 1976, too, in another California city, San Francisco, another organization was being born to combat pornography: Women Against Violence in Pornography and Media (WAVPM). This one started with a march down a San Francisco pornography strip, but soon began staking out educational turf with a newsletter and a series of speaking engagements at libraries and colleges, using a portable slide show. Like WAVAW, WAVPM came out in support of freedom of speech. But where WAVAW pursued boycott rather than censorship, WAVPM issued a more ambiguous statement—a precursor of the more explicit calls for government action which were to come later from members of this movement—in a Q & A newsletter article that the organization distributed as a reprint by the thousands. To the question, "But wouldn't banning pornography jeopardize some people's freedom of speech?" WAVPM answered:

> We think not. WAVPM stands firm in our dedication to freedom of speech. Pornography is an *abuse* of the right to freedom of speech, and the First Amendment was never intended to protect material that condones and promotes violent crimes against any group—be it women, children, Third World people, Jews, old people, etc. The fact that the issue of "censorship" is raised so readily when women are the victims, in contrast with other groups, suggests that a political ploy is being used to confuse and intimidate us.[8]

Reaching Out to the Right?

In 1977 an article by novelist Lois Gould, syndicated by the *New York Times,* revealed what may have been the beginning of an awareness of the consensus that might be formed. She quoted herself as saying, "I wish we had Anita Bryant on our side," in a meeting of feminists who were trying to decide on specific actions against pornography. (Anita Bryant had started a conservative "save our children" campaign against homosexual rights.) The reactions she got ranged from bemused laughter from those who thought her statement "really not funny," to shock. But she tried to explain.

> Of course I deplore what "that woman" stands for; of course I stand against her. But the Bryant constituency is ours too, at least some of the time. We even have identical goals in some crucial areas—pornography, violence, wife-battering, child abuse. So wouldn't it help if we could begin, finally, to see—and to use—the connection?

This was greeted with protest from the others, because "where we diverge is too sharp; where we meet or overlap, too slippery." But Lois Gould's article goes on to explore the value of consensus. Men, she points out, are willing to band together with people they don't like in order to form a team, to win. But women often "grow up thinking that enemies who shake hands over bargaining tables and start helping each other are hypocrites. Even when . . . that help can mean the difference between winning and losing." Longtime feminist writer and editor Robin Morgan was in the meeting and seemed to understand the point. " 'Women who love their children,' she began, 'women who are deeply religious, they don't feel at one with us. . . . The fact is, Anita Bryant can reach and move those women—but we can't.' "

Lois Gould wraps up the article by invoking the diversity of consciousness-raising groups. "We used to come together . . . to find the connective tissues, without ever disowning our differences. Therein used to lie our strength."[9]

This is a very appealing article with a lot of truth to it—a lot of celebration of the individual woman that, for an individualist feminist, is at the center of feminism. The problem I have with it is perhaps idiosyncratic. I am convinced that politics has to be a matter of principle, and Lois Gould sounds willing to compromise with ideological enemies in order to win. Suggesting the use of an ideological enemy in order to reach other ideological enemies who wouldn't otherwise be reached is not a good long-term strategy. If pornography were one of my burning issues (which so far it is not) and I were trying to build a group like WAVAW to boycott and protest certain merchandising of it, I wouldn't have to hold my nose in order to get together a lot of diverse people. The diversity would be a value, because I would not be trying to promote a particular interpretation of pornography but *to organize as wide as possible a boycott*.

But for many other schools of feminism, pornography is connected to a specific social analysis and an analysis of sex relations that may or may not be articulated in any particular campaign or forum: that we live in a patriarchal society, for instance, which means that all heterosexual relations are inherently violent and in some sense "forced" on women by society, if not by individual men. In this view, any commercial, phallic, sexual material exploits women, and therefore is objectionable, even if it isn't violent. This is the hidden agenda in many feminist pornography protests. While they may think they resisted joining with right-wing women because they feel the right wing dislikes any sexual behavior that isn't the "missionary position," many of them have the strongest possible ideological objection to the missionary position and the acceptance of conventional relationships that they think it implies.

I'm not trying to use code language to say they are lesbians—some are and some aren't, but I don't think that's the issue. The issue is what they think is political principle and what they think is compromise.

Political realism is all very well, but we have all seen the current fragmentation of the Democratic Party into a series of *ad hoc* appeals to a multiplicity of special interest groups (Jesse Jackson perhaps *deserves* a presidential nomination for his political brilliance in calling this a "rainbow coalition"). If such a tactic is meant to promote winning, it doesn't seem to work.

And Losing the Liberals

The antipornography movement soon jettisoned much allegiance to the First Amendment, and in the process lost all support but lip-service from many influential liberals in the movement. In 1978 Susan Jacoby wrote in the *New York Times,*

> Feminists who want to censor what they regard as harmful pornography have essentially the same motivation as other would-be censors. They want to use the power of the state to accomplish what they have been unable to achieve in the marketplace of ideas and images. The impulse to censor places no faith in the possibilities of democratic persuasion.
>
> It isn't easy to persuade certain men that they have better uses for $1.95 each month than to spend it on a copy of *Hustler*? Well then, give the man no choice in the matter.[10]

In 1979 an organization called Women Against Pornography (WAP) started conducting sightseeing tours of pornography available in the Times

Square area of New York City. It organized a two-day East Coast conference against pornography and, on October 20, sponsored a march and demonstration against the pornography district in New York City that attracted more than 5,000 demonstrators (they had hoped for 20,000) and a motley crew of backers, including OTB, the city-wide agency that has a monopoly on Off Track Betting, and a league of theatre owners and producers, both of which wanted the area to be cleaned up for tourism by the urban renewal of the area. At these events and elsewhere, leaders and speakers of Women Against Pornography supported the idea that pornography is "nonspeech" and, therefore, outside of First Amendment protection, a position that the American Civil Liberties Union, for one, vigorously opposes.[11]

Susan Brownmiller, prominently associated with WAP, had made several public statements that pornography is not protected by the First Amendment—in *Newsday,* she quoted Chief Justice Warren Burger:

> To equate the free and robust exchange of ideas and political debate with commercial exploitation of obscene material demeans that grand concept of the First Amendment and its high purposes in the historic struggle for freedom. It is a misuse of the great guarantees of free speech and free press.

Brownmiller said she wished she had said that, "for I think the words are thrilling."[12]

At the October WAP demonstration, Bella Abzug reiterated this message that pornography isn't covered by the First Amendment, and Lynn Campbell, organizer of the march, echoed the ambiguities of the early WAVPM statement in saying, "I think the issue of censorship is false. Our group is demanding awareness, not censorship. If legislation grows out of our actions, we'll comment on the specific legislation at that time."[13]

It wasn't just the threat to civil liberties that disturbed more and more feminists, it was also the puritanical aspects of the feminist antipornography analysis. In 1980 Lindsy Van Gelder wrote an account of the activities of the antipornography movement to date for *Ms.* She took the Times Square tour with WAP and attended not only the October march but the September conference, which, she reported, attracted some 280 people (35 percent of the attendees) who had "never been active in the movement before."

But Van Gelder found she had reservations: about what "violence" is; about the attack on "offensive" public displays, an offense, which may be, she points out, in the eye of the beholder. She found it very difficult to adequately classify what sexually explicit material is acceptable.[14]

A long article by Ellen Willis in the *Village Voice* also had little sympathy for "the moralistic rhetoric and the conventionally feminine sexual politics of the antiporn campaign." She called for more open discussion of sexuality within feminism and a more sophisticated analysis of sexual choices and sexual pleasure, including recognizing that some feminists have a positive personal response to pornography and sadomasochism. The antipornography campaign takes the line that these are a form of violence rather than sex, only appealing to men because of their patriarchy; but how then should one appraise feminist women admitting to such fantasies? As traitors to the movement? As sick? As people with unconventional sexual habits?

Willis concludes that the right of sexual partners to consent to what pleases them is "axiomatic," but "a truly radical movement must look . . . beyond the right to choose, and keep focusing on the fundamental questions. Why do we choose what we choose?" It is the "antiporn" answers to these questions that she found superficial.[15]

Nineteen eighty-four was a banner year for feminists against pornography. In January 1984 feminists persuaded the Minneapolis City Council to pass an ordinance, coauthored by Andrea Dworkin and Catharine MacKinnon, labeling pornography discrimination against women (Mayor Donald M. Fraser, a liberal Democrat, vetoed it on constitutional grounds). In May of the same year, wrote Walter Goodman in the *New York Times,* "an ordinance banning pornography on the ground that its effect is 'to deny women equal opportunities in society' was signed into law in Indianapolis," with the support of fundamentalist religious groups. (This ordinance didn't last either; it was declared unconstitutional by the federal courts in 1985 in a decision by Reagan appointee Frank H. Easterbrook.) The National Organization for Women said at its 1984 annual conference that pornography was a "factor in creating and maintaining sex as a basis for discrimination. . . . [It] violates the civil rights of women and children."[16]

And Ronald Reagan called for a national commission on pornography. The 1970 Commission on Pornography and Obscenity had found no provable connection between pornography and criminal action and so had recommended that most laws against pornography be repealed. President Nixon had rejected this commission's report, and President Reagan said he thought it was time to look at any new evidence about a relationship between pornography and criminal behavior.

But liberal and conservative intellectuals alike were starting to express their alienation from some of the feminist positions in this campaign— the outreach was not reaching mainstream intellectuals of both persuasions. Aryeh Neier, a past executive director of the American Civil Liberties

Union, called the campaign "the new censorship." Meanwhile, feminists got negative reactions from Ernest van den Haag, an outspoken conservative advocate of censorship who found the feminist research unconvincing, and from conservative columnist George Will, who thinks pornography should be banned "out of concern for society as a whole," rather than from an appeal to the individual rights of women.[17]

The Meese Commission

But although intellectuals were not buying the feminist analysis that pornography directly incites rape and degrades women, politicians were beginning to. The Minneapolis and Indianapolis city councils had been impressed. And after the Attorney General's Commission on Pornography (first established by William French Smith in February 1985; later to be known as the Meese Commission) held its hearings, Catharine MacKinnon said, in a letter to the *Times Book Review,* "We did our best to influence former Attorney General Edwin Meese 3rd's Commission on Pornography to listen to women, with some success."[18] What happened, according to *Time,* is that "the Meese Commission recommended hearings on a national version of the Dworkin-MacKinnon proposal."[19]

But when the Commission delivered its two-volume, 1,960-page report to Attorney General Meese on July 9, 1986, although Catharine MacKinnon and Andrea Dworkin were perhaps pleased, the general tone of the document was more conservative than feminist. Feminists might have begun this campaign hoping to co-opt conservative and religious strategists, but the Meese Commission's report reads as if it were the feminists who were co-opted. The report did reach a conclusion opposite to that reached by the 1970 Commission, whose report it called "starkly obsolete": it found a causal link between violent pornography and sexual violence. But, in condemning the effects of pornography, the report went on—"A larger issue [than acts of sexual violence] is the very question of promiscuity. . . . Although there are many members of his society who can and have made affirmative cases for uncommitted sexuality, none of us believe it to be a good thing."[20] And as for erotica, explicit material that is neither violent nor degrading, "none of us think the material in this category, individually or as a class, is in every instance harmless."[21]

Two women on the panel, Judith Becker, director of the Sexual Behavior Clinic at the New York State Psychiatric Institute, and Ellen Levine, editor in chief of *Woman's Day,* disagreed with the statement that there was evidence that violent pornography causes sexual violence and wrote an eighteen-page rebuttal to the report.

The report contained thirty-seven pages of suggestions for citizen action against pornography, as well as suggested actions for Congress, state legislatures, state and local prosecutors, and federal agencies. Although disclaiming any interest in censorship, the Commission, of course, endorsed the existing obscenity laws that the Supreme Court had already said did not violate freedom of the press and suggested ways to augment their implementation. It was this Commission, for instance, that suggested that the Racketeer Influenced Corrupt Organization (RICO) Act be used against suspected pornographers and that state legislatures should enact similar acts. If this is not censorship, it looks like a duck and walks like a duck.

So what should one's perspective be toward pornography? Especially for a woman, it doesn't create an inviting environment. In contemporary America, it's sometimes hard for a romantic to know where to look. From paperback racks in the drugstores of resort hotels to newsstands on Fifth Avenue, we are barraged, not just with images of nudity and copulation, but images of beatings, of bondage, and of the sexual exploitation of children. Those with eye trouble peer to see what is playing at the movie house they are passing at their peril: it's apt to be "See the Native Virgins Sacrificed."

What's a nice instinct like sex doing in a place like this? That is a psychological question I can't fully answer, except to say that it seems as if one of the appeals of pornography is that it must be wicked. So, as our society became more permissive and labeled most sexually explicit material as not wicked at all, the issue of pornography didn't disappear—but the pornography publicly available became kinkier. Where once the pastoral romance of Lady Chatterley and her husband's gamekeeper violated marital and class taboos as well as taboos against sexual description and vulgar language, now those who need to imagine forbidden indulgences have to seek images of women being run through meat grinders—as appeared on an infamous cover of *Hustler* magazine in the 1970s.

The Argument for Censorship

The argument feminists have raised is that women as a group are being vilified by such images, just as Jews as a group were vilified by cartoons depicting them in hostile terms in early Nazi Germany. We know that reported instances of rape, wife beating, and child abuse have increased in the culture over the same period in which these degrading images of women have appeared with increasing frequency. We may not be able to establish a causal relationship between violent behavior and violent pornography, but if we as a culture look with equanimity on the depiction of the debasement and torture of any group of people—as a "healthy release," no less—aren't we implying that the group is somehow subhuman and deserves such treatment? And if this kind of depiction goes on indefinitely without protest, even if it's not causing violent action now, won't it lead to a sanctioning of violent action, as it did in Nazi Germany?

Local governments have a tradition of enforcing community standards—shouldn't our communities be allowed to protest the public displays of such offensive materials? Would we allow pictures of men in white hoods hanging terrified blacks, or titillating descriptions of Auschwitz from the Nazi point of view to be similarly publicly displayed and sold?

In fact, at one time a Supreme Court decision held that statutes making it illegal to defame racial or religious groups are constitutional. The right to utter slander or print libel is not considered protected by the First Amendment from lawsuit or damages. And before the Court clarified its position on libel, a 1952 case, *Beauharnais* v. *Illinois,* had held that libeling an ethnic group is equivalent to libeling an individual and therefore not protected speech—*if* there is a specific statute enacted that makes it a crime to defame racial or religious groups.[22] (Common law is the basic law of all the states except Louisiana, and there is no common-law concept of group libel; hence, the need for a statute.) So what about defaming an entire gender by depicting it as masochistic and subservient?

On the Other Hand . . .

This, basically, is the feminist argument for action. The civil libertarian argument points out that the *Beauharnais* decision has been implicitly overruled by subsequent decisions on libel, especially by the 1964 decision, *New York Times Co.* v. *Sullivan,*[23] and the First Amendment guarantees freedom of the press, not just for acceptable material, but, as Justice Oliver Wendell Holmes put it, for "the expression of opinions that we loathe."[24] In the name of freedom of speech, Nazis were allowed to march on the streets of Skokie, Illinois, where Jewish refugees from the Nazis had settled. In the name of freedom of speech, books critical of the government are published. Because of freedom of speech, no serious social or religious doctrine, no matter how pernicious, can be suppressed.

The Supreme Court didn't directly consider the issue of freedom of speech until 1919. In *Schenck* v. *United States,* the Court unanimously upheld the conviction of socialists who had printed a pamphlet arguing that the draft was unconstitutional and had distributed it to men awaiting induction as draftees.[25] This is the case in which Justice Oliver Wendell Holmes said you can't falsely shout "Fire!" in a theatre and cause a panic;

if speech or writing will create a "clear and present danger" of bringing about evils that Congress has a right to prevent, they are not protected by the First Amendment.

After this decision, the history of free speech goes uphill. The clear-and-present-danger concept was later used to strike down convictions of a Jehovah's Witness for breaching the peace by playing an anti-Catholic record in public (*Cantwell* v. *Connecticut,* 1940)[26] and of an unfrocked Catholic priest who made an anti-Semitic speech to an audience of eight hundred people (*Terminiello* v. *Chicago,* 1949),[27] both on the grounds that any danger was not "clear and present."

The late Justice Hugo Black, who sat on the Supreme Court from 1937 to 1971 and held that the words "no law" in the First Amendment *mean* "no law," is credited with shifting the legal discussion about speech from the question, "what are the limits to free speech?" to "are there any?" Gradually, the clear and-present-danger test, as well as other tests the Court had applied to decide whether a restriction on speech was "reasonable," fell into disuse as far as political and religious ideas go. Three categories of speech are still considered exempt from First Amendment protection—libel, "fighting words," and obscenity. (A fourth category, commercial speech, is in a more amorphous position—sometimes protected, sometimes not.) There have been two major Supreme Court decisions defining tests to be applied to questionable material to determine if it's obscene.

In *Roth* v. *United States* (1957), the test was "Whether to the average person applying contemporary community standards, the dominant theme of the material taken as a whole appeals to prurient interest."[28] In *Miller* v. *California* (1973), the Burger Court gave a new definition: "whether the work, taken as a whole, lacks serious literary, artistic, political, or scientific value" as well as appealing to "prurient interest" and depicting sexual conduct "in a patently offensive way"—both to be determined by community values.[29] This is still basically the standard by which obscenity and pornography are legally judged today.

Those who agree with Justice Black that *no law* means no law do not think there should be an exception to the First Amendment coverage of written material because of sexual content—or because, as a number of decisions have held, sexual interest was being "commercially exploited" and commercial interests are not protected. (Perhaps the most horrendous of such cases was the 1966 upholding of the conviction of Ralph Ginzberg, who went to jail for five years for *advertising* his publications as pornographic, even though they were not.) The civil libertarian argument in its purest form is that there should be no legal category of obscenity, which has always been almost impossible to define.

But Then . . .

If I were speaking on behalf of an organization to suppress pornography, I would answer by saying that although such organizations have tried (so far in vain), to have the spirit of the *Beauharnais* decision applied to women through ordinances declaring that pornography violates women's civil rights, by far the most widesweeping and effective actions that have been taken have been those of boycott.

Surely groups that band together to withhold buying power in order to apply economic pressure in accordance with their values are exercising their property rights? That is what a coalition of feminists and fundamentalists have been doing, on a nationwide basis. To quote from an editorial by Marty Zupan, former editor of *Reason,* in 1986, "Why was it perfectly okay, even virtuous, for grocery stores to refuse to stock non-union grapes and lettuce in response to pressure from Cesar Chavez and his followers, but it's not at all okay, it's downright un-American, for convenience stores to pull *Playboy* and *Penthouse* from their shelves in response to pressure from Jerry Falwell and his followers?"[30]

I can't quarrel with that point—boycotts are an expression of opinion, too, and should be allowed even when they might be wrongheaded. I'm afraid that when Marty Zupan's question gets a different answer, it's based on the increasingly common assumption that the First Amendment guarantees something to the reader as well as to the writer. Not only are we free to write and publish, this theory goes, but we should have *access* to the ideas that we might value. This is the assumption behind the Fairness Doctrine in television, and the increasing pressure to force newspapers to also grant "equal time" to the opinions of those that their editors or owners disagree with. This is not a rights-oriented view of the First Amendment, certainly not a property-rights view of newspaper ownership; it is the view that we allow diversity of opinion, not because people have the right to express ideas, but because society benefits from a marketplace of ideas.

If people have individual rights by their very nature, as the Declaration of Independence postulates ("they are endowed by their Creator with certain unalienable rights"), then any benefit to the group arising from individuals exercising their rights is a secondary, derivative benefit. To be sure, we expect such benefits to follow, but the rights would exist even in the absence of a benefit to society. But if we use society's benefit as a *standard* by which to evaluate the importance of individual rights, then when a case can be made that the exercise of one person's right does *not* benefit society, that is a powerful argument for abridging that exercise. The distinction may not seem important—*until* the time when the ideas that win out in the marketplace may be judged potentially harmful to society. Then, those who hold to the social-value view of speech will want them suppressed.

And we have had examples of this. Unpopular or dangerous political ideas are always a target for suppression, especially in times of war or threat of war—consider the anticommunist legislation after both World Wars. Religious ideas have been targets, too. Mormons in the Territory of Utah were refused the right to vote because they adhered to a religion that advocated the practice of polygamy, and the Supreme Court upheld that refusal in 1890.[31] And obscenity and pornography have a long history of being attacked as dangerous—van den Haag and George Will are only the most recent examples of those who want pornography suppressed, for the good of society.

Meese Commission Revisited

If we want to uphold an absolute right of free speech and press, even for offensive "speech" like pornography, we still have a right to speak against it. So, if much pornography is vulgar, demeaning, and hostile to women, and if boycott is a proper way of trying to effect one's values, why are we talking about censorship at all? Censorship is government action, not private action, no matter how effective it might be. Well, there was some government action lurking in the wings in the Meese Commission activities.

Let's go back to the Meese Commission recommendation that "the Department of Justice and United States Attorneys should use the Racketeer Influenced Corrupt Organization Act as a means of prosecuting major producers and distributers of obscene material."[32]

In October 1988, a talk given by attorney Richard Corn-Revere at the Fourth Annual Conference of the Free Press Association, held in Brooklyn, focused on the expanded use of this statute, generally called RICO, to seize and dispose of all the business assets of convicted porn dealers. Corn-Revere reported one case (*United States* v. *Pryba*) in which the government seized and sold over one million dollars worth of videotape inventory, most of which was nonpornographic, after defendant Pryba was convicted of selling "obscene materials" valued at less than one hundred dollars. The seizure was being appealed, but even if the appeal was won, only the sale proceeds—"about ten cents on the dollar"—could be recovered.[33]

And the Commission was not above doing a little strong-arming itself. While it was meeting, it sent out an official letter to publishers, bookstores, and convenience stores. The letter, signed by the commission's director, told recipients that they had been accused by an unnamed witness, offered a chance to rebut the accusation, and warned that refusal to reply would be interpreted as acquiescence to the charges. *Time* magazine reported that more than 10,000 stores stopped selling softcore magazines like *Playboy* and *Penthouse,* at least for a time, when they received a letter telling them that the commission might cite them for distributing pornography. A federal district judge later ordered the commission to send out another letter retracting the implied threat, calling it "a prior restraint on speech."[29]

The Meese Commission report had indirect effects as well. It called for a great deal of state legislation, including the creation of state RICO acts. *Time* cited Steve Hallman, director of Citizens Concerned for Community Values of Greater Cincinnati, as saying that the report "will give momentum nationwide to obscenity-law enforcement."[35] This seems a reference to the report's call for strong legal action against those publications that can be considered legally obscene, as well as for citizen action against publications that are not legally obscene—such as *Playboy* and *Penthouse.* A new climate of opinion was created.

In this new climate of opinion, the definition of obscenity was stretched out of recognition. The City Council of Tyler, Texas, passed an anti-obscenity statute ordering retailers to put all magazines that featured pictorial nudity behind the counter in plain brown wrappers. Since many magazines rely heavily on so called impulse sales in stores or newsstands, the editors of *Cosmopolitan* were concerned when policemen in Tyler began ordering stores to put the July issue of the magazine in plain brown wrappers because of an illustrated story on cosmetic surgery that included before and after photos of breast surgery and tummy tucks. There was a legal controversy, *Cosmopolitan* won, but, as a side effect, at least one chain of convenience stores, Brookshire Food Stores, not only pulled the July *Cosmo* from all its stores (not just those in Tyler) but decided to permanently discontinue carrying the magazine.[36] A decision not to stock a product after police action against it is hardly a response to a boycott!

The boycott front was moving toward the mainstream. The real target of the feminist boycott was supposed to be the hardcore stuff, but that material isn't sold in convenience stores and other places mainly patronized by women, it is sold in adult bookstores. So boycotts were organized against nonobscene targets, because that was where they could be effective. And they were.

An issue of *American Photographer* was pulled off some racks in Kansas because of a photo that showed a woman's breast. Magazine distributors reported complaints about the annual swimsuit issue of *Sports Illustrated; Good Housekeeping* got complaints about a jockey shorts ad. The University of Wisconsin Union, attacked for carrying *Playboy* and

Penthouse, discontinued sixty-seven other magazines, including *Vogue.*

Economic boycott can be a powerful tool, but it has unexpected side effects. If feminists are going to strengthen the clout of fundamentalist forces, they can expect three results. First, this clout will be used to try to ban discussions that feminists might not want to ban, for instance, as part of the antipornography boycott the National Federation for Decency picketed a store in Tampa to get it to remove copies of *National Lampoon* and *Mad,* because they felt those magazines promote rebellion against parental authority. Does that sound like a feminist issue?

Second, such boycotts, if successful, will economically harm magazine distributors, who might then not be able to carry the variety of publications they had in the past. This may affect opinion magazines that feminists like, but it won't affect the giants, like *Playboy* and *Penthouse,* at least not enough to put them out of business. What *Playboy* and *Penthouse* actually did, whether as a result of the boycotts or not, was to diversify into X-rated videotapes.

The third problem that feminists who join the religious-right anti-pornography crusade face is illustrated by history. The laws against obscenity invoke, as I mentioned before, a prejudice against commercial activity. The federal government got into the act in the first place through the power to run a postal service and the power to establish customs regulations. Until this century, obscenity laws were concerned not primarily with books, but with conduct and with articles of commerce.

The first effective antiobscenity federal statute was the Comstock Act of 1873, which made it a crime to mail an "obscene, lewd, lascivious, indecent, filthy or vile article, matter, thing, device or substance" or to inform someone through the mails where such illegal objects may be obtained, directly or indirectly, through a "written or printed card, letter, circular, book, pamphlet, advertisement, or notice of any kind." Since *book* is mentioned, it was stretched to include books, but from the time of its passage, it was enforced against contraceptive devices and contraceptive information.[37]

Anthony Comstock, who designed the law and even worked as an unsalaried postal inspector in order to enforce it, entrapped doctors and birth control advocates by claiming to be a desperate woman whose life would be endangered by childbirth and asking for information through the mail. According to an article in *Playboy* in 1976, "In 1913 he boasted of having convicted some 3600 persons and of having driven at least 15 to suicide."[38]

The religious right often connects campaigns against pornography and against abortion, and some fundamentalists would also like to see legal limits on birth control, at the very least. Do those of us who deplore violent hardcore pornography want to run the risk of actions that might end in a move to revive the original meaning of the Comstock Act, which is still on the books? In 1978 something like that almost happened, according to an op-ed piece by Linda Bird Francke. According to Francke,

> The Senate passed a bill that contained a section titled "Mailing, imparting or transporting obscene matter." If this bill passed the House, any person or organization sending information on abortion facilities and availability will be guilty of a Class O felony, subject to five years in jail and a fine of $100,000.[34]

We all have an undoubted right to express our values, in speech *and* through economic and political action. But we had better make sure that is really what we are doing.

Seeming political expediency can lead us down strange paths and take us to entirely unintended goals. There is a temptation to do something *effective* at all costs in politics, even if important principles are lost sight of for a while. But, we discard our ideals at our peril. Feminists can't afford to take themselves out of the mainstream of rights; our lives and happiness depend on supporting a noncontradictory vision of equal rights for all.

CHAPTER THIRTEEN

The Temptation of Political Expediency: Social Feminism

If action against pornography divides feminists by raising concerns about First Amendment rights, there is another recent attempt at coalition that has deeper historical roots and may have more mainstream appeal.

Feminists versus the Family

One of the most successful anti-ERA efforts by conservatives depicted it as an amendment that would be antifamily in its impact. Speakers from Stop ERA aroused fears that married women would be "forced" to enter the labor force and that husbands would no longer have to support their wives. Feminists didn't do much to counter the wider image of being antifamily as they labored to set the record straight on what the actual impact of the ERA would be.

At the end of 1979, perhaps in a belated attempt to gain back some of the audience swayed by the anti-ERA activists, NOW's Legal Defense and Education Fund held an all-day meeting at the New York Hilton on the "Future of the Family."[1] Betty Friedan was one of the speakers and delivered what turned out to be a highly controversial preview of the message in her book *The Second Stage,* which was to come out in 1981. In an article published in the *New York Times Magazine* the day before the conference, Friedan addressed "the myth that equality means death to the family" and called for new family forms and for feminists to speak from those "elements of their personal truth" that valued husbands and children. She said,

The underlying reality is no different for the bitterest feminists and most stridently fearful defenders of the family. None of us can depend throughout our new, long lives on that "family of Western nostalgia" to meet our needs for nurture and support, but all of us still have those needs. . . .

The new urge of both women and men for meaning in their work and life, for love, roots and family—even though it may not resemble the ideal family that maybe never was—is a powerful force for change.[2]

This, said Friedan, is what the second stage of the feminist movement must support—human liberation.

Friedan's Second Stage

Two years later, when *The Second Stage* was published, she was even sharper, saying that the women's movement must rid itself of a new "feminist mystique," that was replacing the "feminine mystique" she had originally exposed in 1963. "There are *not* two kinds of women in America," she wrote. "The political polarization between feminism and the family was preached and manipulated by extremists on the right—and colluded in, perhaps unconsciously, by feminist and liberal or radical leaders—to extend or defend their own political power." (Emphasis in original)[3]

Almost all women, she pointed out, want to be treated as individuals and also believe in the family: "that last area where one has any hope of . . . nourishing that core of personhood threatened now by vast impersonal institutions and uncontrollable corporate and government bureaucracies."[4]

And how should this new stage of human liberation be achieved? Friedan has her roots in New Deal liberalism. So at the time of the Future of the Family conference she called for strong government programs, saying, "the United States is one of the few advanced nations with no national policy of leaves for maternity, paternity or parenting, no national policy encouraging flexible working arrangements and part-time and shared employment, and no national policy to provide child care for those who need it."[5]

But she has also built her life on the importance of organizations of individuals. She was, after all, a founder of the earliest and most enduring feminist political organizations—NOW, NARAL, and the National Women's Political Caucus—and it was this importance of movement activity that she stressed when it came to *The Second Stage*. Unions and companies should be persuaded to provide for flextime, job sharing, and child care. She also called for flexible benefit packages, a relaxation of zoning laws so that people unrelated by either blood or marriage could buy housing together, and a "voucher system" for people who care for children or elderly relatives in the home, perhaps in the form of a tax rebate.

All of this, she said, will create a new social movement, which must include men and which will be based on volunteerism.

> The voluntary organizations will be the only way to provide the services essential to further social change, and the living of equality—now that it appears we will have to rely less and less on Government agencies and the courts. And in organizing for those services which we need communally and cannot afford or provide, even as superwomen, by ourselves . . . we will build a new political force.[6]

(In an interview at the time *The Second Stage* was published, Friedan pointed out, "The women's movement itself was the best volunteerism I've seen.")[7]

Betty Friedan has always had her finger on the pulse of what's happening in women's lives. *The Feminine Mystique* sparked a tremendous feeling of recognition among women who had been taught that service to others was the only way for a woman to achieve satisfaction, and who had discovered that service was not enough for them. Over the ten years between 1981 and 1991, it has become more clear that the feelings that Friedan discovered and explored in *The Second Stage* are of growing importance to young women—the desire for individuality *and* family, concern for the "biological clock," the sense that a satisfying life needs both work and relationships, and above all, perhaps, the libertarian realization she articulated in *The Second Stage,* that family is the cradle of individualism, and the antithesis of both of them is bureaucracy.

At the time the book was published, however, the message that feminists had much in common with supporters of the family did not get good reviews from some feminists. Ellen Willis wrote in a letter to the *Times,* "Betty Friedan would destroy feminism in order to save it, and beat the Moral Majority by joining it."[8] But others were listening. Megan Marshall in the *New Republic* thought that Friedan's reforms were "unquestionably appealing," but did question "Friedan's notion that such reforms can and will be accomplished through a quiet, community-based movement of 'job protestors' of both sexes."[9]

The Search for Economic Legislation: Comparable Worth

By the time the ERA went down to defeat in June of 1982, Friedan's vision of ways in which the right and the left could join together to promote economic change of benefit to women had been duly noted by politically activist feminists.

And they tried to find an economic goal that would echo the appeals of their failed ERA campaign. At NOW's first national convention after ERA in the fall of 1982, Judy Goldsmith, the new president of NOW, announced that the organization would have a "strong economic focus," agitating for, among other goals, equal pay for work of "comparable worth."[10]

(This was a relatively new outgrowth of the issue of "equal pay for equal work," which nonfeminists had said in recent political campaigns that they, of course, supported. In the 1980 presidential election, Rep. Barbara Mikulski counseled that economic issues widened the base of the feminist movement. "Women come up to me," she said, "and say, 'I'm not one of those women libbers, but I sure want to earn the same salary as the guy next to me.' "[11])

The issue of equal pay for work of comparable worth had begun to surface as far back as the 1970s, when local government employees began to analyze the job evaluation systems that determined their salaries. Unions got into the act and began to find that jobs held mainly by women generally paid less than jobs held mainly by men, even when such jobs seemed to be evaluated as requiring similar levels of skill, effort, responsibility, and similar working conditions. Nurses working for the city of Denver brought an unsuccessful suit against the city claiming that the classification system used by the Career Service Authority discriminated against them because they were women. Unions brought suits against universities and some private companies. The National Research Council did a study under contract to the EEOC that was published in 1981. A committee on occupational classification and analysis was given the task of studying "the principles and procedures used in determining compensation for work in the United States" particularly to see if pay differences between jobs are caused by discrimination (defined by result, not necessarily by intent). The committee decided that they were, as the various criteria and systems used to set pay resulted in "women earning substantially less then men," and an important reason for this was "the ghettoization of women in the economy."[12]

A minority report by Professor Ernest J. McCormick of Purdue University disagreed with the economic assumptions that underlay the report's conclusions in the following words:

> The committee report views the labor market as one that tends to undervalue "women's jobs" relative to "men's jobs" and concludes that the market is discriminatory and therefore should be disregarded in establishing rates of pay. Such a view of the labor market seems to me to be naive and unrealistic. The labor market is the generic term for a value system rooted in the hierarchy of skills, effort, responsibility, and work activities (and to some extent working conditions) that comprise jobs, and the supply and demand

forces that operate as organizations and workers compete in our economy. As a matter of interest, statements of female or minority "undervaluation" seem to be based upon the concept that there is a value system but that some types of individuals in certain jobs are not paid according to the underlying system. If there is no available hierarchy of worth, there is no objective basis upon which to make claims of bias. Accordingly, I am convinced that the labor market must be the arbiter of basic rates of pay.[13]

There is a long tradition of comparing the quality of certain occupations or products and finding a cosmic injustice in the way the market values them. Why do vintage wines cost more than water, when we need water to stay alive? (They are scarcer.) Why does a star athlete earn more than an Einstein? (More people are interested in what she does.) In the early eighties, feminists extended this approach to the earning power of different jobs. And it wasn't only feminists; bureaucrats and particularly public service unions with their clients (governments, which could ignore the market because their revenue depended on taxation) became converts to the new approach. For a while, the comparable worth issue became a matter of great political concern. The state of Washington initiated a study to compare pay for state jobs held by men with those held by women and found that those held mainly by men paid more on the average than those held mainly by women. The Washington Federation of State Employees then brought suit charging the government with sex discrimination, and in 1983 a federal judge ordered the state to pay millions—perhaps hundreds of millions—of dollars in back pay to women workers. (On September 6, 1985, the U.S. Court of Appeals for the Ninth Circuit finally reversed this decision, saying that the evidence had not established discrimination in this case. Shortly before this reversal, Governor Booth Gardner of Washington had agreed to bargain with the union to establish "a program of pay equity" for men and women, and a $482 million agreement was signed in the state on the last day of December 1985.[14])

Who Dares to Disagree?

By 1984 the concept of "pay equity" had become an accepted part of the political landscape. In that year the first National Conference on Women, the Economy and Public Policy was held in Washington. This was not a conference that involved some marginal—or even mainstream—feminist group. Its announcement said: "Believing that the need for creation of a new economic policy to fit the changing role of women is urgent, all the women members of Congress have joined with almost 100 concerned organizations and 60 national leaders to explore the issues and the possible policy changes."[15]

This was a conference for women in politics. Among the sponsors were the vice Chair of the Democratic National Committee; the Co-Chair of the Republican National Committee (as well as its former Chair); and the heads of such organizations as the League of Women Voters, the American Association of University Women, the National Federation of Republican Women, the National Women's Political Caucus, the Coalition of Labor Union Women, the Congressional Caucus on Women's Issues, the National Education Association, the National Association of Women Business Owners, the Girl Scouts of America, and the YWCA. It was also sponsored by the presidents of several women's colleges, a state lieutenant governor, a couple of women bank executives, Mary Louise Smith (former chair of the Republican National Committee), and former political appointees such as Eleanor Holmes Norton and Juanita Kreps.

All in all, there were sixty-nine endorsing organizations and thirty-nine funders—businesses, foundations, and unions.

There were a number of workshops and debates, as well as presentations. And of all these prestigious people, *no one,* with the exception of economist June O'Neill of the Urban Institute who had been invited specifically to debate the issue, criticized the concept of pay equity or comparable worth. Senator Nancy Kassebaum avoided endorsing it during a question period; the official Republican greeter did not mention it; but the greeter from the Democratic Party, Nancy Beaver, made it a ringing part of the changes in economic policy that she called for. And this call became a continuing theme of the conference.

Nevertheless, the Concept has Grave Problems

Later in 1984, a Roundtable Discussion at the Manhattan Institute in New York among people more informed about economics, which was later published in the *Manhattan Report,* produced more diversity of opinion. Mark Killingworth, professor of economics at Rutgers, pointed out that instituting comparable worth pay scales would "amount to a tax on low-wage female labor," that "will simply lead to women losing jobs," whereas Pamela Cain, professor of sociology at Hunter, said that women had not been able to get a fair wage because they hadn't organized.[16]

This exchange raises an interesting question, to my mind. In all of the comparable worth job evaluations that were pointed to during this period as showing discriminatory practices, it was usually nonunionized jobs mainly held by women (such as that of secretary) that were compared to unionized jobs mainly held by men (such as that of truck driver). This points to the possibility that the comparable worth movement, despite its strong union component, might have been unintentionally protesting a previous tampering with the market rates of pay that had been instituted by unions. And there is evidence of such tampering having caused economic problems. In heavy industry, for instance, it has become clear in recent years that union activity did raise wages above what turned out to be the market rate. Companies faced bankruptcy and had to lay off workers. Others established overseas operations where wage rates let their prices compete on a world market. So it looks as if those feminists who saw wage rates for blue collar work as overvalued may very well have been absolutely correct in that assessment! Despite this possibility, the one major group apart from the Democratic Party that joined women's groups in advocating comparable worth policies was labor unions (who thereby attracted more women members in a time of attrition for union membership).

What remains questionable in their analysis is the assumption that where you cannot assign a specific cause for a difference in wage rates, there must be discrimination against the recipients of lower wages. As Professor Jennifer Roback, author of the Twentieth Century Fund pamphlet, *A Matter of Choice: a Critique of Comparable Worth by a Skeptical Feminist,* said in the Manhattan Institute Roundtable,

> The statistical evidence of discrimination usually relies upon the use of some statistical residual. That is, once you've considered every factor that can explain wage differences, what's left? But if you just took a population of white men and considered all the factors that could account for differences in their earnings, you'd find that only 40 percent of their variance in earnings could be explained—while some 60 percent of the variance in earnings is attributable to factors that we cannot inherently measure. And this is a population in which discrimination shouldn't be an issue.[17]

Although by 1985 more than forty states and fifty-two municipalities had established pay equity to some degree, the question seems to have ceased in the nineties to be important politically. First, the "pay gap" between men and women had narrowed by 1986—the average woman was earning 70 percent of the salary of the average man.[18] Then, the recession of the early nineties resulted in a further lowering of the gap, not necessarily because women's wages have increased, but because the wages of many blue collar jobs have dramatically fallen.

It's too bad, in a way, that feminist voices have supported instead of attacked comparable worth, because it is another, disguised form of the protective legislation that feminists repudiated in the seventies. All comparable worth schemes depend on someone "evaluating" the worth of different jobs, which means they depend on another way of interposing a subjective value judgment between the individual woman and her economic possibilities. That's exactly what happened in protective labor legislation—under the claim that night work was dangerous for them, women were "protected" from jobs such as bartender or night elevator operator that paid quite well, but not from low-paying jobs requiring the same hours such as scrubwoman.

If we do away with the impersonal forces of the market and substitute job evaluations to set pay standards, *just who do we think is going to do the evaluating?* In the present political climate, the evaluations might very well find that jobs held mainly by women are undervalued, although even that is not certain during a recession. And suppose the climate changed?

The Search for Economic Legislation: Another Proposal

A strong call to find more issues on which to build an alliance, not just among women's groups, but between women's groups and organized labor, came in 1986. That spring saw the publication of *A Lesser Life* by Sylvia Ann Hewlett, who was at the time the vice president for economic studies at the United Nations Association.

It is the feminist movement, says Hewlett, that was largely responsible for the plight of women in America in the mideighties. She considered herself to be a feminist when she came from England to work as an assistant professor of economics at Barnard College in 1974, partly because she wished to be in the country that was the center of contemporary feminism. She stayed there until 1981, combining teaching with marriage and family life, and it was her difficult experiences in trying to do this that led to this book.

How did the feminist movement help to create her problems? Conservatives who think of it as a socialist movement may be surprised to hear that Hewlett thinks it is because feminism as it was promoted in the United States, with its emphasis on consciousness raising, abortion rights, and the ERA, has been too individualistic. This is how she put it.

> The problem is that consciousness raising tends to shift the burden for change away from society and toward the individual woman. It encourages women to look to themselves, or to that small group of women with whom they share consciousness, as the source of their "liberation." In short, consciousness raising is an approach that de-emphasizes broad-based social action in favor of personal redemption. . . . Because it shifts responsibility away from society and toward the individual, it tends to de-emphasize political action in favor of highly personal transformation experiences.[19]

According to Hewlett, Eleanor Roosevelt and the Women's Bureau of the Department of Labor were correct when they opposed an Equal Rights Amendment on the grounds that women didn't need equality before the law, they needed special protective legislation. This is why she endorses "social feminism" as it has been practiced in contemporary Western Europe. She interviewed "hundreds of working parents in five different countries" and concluded that only ever-expanding government programs could solve their problems. Further, she holds that, by her definition, American women are less liberated than their European counterparts because European countries have more protective legislation than we do. The problems of women, says Hewlett, are problems the market cannot solve, and American women, by trying to solve their problems themselves, are relieving what would otherwise be pressure on government to seek collective solutions to these problems.

Not Rights, but Entitlements

What she is suggesting, of course, is that the American women's movement should abandon its classical liberal goal of individual rights for women and join those democracies that substitute entitlements for rights. In Europe "advanced democracies have instituted family support systems such as paid maternity leaves, child allowances, subsidized day care, and free health services, all of which considerably ease the lives of working parents."[20]

Hewlett owes a debt to Betty Friedan's *The Second Stage*. Like Friedan, she sees the plight of the American family and the need for solutions to the problems of organizing work and family that face the contemporary mother. And, like Friedan, she sees that both feminist and antifeminist women have family needs in common. But, unlike Friedan, she looks to the past, especially the recent European past, for inspiration. Since there is no national movement to secure legislation gaining special privileges for working mothers, and since neither the feminist movement nor the antifeminist movement has yet done much to improve women's economic security, she calls for an alliance between women and organized labor to secure some of the entitlements she thinks are owed to women. Such an alliance had already been forged to promote comparable worth policies: an issue she did not discuss except to say that she didn't see why Phyllis Schlafly, with whom she agreed on ERA, couldn't "understand" its value.

Of course, even in the mideighties, the cost of the benefits she proposed would be astronomical. The European countries she cited had relatively homogeneous populations and a much more stable tradition of marriage—"the divorce rate in the United States is now double that in Sweden, Britain, and Germany; triple that in France; and twenty times as high as in Italy"[21]—

and despite this, their social welfare programs were causing them unprecedented budget crises, even as she wrote.

The assumption behind an appeal to people of different political philosophies to unite in a pressure group to lobby for entitlements is that self-interest is more basic than any philosophical difference. It's an appeal that hasn't worked too well for the Democratic Party recently. True classical liberals are immune to such blandishments because they would see them as contradicting the important principle of rights; their view would be that such entitlements would violate the rights of others that had to pay for them. But the individual-oriented woman in the American feminist movement might be tempted, having no such firm political philosophy dealing with economic rights and limited government and having been raised on a group of entitlements, such as social security, that were already in place and taken for granted, whose effects were criticized only by a few unpublicized libertarians.

Do We Want Special Legal Treatment for Pregnant Women?

Nevertheless, one classical liberal principle, that of equality before the law, has become important to a number of feminists. Even as *A Lesser Life* was published, feminists were on both sides of an issue that was coming before the Supreme Court and had to do with one of Dr. Hewlett's desired entitlements.

The case had to do with preferential treatment for pregnancy. Lillian Garland had left her job at the California Federal Savings and Loan Association in Los Angeles in order to have her baby, who was born by Caesarean section on February 12, 1982. Her doctor told her she could return to work on April 21. She had taken a disability leave, which Cal Fed allowed disabled workers to take without guaranteeing them that they could return to the job. When Ms. Garland returned to work, she found that her job had been filled, and the company had no comparable job available.

California, however, had passed a law in 1979 saying that medical disability caused by pregnancy or childbirth entitled a woman to up to four months of unpaid leave, without losing her job. In other words, this law made pregnancy a unique disability that got preferential treatment in California.

(The 1978 Pregnancy Disability Act had required that pregnancy be treated like any other disability. Congress had passed the law to modify a Supreme Court ruling that had allowed companies to selectively refuse to pay for pregnancy expenses, even when they paid for elective surgery for male workers. The 1978 law specifically did *not* require companies that offered no benefits to male workers to offer them for pregnancy.)

Garland sued, saying the 1979 California law required Cal Fed to give her job back to her. Cal Fed's position was that the state law was a form of sex discrimination, an argument that a federal judge accepted, declaring the California law null and void. The decision was appealed, all the way to the Supreme Court.

A lot of different interests were represented in this fight. The Reagan administration's brief said that laws mandating special treatment for pregnancy discriminated against men. Liberal interests likened the argument to the arguments about affirmative action. And feminists were split down the middle. Did they want the law to treat men and women the same, or did they prefer to endorse the position of Linda Krieger of San Francisco's Employment Law Center? She said, "The point isn't that men and women must be treated alike, it's that they must have equal opportunities. When it comes to pregnancy, equal treatment means inequality for women." She also deplored the fact that "we are the only industrialized nation that doesn't provide paid maternity leave as a matter of national policy."[22]

The State of California took a similar position, and so did a number of feminists, including Betty Friedan.

The expedient coalition had not coalesced. The more vocal feminist presence was on the other side. Those who opposed Garland's position said that special treatment had always fostered employment discrimination against women and that it violated Title VII of the Civil Rights Act of 1964. That was what NOW's amicus brief said. And Dianne Feinstein, who was Mayor of San Francisco at the time, agreed.

> What we women have been saying all along is we want to be treated equally. Now we have to put our money where our mouth is. What we were asking was to create a special group of workers that, in essence, is pregnant women and new mothers. I just don't happen to agree with that.[23]

In a letter to the *Times Book Review* on June 8, 1986, Isabelle Katz Pinzler and Joan E. Bertin of the ACLU Women's Rights Project warned,

> Those who urge a preferential approach for pregnancy based on its unique and incomparable qualities forget that the idea that pregnancy is unique does not always (or even usually) lead to its receiving preferred treatment. In fact, in 1974 the Supreme Court of the United States used such a notion to justify a California disability insurance law that excluded only pregnancy from coverage, thus illustrating once more that the failure to insist on legal equality between the sexes always has the potential to deprive women of rights and concrete benefits.[24]

Well, we who believe in legal equality lost that one. On January 14, 1987, the Supreme Court upheld California's law, six to three, saying it allowed "women, as well as men, to have families without losing their jobs" and promoted equal employment opportunities.[25]

A Wave of the Future?

There really isn't a wave of support for entitlements for family women. While the Garland case was wending its way to a Supreme Court decision, Reps. Patricia Schroeder of Colorado and William Clay of Missouri were sponsoring a Parental and Medical Leave Bill that would sidestep the gender equality issue. Their bill required employers with more than five employees to give up to eighteen weeks of unpaid leave to any employees, male or female, who wanted to care for newly born, newly adopted, or seriously ill children (or parents), and to guarantee them their jobs back. NOW was in favor of this one, since on the face of it, it applied to both sexes—although everyone could guess *which* sex was more likely to avail themselves of its provisions. But this was another proposal on which women split. The National Association of Women Business Owners strongly opposed the bill, saying that it would place an enormous burden on small companies, and particularly on their members, who employed a disproportionate number of women of childbearing age. At the same time, the Bureau of National Affairs showed that 90 percent of the companies in the United States already granted maternity leave, and 40 percent of them also granted leave to new fathers.

The bill passed, but was vetoed in 1990 by President Bush. Other legislators have tried to introduce federal day-care bills, and Rep. Schroeder has even asked for an examination of the feasibility of *paid* parental leave. But the Republican administrations of Reagan and Bush, together with the great attention the federal deficit has received from politicians and media alike, has ensured that, at least so far, the time has not yet come for the social feminist agenda. The individualist (if divisive) politics of keeping multiple kinds of choice legally alive is clearly the most practical agenda for political feminism in the nineties.

CHAPTER FOURTEEN

Back to Our Roots: How We Might Grow

Individualists are not speaking out in the name of feminism. In America today, uncounted numbers of women who would have been feminists like the abolitionist women or like the early twentieth-century feminists are not claiming to be feminists. On the contrary, they often look on many of the feminists they meet as bitter, as unhappy, as narrow. These women, like their predecessors, know they can do anything, try to do it, and want not to be hampered by state and society while they are trying. And there are men who would like to help such women.

One such man wrote a letter to the editor that was published in the *New York Times* in December of 1985. He claimed that the definition of a feminist as "a person who advocates the same rights for women as for men" is "exhaustive" and that he felt an article by a feminist the previous month excluded feminists who were conservative Republicans, or conservative Democrats, as well as all the women who had voted for Reagan, because the article "offers a platform only for women (and men) who embrace the philosophy of the liberal wing of the Democratic Party." But he insisted he is still a feminist. He concluded by saying, "The women's movement will start moving again only when it escapes the bondage of its liberal baggage and strives to unite both conservatives and liberals in the important but limited fight against a common enemy: the remaining barriers to true equality between women and men."[1]

As for a nonfeminist who honors this individualist tradition of feminism, take Midge Decter, one of the most vocal critics of contemporary feminism. She wrote in a *Policy Review* article, "The Intelligent Woman's Guide to Feminism,"

> Feminism properly understood is a view summed up in the simple proposition that women are the equals of men; that they are as intelligent,

as competent, as brave, and above all, as morally responsible. It was this proposition, for example, that earlier in the century secured for women the right to vote, to educate themselves, to have and to spend their own money, and in general, to take upon themselves a share of the burden of civic responsibility.

And she finds that these are not the characteristics of the contemporary women's movement as she sees it. "Women," writes Decter,

> have indeed reached a new, if you will a revolutionary, condition. In the last fifty years, the combination of birth control, medical science, and modern technology have made it possible for them both to pursue careers and to have families. Now they are faced with an altogether new choice: Do I wish to have children or do I not wish to have children? This is both a new freedom and a tremendous new anxiety. The same is true with respect to the pursuit of careers. . . .
>
> A true feminist movement under these circumstances would have said to women in effect: Yes, indeed, life does have new difficulties; yes, indeed, it is full of new burdens and anxieties; yes, indeed, it is very hard. On the other hand, your new freedom can be very gratifying. You will need a lot of courage to secure its gratifications, but you *can* do so. . . .
>
> If the movement had been addressing itself to the real difficulties of women, we should have seen an analysis of the condition of women today as one actually recognizes that condition to be. Such a movement would not have produced a literature which said that the educated American woman is a useless, helpless, brainwashed victim; for she is no such thing. If this movement had addressed itself to the problems of how much new will and courage it takes for her to deal with her new life as a person facing an altogether new kind of freedom, it would perhaps not have enjoyed such a wide response. But it would have been speaking truthfully, and it might in the long run have produced new vital juices instead of poison.[2]

At this point I disagree with Midge Decter—I think it is precisely the extent to which feminism *has* spoken to the truth and difficulty of the new choices facing women that is responsible for the movement's "wide response," and I think a lot of the material in this book has shown that to be true. My grassroots friends and I read a lot of the literature of "oppression," in the seventies, but we also read the newly available reprints of feminist classics and biographies of women of achievement. The point of reading all these books was to think for yourself—and most of us found no trouble with being feminists and not taking to radical theories of oppression, let alone theories of brainwashing.

When I read "The Intelligent Woman's Guide to Feminism," its negative strictures on contemporary radical feminism seemed to apply to a marginal group, but its positive vision of "feminism properly understood" was inspiring. It was my vision of what feminism has been in my life, and I wondered why anyone would settle for anything less. We feminists who believe in the inspiring history and classical liberal mainstream of American feminism should not give up our claim to the name *feminist,* any more than institutions supporting limited government should give up their claim to the name *liberal.*

Victimization

I can't end this book without saying at least a word about victimization, which, at least at one time, was a treasured concept of radical feminists. Several of the people I have quoted have mentioned this concept disparagingly. You may remember Virginia Postrel's *Reason* editorial that referred to feminism's "whine of victimization." Midge Decter characterized the entire movement as one in which "a group of the freest, most vital and energetic—and most economically and physically privileged—young women in the history of the race rose up and proclaimed themselves to be the victims of intolerable oppression."[3] And Colette Dowling admitted in *The Cinderella Complex,*

> I became quite fascinated with the new view of women as oppressed. Unfortunately, the trendier aspects of the feminist movement meshed with and reinforced my own personal paralysis. I used feminism as a rationalization for staying right where I was. Instead of concentrating on my own development, I focused on "them." "They" were keeping me down. Women couldn't get it together because men wouldn't *let* them, period.[4]

This attitude is not characteristic of all women who consider themselves feminists any more than it is characteristic of all African Americans who join civil rights organizations. The attitude and what is wrong with it was eloquently discussed by Shelby Steele in his 1990 book, *The Content of Our Character: A New Vision of Race in America,* as well as in a 1988 *Commentary* article on which much of the book is based, "On Being Black and Middle Class."

The "party line" of racial identification in the sixties was redefined, he says, to present "blacks as a racial monolith, a singular people with a common experience of oppression. . . . If the form of this racial identity was the monolith, its substance was victimization."[5] But the middle-class values by which Steele had been raised—education, self-reliance, the work ethic—pushed him in another direction, "toward the entire constellation of qualities that are implied in the word individualism," rather than toward taking what he called an adversarial stance toward the mainstream.[6]

Since perhaps the majority of radical feminists were middle-class white women, they were caught in a similar bind, with their self-identification as victims at war with the individualist values of their backgrounds, which is what would enable them to achieve individual success. For middle-class women as well as middle-class blacks, the result was inner conflict. Steele said, near the end of his article,

> Hard work, education, individual initiative, stable family life, property ownership—these have always been the means by which ethnic groups have moved ahead in America. Regardless of past or present victimization, these "laws" of advancement apply absolutely to black Americans also. There is no getting around this. *What we need is a form of racial identity that energizes the individual by putting him in touch with both his possibilities and his responsibilities.* (Emphasis added)[7]

I say that we need a similar form of feminism. And that we have had it, and still have it, more than we know. When there has been inner conflict between the appeal of victimization and the values of individualism, individualist values have won most often.

Policy Futures

So we come to the nub of it all. What does what I have said imply about what feminists should do in the future?

We should make it clear to ourselves and others that individualism includes both responsibility and community.

We should revive consciousness raising and conscious community, and support the idea of similar groups for men. This involves articulating the interdependence of separatism and interaction between men and women, as similar to the interaction of individual and community. We are going to find a new way, in the nineties, to be friends with both women and men.

And we should admit what we don't know about sameness and difference between the sexes and stress that this makes no *political* difference as to how people should be treated. This implies that we should realize that the largest political constituency is the individual rights one and give up searching for political expediency.

In the area of policy, feminists need to hold on to the realizations that they came to in the long battle between equal rights and protective legislation. Legislation to help and protect the members of a group generally hinders them. Subjective legal standards of "health" and "need" and "assistance"—or "value"—must be interpreted, and the interpretations are just as likely to be against the interests of a specific individual as for them. Also, a departure from equality in the direction of privileges for a class is not going to affect members of that class equally. In other words, if our standard is the individual, that individual is best served by not being treated as an interchangeable member of a class. Feminists astounded politicians who were sure that they would stop asking for the Equal Rights Amendment in the seventies when they learned that their "protective" laws would be lost by criticizing those laws instead.

If we have seen so clearly that these laws worked to our economic disadvantage, can we broaden the application of that principle when we look at questions of discrimination, resisting all forms of government discrimination, but also speaking out against affirmative action laws and even social pressure in favor of numerical affirmative action *practices,* in order to preserve our own interests and our own institutions? Can we see that ideas of legislation to impose equal pay for work of "comparable worth" is a similar imposition of bureaucratic subjective decisions on bargains that individual employees are perfectly capable of making, needing no more protection against such bargains than they needed against working in the mines or working overtime?

It's relatively easy to know how to respond when government invades our rights—when laws are passed to make home births a form of child abuse, for instance. It's more complicated when government purports to convey a benefit. But we should take to heart our painfully won understanding that when government violated its own principles of equal protection to pass protective labor legislation, supposedly to protect women, it was *not* in our interest, and apply this lesson to affirmative action preferences and ideas of pay equity. The problem with affirmative action, pay equity, and protective labor legislation is in essence the same: they all treat women as interchangeable, and helpless, members of a group. Some women can lift weights and some cannot, but protective laws said those who could were *not allowed* to be hired. Now affirmative action takes the opposite tack—even some who cannot lift weights *must* be hired, if the employer doesn't have what authorities consider to be "enough" women on the payroll. And pay equity, in trying to raise the wages of women in some employments, will "protect" them out of jobs just as laws protecting them from overtime did.

As for the "remedies" that affirmative action laws offer for past discrimination, redress is appropriate when an individual is mistreated—

but what kind of redress is it, if one individual has been discriminated against, to require the hiring of other members of the same group in the future? In any case, my contention is that women should scrutinize very carefully claims that sexual "discrimination" is mistreatment—we (as do African Americans) want to keep the option of having our own meetings, schools, and clubs.

I remember in my libertarian consciousness-raising group in San Francisco, a libertarian man insisted on trying to join, saying that we were violating our own statement of principles—something about being for equality and against sexism—if we didn't include him. I told him he was absolutely correct, and, therefore, I would resign and suggested that the other women should, too, since clearly we didn't want to be in the position of discussing on a regular basis his experiences of being a woman. But it was our own fault that we got into that position. One of the *purposes* of our formation was sexual separation. But we were too chicken to spell it out in our organizing papers.

The other political area that I see as important for feminists in the nineties is a continuing political crusade on the issues of police protection and bodily choice. If, as seems likely at this writing, the Supreme Court is going to modify and perhaps overrule the *Roe* v. *Wade* rule that individual states may not outlaw abortions, we may be faced with a state-by-state fight to protect the right to abortion. If so, we would be politically smart to take into account the concern that this issue has aroused nationwide and to promote wording such as the NARAL resolution in New Hampshire, discussed in Chapter Eleven. We need to promote both sides of reproductive choice and to generate interest, not only in abortion clinics, but in an increasing diversity of individual and community programs and organizations to help women who want to have babies.

Feminists should promote laws to keep the states out of the business of regulating childbirth and abortion as well as laws and police practices to protect the victims and potential victims of wife beating and rape. We should promote the repeal of laws limiting fetal research, or new methods of contraception, or new approaches to fertilization. We should support the work of the Women's Project of the ACLU and other organizations defending the right of women not to become second-class citizens once they become pregnant, subject to forced operations and procedures. Since such a political crusade would be based on the importance of the individual, it's not surprising that supporting these feminist issues of police protection and various kinds of choice is also the move that will win us the most popular political support.

We also need to make a start on the volunteerism that Betty Friedan has spoken about, not just because government cutbacks make it imperative, but because that is the best way to discover what actions can be really helpful. We need more battered women's shelters, and help lines, and rape crisis counseling. But we also need assertiveness training for women who have become victims, we need entrepreneurship training for girls growing up inner cities, we need businesses to be even more innovative in flexible time and benefits and training.

But especially, feminists should reach out to enlarge their community. Too often the feminist community seems to be limited to a network of people with similar interests and background. But in the seventies, for all of the positions of radical feminism that I do not share, feminists were reaching out to recruit disparate women. Now we need to identify the voids in our society that need a feminist input. We should reach out in the area of sex education for young women tempted to become early mothers and try to bring hope to those who do become young mothers. Perhaps this is the new ground for consciousness raising—just as the mothers in the sixties who didn't know what to do with their lives helped each other to change through consciousness raising, perhaps inner-city girls and women might build similar community structures of their own to enable them to help each other to be a little less isolated. Some of such activity is going on already—programs that match intact families with broken families, for instance, in which the intact family teaches such basic skills as paying bills, shopping, and keeping an apartment clean. But if ways could be found to bring young women with similar problems and the potential for similar goals to talk to each other, not just to mentors, that would be a big beginning.

Community has been a buzz-word for politicians; Robert B. Reich has pointed out that often it means *economic enclave* and that the top economic 20 percent is able to form "communities" because it can afford to withdraw from the influence of government by funding alternate services—in the process, withdrawing from any responsibility for poorer communities.[8] That's not what I'm suggesting. I am suggesting an outreach that puts together those who can benefit from giving help with those who can benefit from receiving it, so that we can experience the common bond of sisterhood (and incidentally, motherhood, daughterhood, even fatherhood and brotherhood). That, to my mind, is the true feminist experience of individualism in community.

Not NOW

There is a role for nationally based as well as community-based feminist action. Unfortunately, the organization that began in forming communities by trying to promote consciousness raising, the National Organization for Women, has adopted an increasingly narrow political agenda. L. A. Kauffman, in the March 1984 *Progressive,* reports that NOW has become increasingly bureaucratized and impersonal. She complains that "sisterhood" is used today as "a code word for cultural feminist separatism," instead of what individual women's lives have in common. The result, she says, is that today,

> NOW is feminism impersonalized, divorced from its grass roots base; feminism institutionalized, rigidly structured, with an internal agenda of its own; feminism professionalized, dominated by a small group of full-time activists. And it is feminism legitimized, locked within the narrow confines of electoral and legislative politics.[9]

Kauffman goes on to suggest a need for a new radical feminism, establishing some community action, beginning in smaller communities rather than trying to be national in scope, not stereotypical or simplistic like the seventies radicalism—perhaps "a network of community and campus activist groups" that could experiment with different approaches and meet in existing women's bookstores, bars, and cafes. Although she seems to advocate "politically correct" campus activism that I would not endorse, she is very right that one of the consequences of a shift from a vital, individualist feminism interested in personal transformation to a narrow, outwardly focused social feminism is the loss of a sense of connectedness, which is a real loss for the feminist movement today.

Kauffman is not the only one suggesting grassroots feminist action—an article in the June 1990 *Radcliffe Quarterly* suggests that one of the biggest needs of working women is the establishment of some sort of "caring Communities" that will increase the sense of interdependency that used to exist in extended family networks and will take some of the burden off nuclear families and single parents.[10]

An associate professor of human services at Massasoit Community College in Brockton, Massachusetts, Rebecca Shipman Hurst, suggested in a letter to me that feminists can join women's networks, such as women's health cooperatives, or counseling cooperatives. Other volunteer projects that are important in her opinion are helping crime victims and immigrants. She also says shelters for battered women are particularly in need of help, since they often try to phase out government money because they don't like the bureaucracy and control the government requires of them.

The Past as Vision of the Future

The political agenda of feminism has been to protest and try to change the respects in which the law has subjected women as a class to society and, at times, required the subjection of individual women to individual men. The cultural agenda of feminism has changed over the years, but it has always been to encourage women to fulfill themselves as individuals, whether this be through occupation, avocation, or relationship. The selective emphasis given each of these areas has, of course, shifted in different periods, depending on the climate of the time.

What I would like to see is a feminist movement that is more self-consciously individualistic, but also understands that individual action includes cooperation and association, which doesn't tie feminism to positive government programs but to taking action together to solve problems. If, like LaFollette and Elshtain, we don't feel it is helpful to consider government "Mr. Right" and if, like Friedan, we think the only way to achieve the institutions we want is by a "passionate volunteerism," then we will have to rely on ourselves and on each other. Because we still need to expand our own options, to make our lives a little easier, to learn even more to help each other.

The classical liberal has moral objections to using government power to impose change on people by force. But there are also practical objections—no one knows what will work and what won't. Even the spontaneous changes that affected American women so profoundly since the 1960s brought problems that no one could have predicted. I've quoted Betty Friedan in 1963 saying that it would be no big deal for women to combine motherhood and work—and in 1981 saying that how to achieve such a combination happily was the problem of the second stage of feminism. Some people have felt that this was an indication that she was being revisionist or a turncoat, but the plain fact is, *she didn't know,* in 1963. Many women have complained that they weren't warned in advance of how complex their lives were going to become—but no one knew how hard it was going to be for women to change their lives. If women had then, in the late sixties, the unlimited political power to put into effect any government programs they wanted, no one would have known what government programs to design.

There's another reason to stick to the original vision of feminism, instead of adopting one or another version of social feminism. Who is really inspired to join a movement to be a special interest? To seize the power of government and use it to create a spoils system to reward our own group? The only argument that can remotely justify such actions on moral grounds is the argument of past victimization, and that is not only a very specious argument, but, as we have seen, a personally destructive one.

The ERA was lost when the women supporting it turned away from the vision of equal rights to a search for political dominance; to get a large enough voting block to wrest privileges from society. Do we really want to go from a subordinate to a dominant legal position? To get legislation to try to make the taxpayers in general make our domestic lives easier with child allowances and subsidized day care? Despite the blandishments of some government-enamored feminists, people in the welfare democracies of Europe are not happier than people here. They think they like their benefits, but they have to work very hard to pay for these supposedly "free" advantages. And now they are faced with changes and cuts, with no lessening of the work or the taxes, as these states, too, run out of money. This is a self-defeating and ultimately puny vision of democracy as a way of using the vote to get things from others. Our heritage is grander than that.

In her last public address, in 1892, "The Solitude of the Self," Elizabeth Cady Stanton said that the strongest reason for all the reforms to benefit woman that she had spent her life advocating—access to higher education; a voice in government, religion, and social life; the right to earn a living— was because of "her birthright of self-sovereignty; because, as an individual, she must rely on herself. . . . Seeing then, that life must ever be a march and a battle, that each soldier must be equipped for his own protection, it is the height of cruelty to rob the individual of a single natural right."[11]

An internally contradictory view of liberty will not work. We have to choose between trying to build a special interest group, out for our own aggrandizement, and this view of the importance of rights. In a review of a collection of the correspondence, writings, and speeches of Elizabeth Cady Stanton and Susan B. Anthony, Vivian Gornick wrote, "The subject of Stanton's lifelong speculation was the nature and meaning of natural rights—women's rights was a euphemism—and her thinking took her ever more inward, to the psychological heart of the matter."[12]

It is that psychological heart of the matter that we are still discovering. We have to give up the idea that we can force others, either personally or by using the power of government, to treat us as we would wish. Instead, we have to live our lives as equal citizens of the world, establishing our networks of relationship, our ways to earn a living, our values, and our goals, by relying on ourselves and each other. There's a lot we don't know. We don't know how alike, or different, men and women really are. We don't know how to solve all the problems of living together and bringing up children. We don't know what institutions we really need to form or how to solve the problems of the inner cities, or the homeless, or the environment.

We do know that the idea of equal rights is a very powerful engine and that if enough individuals are inspired by it to transform their lives, they can make unforseen changes together that will change a lot of their world. Feminists have done that, over the last thirty years. Some of the changes have been wonderful, and some have been hard. But we don't have to stop changing. Individuals inspired by a grand, idealistic tradition to link together in a community can do remarkable things.

Notes

Chapter One: So You Think You're Not a Feminist?

1. Elizabeth Fox-Genovese, *Feminism Without Illusions: A Critique of Individualism* (Chapel Hill and London: The University of North Carolina Press, 1991), 7.

2. Fox-Genovese, *Feminism Without Illusions,* 111.

3. Herbert Spencer, *Social Statics: or, The Conditions Necessary to Human Happiness* (1851; reprint, New York: Augustus Kelley Publishers, 1969), 78.

4. Spencer, *Social Statics,* 173.

5. Spencer, *Social Statics,* 173–74.

6. Spencer, *Social Statics,* 188.

7. David L. Kirp, Mark G. Yudof, and Marlene Strong Franks, *Gender Justice* (Chicago and London: The University of Chicago Press, 1986), 100.

8. Kirp, Yudof, and Franks, *Gender Justice,* 97–98.

9. Kirp, Yudof, and Franks, *Gender Justice,* 112.

10. Kirp, Yudof, and Franks, *Gender Justice,* 204.

11. Vivian Gornick, "Who Says We Haven't Made a Revolution?" *New York Times Magazine,* 15 April 1990, 27.

12. Wendy McElroy, "The Roots of Individualist Feminism in 19th-Century America," in *Freedom, Feminism, and the State: An Overview of Individualist Feminism,* ed. Wendy McElroy (Washington, D.C.: Cato Institute, 1982), 11–12.

13. William L. O'Neill, "The Fight for Suffrage," *Wilson Quarterly,* vol. 10, no. 4 (Autumn 1986): 103.

14. McElroy, "The Roots of Individualist Feminism in 19th-Century America," 20.

15. O'Neill, "The Fight for Suffrage," 99.

16. O'Neill, "The Fight for Suffrage," 108.

17. L. A. Kauffman, "Three Women: The LaFollettes Espoused an Early Feminism," *Progressive,* July 1984, 74.

18. Quoted in Sharon Presley, "Suzanne LaFollette: The Freewoman," Libertarian Feminist Heritage Series, Paper 2 (New York: Association of Libertarian Feminists).

19. Quoted in Presley, "Suzanne LaFollette."

20. Quoted in Presley, "Suzanne LaFollette."

21. Jean Bethke Elshtain, "Antigone's Daughters," *democracy,* April 1982, 46.

22. Betty Friedan, *The Second Stage* (New York: Summit Books, 1981) 229–30.

23. Quoted in *Libertarian Familist*, vol. 10, no. 5 (Summer 1991): 3.

24. David T. Beito, "Mutual Aid for Social Welfare: The Case of American Fraternal Societies," *Critical Review*, vol. 4, no. 4 (Fall 1990): 711.

25. Beito, "Mutual Aid for Social Welfare," 715.

26. Alexis de Tocqueville, *Democracy in America*, quoted in Anne Firor Scott, "On Seeing and Not Seeing: A Case of Historical Invisibility," *Journal of American History*, vol 71, no. 1 (June 1984): 8–9.

27. Scott, "On Seeing and Not Seeing" (see n. 26), 9.

28. Scott, "On Seeing and Not Seeing," 10.

29. Scott, "On Seeing and Not Seeing," 19.

30. Virginia Postrel, "Why Women Can't Commit," *Reason*, vol 23, no. 2 (June 1991): 4.

31. Stephen Koch, "Journey's Beginning: A Talk With Diana Trilling," *New York Times Book Review*, 19 February 1989, 26.

Chapter Two: Inside Every Socialist is an Individualist Trying to Get Out

1. *A Vindication of the Rights of Men*, quoted in Charles W. Hagelman, Jr., "Introduction," in Mary Wollstonecraft, *A Vindication of the Rights of Woman*, edited by and with Introduction, Chronology, and Bibliography by Charles W. Hagelman, Jr. (New York: The Norton Library, 1967), 8.

2. Wollstonecraft, *Rights of Woman*, 33–35.

3. Wollstonecraft, *Rights of Woman*, 82-83.

4. Wollstonecraft, *Rights of Woman*, 73.

5. Wollstonecraft, *Rights of Woman*, 33.

6. Wollstonecraft, *Rights of Woman*, 218–19.

7. Wollstonecraft, *Rights of Woman*, 223–24.

8. Margaret Fuller, *Woman in the Nineteenth Century*, with an Introduction by Bernard Rosenthal (New York: The Norton Library, 1971), 14.

9. Fuller, *Woman in the Nineteenth Century*, 24.

10. Fuller, *Woman in the Nineteenth Century*, 169.

11. Fuller, *Woman in the Nineteenth Century*, 169.

12. Fuller, *Woman in the Nineteenth Century*, 170–71.

13. Fuller, *Woman in the Nineteenth Century*, 95.

14. Fuller, *Woman in the Nineteenth Century*, 172.

15. Fuller, *Woman in the Nineteenth Century*, 174–75.

16. Fuller, *Woman in the Nineteenth Century*, 29.

17. John Stuart Mill and Harriet Taylor Mill, *Essays on Sex Equality*, edited by and with an Introductory Essay by Alice S. Rossi (Chicago and London: The University of Chicago Press, 1970), 125.

18. Mill, *Essays on Sex Equality*, 148.

19. Mill, *Essays on Sex Equality*, 155.

20. Mill, *Essays on Sex Equality*, 190.

21. Mill, *Essays on Sex Equality*, 186.

22. Mill, *Essays on Sex Equality*, 220.

23. Mill, *Essays on Sex Equality*, 221.

24. Mill, *Essays on Sex Equality*, 233.

25. Mill, *Essays on Sex Equality,* 235–36.

26. John Stuart Mill, *Autobiography,* ed. Jack Stillinger (Boston: Houghton Mifflin Company, 1969), 138.

27. Alice S. Rossi, "Sentiment and Intellect: The Story of John Stuart Mill and Harriet Taylor Mill," in Mill, *Essays on Sex Equality,* 45–46.

28. Mill, *Autobiography,* 158.

29. Charlotte Perkins Gilman, published as Charlotte Perkins Stetson, *Women and Economics,* 3d ed. (Boston: Small, Maynard & Co., 1900), 5.

30. Gilman, *Women and Economics,* 37–38.

31. Gilman, *Women and Economics,* 13.

32. Gilman, *Women and Economics,* 43, 51.

33. Gilman, *Women and Economics,* 70.

34. Gilman, *Women and Economics,* 110.

35. Gilman, *Women and Economics,* 152.

36. Gilman, *Women and Economics,* 157.

37. Gilman, *Women and Economics,* 242.

38. Gilman, *Women and Economics,* 243.

39. Gilman, *Women and Economics,* 314.

40. Gilman, *Women and Economics,* 242.

41. Gilman, *Women and Economics,* 243.

42. Quoted in Nancy F. Cott, *The Grounding of Modern Feminism* (New Haven and London: Yale University Press, 1987), 49.

43. Cott, *The Grounding of Modern Feminism,* 48.

Chapter Three: The Rights of Man—Are Women Included?

1. Quoted in Roger Langley and Richard C. Levy, *Wife Beating: The Silent Crisis* (1977; reprint, New York: Pocket Books, 1978), 51.

2. Gilbert Hobbs Barnes, *The Antislavery Impulse: 1830–1844* (New York and London: D. Appleton-Century Co., Inc., 1933), 140–41.

3. Charles A. Beard and Mary R. Beard, *The Rise of American Civilization: New Edition, Two Volumes in One Revised and Enlarged* (New York: The Macmillan Company, 1944), 755.

4. Quoted in Eleanor Flexner, *Century of Struggle: The Woman's Rights Movement in the United States* (1959; reprint, New York: Atheneum, 1974), 74.

5. Flexner, *Century of Struggle,* 76.

6. Beard and Beard, *The Rise of American Civilization,* 758.

7. "Declaration of Sentiments and Resolutions, Seneca Falls Convention (1848)," as reprinted in *Up From the Pedestal: Selected Writings in the History of American Feminism,* ed. Aileen S. Kraditor (Chicago: Quadrangle Books, 1968), 183–86.

8. Betty Friedan, *The Feminine Mystique* (1963; reprint, New York: Dell Publishing Co., Inc., 1970), 87.

9. Beard and Beard, *The Rise of American Civilization,* 562.

10. Katherine Anthony, *Susan B. Anthony: Her Personal History and Her Era* (Garden City, N.Y.: Doubleday & Company, Inc., 1954), 195.

11. Anthony, *Susan B. Anthony,* 252.

12. Anthony, *Susan B. Anthony,* 278.

13. *Minor* v. *Happersett,* 21 Wall. 162 (1874).

14. Barbara Deckard, *The Women's Movement: Political, Socioeconomic, and Psychological Issues* (New York, Evanston, San Francisco, London: Harper & Row, Publishers, 1975), 254–56.

15. Robert W. Smuts, *Women and Work in America,* with a new Introduction by Eli Ginzberg (1959; reprint, New York: Schocken Books, 1971), 50–51.

16. Quoted in Smuts, *Women and Work in America,* 114.

17. Smuts, *Women and Work in America,* 115.

18. Quoted in Karen DeCrow, *Sexist Justice* (1974; reprint, New York: Vintage Books, 1975), 30.

19. Deckard, *The Women's Movement,* 161–62.

20. Caroline Bird, *Enterprising Women* (New York: W. W. Norton & Company Inc., 1976), 110.

21. Flexner, *Century of Struggle,* 113.

22. Smuts, *Women and Work in America,* 126–27.

23. Smuts, *Women and Work in America,* 131–32.

24. Deckard, *The Women's Movement,* 266.

25. Philip S. Foner, *Women and the American Labor Movement: From Colonial Times to the Eve of World War I* (New York: The Free Press, 1979), 219.

26. Quoted in Foner, *Women and the American Labor Movement,* 129.

27. Foner, *Women and the American Labor Movement,* 129.

28. Anthony, *Susan B. Anthony,* 226.

29. Quoted in Foner, *Women and the American Labor Movement,* 126.

30. Foner, *Women and the American Labor Movement,* 130.

31. Foner, *Women and the American Labor Movement,* 130–31.

32. Foner, *Women and the American Labor Movement,* 154.

33. Deckard, *The Women's Movement,* 264.

34. Quoted in Flexner, *Century of Struggle,* 250.

35. Flexner, *Century of Struggle,* 279.

36. Quoted in Flexner, *Century of Struggle,* 173.

37. Anthony, *Susan B. Anthony,* 326.

38. Foner, *Women and the American Labor Movement,* 74.

39. *Muller* v. *Oregon,* 208 U.S. 412. (1908).

40. Jack Greenberg, *Race Relations in American Law* (New York: Columbia University Press, 1959), 48.

41. John Stuart Mill, *On Liberty and Other Essays,* edited by and with an Introduction by John Gray (Oxford and New York: World's Classics, Oxford University Press, 1991), 122–23.

42. Mill, *On Liberty and Other Essays,* 123–24.

43. Quoted in Foner, *Women in the American Labor Movement,* 270.

44. Foner, *Women in the American Labor Movement,* 274.

Chapter Four: The Rise of Feminism

1. Catharine R. Stimpson, "The 'F' Word," *Ms.,* July/August 1987, 80.

2. Cott, *The Grounding of Modern Feminism* (see chap. 2, n. 42), 3.

3. Cott, *The Grounding of Modern Feminism,* 36.

4. Cott, *The Grounding of Modern Feminism,* 37.

5. Cott, *The Grounding of Modern Feminism,* 39.

6. Cott, *The Grounding of Modern Feminism,* 49.

7. Ruth Hale, *The First Five Years of The Lucy Stone League* (New York: Lucy Stone League, 1925), 19.

8. Deckard, *The Women's Movement* (see chap. 3, n. 14), 287.

9. Judith Hole and Ellen Levine, *Rebirth of Feminism* (New York: Quadrangle Books, 1971), 77.

10. Hole and Levine, *Rebirth of Feminism,* 78–79.

11. Cott, *The Grounding of Modern Feminism,* 123.

12. Cott, *The Grounding of Modern Feminism,* 124.

13. Cott, *The Grounding of Modern Feminism,* 125.

14. Cott, *The Grounding of Modern Feminism,* 125.

15. Deckard, *The Women's Movement,* 287.

16. Deckard, *The Women's Movement,* 290–91.

17. Senate Committee on the Judiciary, *Hearings on S.J. Res. 61 and S. J. Res. 231 Proposing an Amendment to the Constitution of the United States Relative to Equal Rights for Men and Women,* 91st Cong., 2nd sess., 1970 (Washington: U.S. Government Printing Office, 1970), 152.

Chapter Five: What Does a Woman Want?

1. Deckard, *The Women's Movement,* (see chap. 3, n. 14), 430.

2. Leah Fritz, *Dreamers & Dealers: An Intimate Appraisal of the Women's Movement* (Boston: Beacon Press, 1979), 274, fn. 4.

3. Anita Shreve, "The Group, 12 Years Later," *New York Times Magazine,* 6 July 1986, 14.

4. Deckard, *The Women's Movement,* 346–47.

5. "The Lee-Lenox-Stockbridge Consciousness Raising Group," *Women: Berkshire Women's Liberation Newsletter,* vol. 1, no. 2 (10 April 1971): 11–12.

6. Rona F. Feit, "Organizing for Political Power: The National Women's Political Caucus," in *Women Organizing: An Anthology,* ed. Bernice Cummings and Victoria Schuck (Metuchen, NJ & London: The Scarecrow Press, Inc., 1979), 205.

7. Jane O'Reilly, "The Housewife's Moment of Truth," *Ms.,* Preview Issue (Spring/ 72): 54–55.

8. Colette Dowling, *The Cinderella Complex: Women's Hidden Fear of Independence* (New York: Summit Books, 1981), 31.

9. Friedan, *The Second Stage,* (see chap. 1, n. 22), 28.

10. Friedan, *The Second Stage,* 229.

11. Shreve, "The Group, 12 Years Later," 17.

12. Trip Gabriel, "Call of the Wildmen," *New York Times Magazine,* 14 October 1990, 37, 39.

13. Gabriel, "Call of the Wildmen," 47.

14. Alix Kates Shulman, review of *Women Together, Women Alone: The Legacy of the Consciousness Raising Movement,* by Anita Shreve, *New York Times Book Review,* 13 August 1989, 10.

Chapter Six: The Workplace: I'm Not a Woman's Libber, But

1. "Female Miners Fight for Acceptance," *New York Times,* 11 October 1982.

2. *TV Guide,* 8 November 1986, 8.

3. *Time,* 19 February 1990, 67.

4. Robert Reinhold, "Cherokees Install First Woman as Chief of Major American Indian Tribe," *New York Times,* 15 December 1985.

5. Perri Klass, "Are Women Better Doctors?" *New York Times Magazine,* 10 April 1988, 32.

6. Pam Mendelsohn, "The College Reentry Phenomenon," *San Francisco Saturday Examiner and Chronicle,* 11 May 1980, 4.

7. Sue Shellenbarger, "Societal Shift: As More Women Take Jobs, They Affect Ads, Politics, Family Life," *Wall Street Journal,* eastern edition, 29 June 1982.

8. "Full-Time Homemaking Is Now 'Obsolete,' " *U.S. News & World Report,* 9 July 1979, 47.

9. Steve Curwood, "Women Encounter the Wage Gap," *Boston Globe,* 25 September 1983.

10. Karla Vallance, "Women: Work and Family, They're Finding a Way, Making a Way to Have Both," *Christian Science Monitor,* eastern edition, 14 April 1983.

11. Maureen Dowd, "Many Women in Poll Value Jobs as Much as Family Life," *New York Times,* 4 December 1983.

12. Friedan, *The Second Stage,* (see chap. 1, n. 22), 241.

13. Shellenbarger, "Societal Shift."

14. William Meyers, "Child Care Finds a Champion in the Corporation," *New York Times,* Business Section, 4 August 1985.

15. Kirsten O. Lundberg, "What's New in Day Care," *New York Times,* Business Section, 26 February 1989.

16. Lundberg, "What's New in Day Care?"

17. Lynda S. Zengerle, "If You Ask Me: Help Wanted," *Washington Post,* 21 September 1982.

18. Susan Dillingham, "Employers Find Advantages in Sending Workers Home," *Insight,* 5 December 1988, 43.

19. Dillingham, "Employers Find Advantages in Sending Workers Home," 40.

20. Deborah Fallows, "The Politics of Motherhood," adapted from *A Mother's Work* (Boston, Houghton Mifflin, 1985), *Washington Monthly,* June 1985, 41.

21. Fallows, "Politics of Motherhood," 49.

22. "Women in the Work Force: The Mommy Track vs. the Fast Track," *New York Times,* Business Section, 21 May 1989.

23. Betty Lehan Harragan, *Games Mother Never Taught You: Corporate Gamesmanship for Women* (New York: Rawson Associates Publishers, Inc., 1977).

24. Barbara Ehrenreich, "Strategies of Corporate Women," *New Republic,* 27 January 1986, 28.

25. "Women Executives: What Holds So Many Back?" *U.S. News & World Report,* 8 February 1982, 63–64.

26. Ehrenreich, "Strategies of Corporate Women," 28.

27. Andrew Hacker, "Women at Work," *New York Review,* 14 August 1986, 31.

28. Enid Nemy, "Networks: New Concept for Top-Level Women," *New York Times,* 29 April 1979.

29. Anna Quindlen, "Women's Networks Come of Age," *New York Times Magazine,*

22 November 1981, 82, 86.

30. Deirdre Fanning, "It's Women, It's Power, But Not Much Is New," *The Executive Life,* Business Section, *New York Times,* 7 April 1991.

31. Ellen Wojahn, "Why There Aren't More Women in This Magazine," *Inc.* (July 1986): 46.

32. Suzanne Gordon, "Every Woman for Herself," *New York Times,* 19 August 1991.

33. Joan Kennedy Taylor, "The Entrepreneurial Alternative," *Manhattan Report,* vol. 4. no. 4, 11.

34. Tom Richman, "The Hottest Entrepreneur in America," *Inc.* (February 1987): 54–56.

35. Barbara Gamarekian, "Envoys' Spouses Learn What a Man's Place Is," *New York Times,* 1 September 1989.

36. Deirdre Fanning, "When She Moves, And He Must Trail Along," *New York Times,* 8 April 1990.

37. Gail Gregg, "Putting Kids First," *New York Times Magazine,* 13 April 1986, 47.

38. Gregg, "Putting Kids First," 50.

39. Jane Gross, "A Women's Resignation Touches a Nerve at Medical Schools," *New York Times,* 14 July 1991.

40. Vallance, "Women: Work and Family."

41. Sara Rimer, "Women Searching for Ways to Balance Children and Jobs," *New York Times,* 27 November 1988.

42. Lisa Belkin, "Bars to Equality of Sexes Seen as Eroding, Slowly," *New York Times,* 20 August 1989.

Chapter Seven: A Funny Thing Happened to Us on the Way to the ERA

1. House Committee on the Judiciary, *Hearings before Subcommittee No. 4 on H.J. Res. 35, 208, and Related Bills Proposing an Amendment to the Constitution of the United States Relative to Equal Rights for Men and Women and H.R. 916 and Related Bills Concerning the Recommendations of the Presidential task force on Women's Rights and Responsibilities,* 92nd Cong., 1st sess., 1971 (Washington: U.S. Government Printing Office, 1971), 98.

2. Senate Committee on the Judiciary (see chap. 4, n. 17), *Hearings,* 76–77.

3. Senate Committee on the Judiciary, *Hearings,* 224.

4. Senate Committee on the Judiciary, *Hearings,* 303–04.

5. Senate Committee on the Judiciary, *Hearings,* 224.

6. Senate Committee on the Judiciary, *Hearings,* 131.

7. House Committee on the Judiciary, *Hearings,* 237.

8. House Committee on the Judiciary, *Hearings,* 59.

9. Senate Committee on the Judiciary, *Hearings,* 410.

10. Senate Committee on the Judiciary, *Hearings,* 11.

11. Senate Committee on the Judiciary, *Hearings,* 424.

12. Senate Committee on the Judiciary, *Hearings,* 31–32.

13. Senate Committee on the Judiciary, *Hearings,* 304.

14. Senate Committee on the Judiciary, *Hearings,* 3.

15. Senate Committee on the Judiciary, *Hearings,* 4.

16. Senate Committee on the Judiciary, *Hearings,* 6–7.

17. Senate Committee on the Judiciary, *Hearings,* 114.

18. Senate Committee on the Judiciary, *Hearings,* 8.

19. Senate Committee on the Judiciary, *Hearings,* 350–51.

20. Senate Committee on the Judiciary, *Hearings,* 375.

21. House Committee on the Judiciary, *Hearings,* 126.

22. Senate Committee on the Judiciary, *Hearings,* 410.

23. Senate Committee on the Judiciary, *Hearings,* 418.

24. Senate Committee on the Judiciary, *Hearings,* 292.

25. Senate Committee on the Judiciary, *Hearings,* 155.

26. Senate Committee on the Judiciary, *Hearings,* 106.

27. Senate Committee on the Judiciary, *Hearings,* 153–55.

28. Senate Committee on the Judiciary, *Hearings,* 392.

29. House Committee on the Judiciary, *Hearings,* 410–11.

30. *United States ex. rel. Robinson* v. *York,* 281 F. Supp. (D. Conn. 1968) and *Commonwealth* v. *Daniel,* 430 Pa. 642, 243, A2d 400 (1968).

31. Phyllis Schlafly, "The Effect of ERAs in State Constitutions," *Phyllis Schlafly Report,* vol. 13, no. 1, section 2 (August 1979).

32. Schlafly, "The Effect of ERAs in State Constitutions," 1.

33. DeCrow, *Sexist Justice* (see chap. 3, n. 18), 302.

34. Ann Scott, "The Equal Rights Amendment: What's in It for You?" *Ms.,* July 1972, 83.

35. Scott, "The Equal Rights Amendment," 83.

36. Elinor Langer, "Why Big Business Is Trying to Defeat the ERA," *Ms.,* May 1976, 104.

37. Phyllis Schlafly, "ERA and Homosexual 'Marriages,' " *Phyllis Schlafly Report,* vol. 8, no. 2, section 2 (September 1974).

38. Phyllis Schlafly, "The Legislative History of ERA," *Phyllis Schlafly Report,* vol. 10, no. 4, section 2 (November 1976).

39. Phyllis Schlafly, "Will ERA Force All Private Schools Coed?" *Phyllis Schlafly Report,* vol. 10, no. 5, section 2 (December 1976).

40. Phyllis Schlafly, "How ERA Will Raise Insurance Rates," *Phyllis Schlafly Report,* vol. 12, no. 7, section 2 (February 1979).

41. Eagle Forum Pamphlet, "Don't Let the Libs and the Feds tear up the Homemaker's Social Security Card."

42. *Wall Street Journal,* 30 May 1979.

43. Unattributed reprint, John W. Gardner, "Some Observations About Women," *In the Public Interest.*

44. *In Oklahoma . . . Just Because They're Women,* Common Cause.

45. *ERA Yes* (Washington: Now National Action Center).

46. Senate Committee on the Judiciary, *Hearings,* 31.

47. F. A. Hayek, *The Constitution of Liberty* (Chicago: The University of Chicago Press, 1960), 85.

48. Hayek, *The Constitution of Liberty,* 195.

49. Hayek, *The Constitution of Liberty,* 85–86.

50. Hayek, *The Constitution of Liberty,* 87.

51. Jane O'Reilly, "Support Your ERA. You Didn't Get Where You Are Alone," *Savvy,* November 1979, 8.

52. Lisa Cronin Wohl, "ERA: What If It Fails?" *Ms.,* November 1979, 64–65.

Chapter Eight: Contemporary Feminism

1. Gail Sheehy, "Hers," *New York Times*, 31 January 1980.

2. Nicholas Davidson, *The Failure of Feminism* (Buffalo, N.Y.: Prometheus Books, 1988), 45.

3. Alison M. Jaggar, review of *Feminism Unmodified*, by Catharine A. MacKinnon, *New York Times Book Review*, 14 June 1987.

4. Janet Radcliffe Richards, *The Sceptical Feminist: A Philosophical Enquiry* (1980; reprint, Boston: Routledge & Kegan Paul, 1982), 1–2.

5. Cott, *The Grounding of Modern Feminism* (see chap. 2, n. 42), 4–6.

6. Deckard, *The Women's Movement* (see chap. 3, n. 14), 414.

7. Kirp, Yudof, and Franks, *Gender Justice* (see chap. 2, n. 42), 47–48.

8. Stimpson, "The 'F' Word" (see chap. 4, n. 1), 80.

9. Fritz, *Dreamers & Dealers* (see chap. 5, n. 2), 7.

10. Fritz, *Dreamers & Dealers*, 164.

11. Friedan, *The Feminine Mystique* (see chap. 3, n. 8), 330–32.

12. Heidi Hartmann, "A Discussion of the Unhappy Marriage of Marxism and Feminism," in *Women and Revolution: A Discussion of the Unhappy Marriage of Marxism and Feminism*, ed. Lydia Sargent (Boston: South End Press, 1981), 2.

13. Carol Ehrlich, "The Unhappy Marriage of Marxism and Feminism: Can It Be Saved?" in Sargent, *Women and Revolution*, 110–11.

14. Quoted in Deckard, *The Women's Movement*, 335.

15. Quoted in Sandra M. Gilbert and Susan Gubar, "Sex Wars: Not the Fun Kind," *New York Times Book Review*, 27 December 1987, 1.

16. Andrea Dworkin, *Woman Hating* (New York: E. P. Dutton & Co., Inc., 1974), 20–23.

17. Quoted in Fritz, *Dreamers & Dealers*, 61.

18. Fritz, *Dreamers & Dealers*, 65–66.

19. Fritz, *Dreamers & Dealers*, 13.

20. Deckard, *The Women's Movement*, 357–58.

21. tanya sharon, farar elliot, and cecile latham, "The National Lesbian Conference: For, By, and About Lesbians," *off our backs*, vol xxi, no. 6 (June 1991): 19.

22. Enid Nemy, "Women's Groups: A forecast for the 80's," *New York Times*, 18 January 1980.

23. Tamar Jacoby, "New Generation of Women's Publications," *New York Times*, 3 March 1986.

24. "The Decade in Review," *Radcliffe News*, Spring 1990, 2.

25. Quoted in Catharine R. Stimpson, "An Interview with Gerda Lerner," *Ms.*, September 1981, 94.

26. Nora Johnson, "Housewives and Prom Queens, 25 Years Later," *New York Times Book Review*, 20 March 1988, 33.

27. Madeleine L'Engle, "Shake the Universe: A Spiritual Vision," *Ms.*, July/August 1987, 182, 219.

28. Ari L. Goldman, "As Call Comes, More Women Answer," *New York Times*, Week in Review Section, 19 October 1986.

29. Charles Austin, "Women Ministers Are Feeling Dual Task," *New York Times*, 10 April 1983.

30. Goldman, "As Call Comes, More Women Answer."

31. "Altar Girls: a Quiet Defiance of Policy," *New York Times*, 6 April 1986.

32. Hans Kung, "Will the Pope Win Over Women?" *New York Times,* 16 November 1983.

33. Derk Kinnane Roelofsma, "Women Making New Trip to Altar," *Insight,* 6 April 1987, 8.

34. "The Decade in Review," 2.

35. Erica Jong, *Ms.,* July/August 1987, 16.

36. Betty Friedan, *Ms.,* July/August 1987, 14.

Chapter Nine: Discrimination, Real and Imaginary

1. Carol Gilligan, *In a Different Voice: Psychological Theory and Women's Development* (Cambridge: Harvard University Press, 1982).

2. Gina Kolata, "In Medical Research Equal Opportunity Doesn't Always Apply," *New York Times,* 10 March 1991.

3. Dorothy L. Sayers, *Are Women Human?* (Grand Rapids: William B. Eerdmans Publishing Company, 1971), 19.

4. Simone de Beauvoir, *The Second Sex,* translated and edited by H. M. Parshley (1953; reprint, New York, Bantam Books, 1961), xv–xvi.

5. *Muller* v. *Oregon,* 208 U.S. 412 (1908).

6. Lilli S. Hornig, "Women in Science and Engineering: Why So Few?" *Technology Review,* November/December 1984, 32.

7. Hornig, "Women in Science and Engineering: Why So Few?" 32.

8. Hornig, "Women in Science and Engineering: Why So Few?" 33.

9. Hornig, "Women in Science and Engineering: Why So Few?" 33.

10. *Brown* v. *Board of Education of Topeka, Kansas,* 347 U.S. 483 (1954).

11. Executive Order 9981, *Federal Register,* vol. 13 (1948), 4313.

12. *Plessy* v. *Ferguson,* 163 U.S. 537 (1896).

13. *Frontiero* v. *Richardson,* 411 U.S. 677 (1973).

14. *Brown* v. *Board of Education of Topeka, Kansas,* 347 U.S. 483 (1954).

15. Quoted in Joan Kennedy Taylor, "The Second American Revolution May Be Here," *Libertarian Review,* July 1977, 17.

16. Editorial, *New York Times,* 3 May 1984.

17. *Green* v. *School Board of New Kent County,* 391 U.S. 430 (1968).

18. *Alexander* v. *Holmes County Board of Education,* 396 U.S. 19 (1969)

19. *Swann* v. *Charlotte-Mecklenburg Board of Education,* 402 U.S. 1 (1971).

20. *DeFunis* v. *Odegaard,* 507 P. 2d 1169 (1973).

21. *McDonald* v. *Santa Fe Transportation Co.,* 427 U.S. 273 (1976), referred to in Henry J. Abraham, *Freedom and the Court: Civil Rights and Liberties in the United States,* 4th ed. (New York and Oxford: Oxford University Press, 1982), 349 fn. 158.

22. *Regents of the University of California* v. *Bakke,* 347 U.S. 483 (1978).

23. *United Steelworkers of America* v. *Weber,* 443 U.S. 193 (1979).

24. Alfred W. Blumrosen, "Affirmative Action in Employment after *Weber,*" *Rutgers Law Review,* vol. 34, no. 1 (Fall 1981): 42.

25. Patrick T. Murphy, review of *Unequal Protection: Women, Children, and the Elderly in Court,* by Lois G. Forer, *New York Times Book Review,* 31 March 1991, 27.

26. "Dispute on Sex Ratio Troubles Women at North Carolina University," *New York Times,* 22 March 1987.

27. "Student Imbalance at Chapel Hill," *New York Times,* 30 August 1987.

28. Stephen L. Carter, *Reflections of an Affirmative Action Baby* (New York: Basic Books, 1991).

29. Deborah Tannen, *You Just Don't Understand: Women and Men in Conversation* (1990; reprint, New York: Ballantine Books, 1991).

30. Charol Shakeshaft, "A Gender at Risk," *Phi Delta Kappan*, March 1986, quoted in Catherine Hunter, "An Invisible Sea of Bias," *Walking the Lane: A Newsletter from St. Timothy's*, vol. 16 no. 1 (Winter 1990): 1.

31. "Why Can't a Woman Be More?" *Time*, 5 October 1987, 76.

32. Susan Chira, "Educators Ask of All-Girl Schools Would Make a Difference in Inner Cities," *New York Times*, 23 October 1991.

33. "Single-Sex Groups Told to Include Members of Other," *New York Times*, 3 February 1991.

34. Annie Gottlieb, "What Men Need That Women Can't Give Them," *McCall's*, October 1983, 166.

35. Margaret Mead, *Male and Female*, quoted in Gottlieb, "What Men Need that Women Can't Give Them," 168.

36. Gottlieb, "What Men Need That Women Can't Give Them," 168–70.

37. Quoted in Sharon Presley and Lynn Kinsky, "Government is Women's Enemy," an ALF discussion paper (New York: Association of Libertarian Feminists, 1979).

Chapter Ten: My Body, Myself: The Right to Protection

1. *Muller* v. *Oregon*, 208 U.S. 412 (1908).

2. "Private Property?—Not a Wife's Body," *Boston Herald*, 13 July 1982.

3. "Jurors in Florida Convict Man of Raping His Wife," *New York Times*, 2 September 1984.

4. Joan Kennedy Taylor, "Females and Rape," commentary syndicated on *Byline*, airdate 7 February 1985.

5. Tina Maddela, "SafeStreets," *Radcliffe News*, Winter 1989, 12.

6. "Reports of Rape Rise by 33 Percent on Irvine Campus," *New York Times*, 5 November 1989.

7. Catherine Warren, "Activists Rally for Girl Who Refused to Testify," *Stamford Advocate*, 6 December 1986.

8. David Finkelhor, *Sexually Victimized Children* (New York: The Free Press, 1979).

9. "The Facts About Rape and Incest" (Washington: The NARAL Foundation).

10. Michael deCourcy Hinds, "Relationships: The Child Victim of Incest," *New York Times*, 15 June 1981.

11. Diana E. H. Russell, *The Secret Trauma: Incest in the Lives of Girls and Women* (New York: Basic Books, 1986).

12. See Janet Hawkins, "Rowers on the River Styx," *Harvard Magazine*, March/April 1991, 43–52.

13. Tamar Lewin, "Archives of Business: A Grueling Struggle for Equality," *New York Times*, Business Section, 13.

14. John Gordon, "The Politics of Harassment," *Inquiry*, March/April 1984.

15. Joan Kennedy Taylor, "The Politics of Harassment II," *Inquiry*, May 1984, 35.

16. "Women's Lib Blamed for Wife-Beating," *Pittsfield Berkshire Eagle*, 15 September 1977.

17. Langley and Levy, *Wife Beating* (see chap. 3, n. 1), 215–19.

18. "Wife Beating Reported Common in America," *(Pittsfield) Berkshire Eagle,* 25 July 1977.

19. Quoted in Langley and Levy, *Wife Beating,* 49.

20. Quoted in Langley and Levy, *Wife Beating,* 54.

21. Terry Davidson, *Conjugal Crime: Understanding and Changing the Wifebeating Pattern,* (New York: Hawthorn Books, Inc. Publishers, 1978), 103.

22. "12 Wives Lose Suit on Court Handling of Beatings," *New York Times,* 6 August 1978.

23. Judy Katz, "Law Aids Beaten Women: Police Prepare to Give Extended Protection," *(Pittsfield) Berkshire Eagle,* 2 October 1978.

24. "Abuser, Not Victim Is Destroying the Family," *USA Today,* 12 December 1983.

25. Dirk Johnson, "Abused Women Get Leverage in Connecticut," *New York Times,* 15 June 1986.

26. "Court Challenged in Massachusetts," *New York Times,* 30 November 1986.

27. "Judges in Massachusetts Studying Spouse Abuse," *New York Times,* 3 May 1987. See *Commonwealth* v. *Paul Dunn,* 407 Mass 798.

28. Langley and Levy, *Wife Beating,* 132.

29. Reported in "Domestic Violence Is Target of Bill," *New York Times,* 16 December 1990.

Chapter Eleven: My Body, Myself: The Many Kinds of Choice

1. James Stark, "Update," *Boston Sunday Globe,* 5 November 1978.

2. Stephen Weeks, "Prostitute Charges Tax Laws Amount to Pimping," *Los Angeles Times,* 19 December 1979.

3. Paul Webster, "A New Journal in Paris by and for Prostitutes," *Press,* June/July 1981, 13.

4. Iver Peterson, "States Assess Surrogate Motherhood," *New York Times,* 13 December 1987.

5. Don Wegars, "Child Safe After Strange Kidnapping," *San Francisco Chronicle,* Home Edition, 9 April 1980.

6. "Baby M: Taking the Money Out of Motherhood," *New York Times,* 7 February 1988.

7. Seth Mydans, "Surrogate Denied Custody of Child," *New York Times,* 23 October 1990.

8. "New Turn in a Couple's Fight Over Embryos," *New York Times,* 27 May 1990.

9. Tamar Lewin, "Medical Use of Fetal Tissues Spurs New Abortion Debate," *New York Times,* 16 August 1987.

10. Philip J. Hilts, "Fetal Tissue Used: Anguish Behind a Medical First," *New York Times,* 16 April 1991.

11. Philip J. Hilts, "Fetus-to-Fetus Transplant Blocks Deadly Genetic Defect, Researchers Say," *New York Times,* 2d section, 21 November 1991.

12. *Roe* v. *Wade,* 410 U.S. 113 (1973).

13. Peter Steinfels, "Catholic Scholars, Citing New Data, Widen Debate on When Life Begins," *New York Times,* Week in Review Section, 13 January 1991.

14. James C. Mohr, *Abortion in America: The Origins and Evolution of National Policy, 1800–1900* (New York: Oxford University Press, 1978), 28.

15. Mohr, *Abortion in America,* 137.

16. Warren E. Leary, "Koop Challenged on Abortion Data," *New York Times,* 15

January 1989.

17. *S.J. Res. 19, Proposing an amendment to the Constitution of the United States guaranteeing the right of life,* 97th Cong., 1st Sess., 22 January 1981.

18. William B. Irvine, "The Right Not to Live," *Freeman,* vol. 41 no. 5 (May 1991): 195.

19. Peggy Simpson, "The Political Arena," *Ms.,* July/August 1989, 46.

20. "Woman Jailed in Florida for Having 2d Baby," *New York Times,* 27 January 1984.

21. Nadine Brozan, "7 Contend Correction Dept. Urged Abortions for Guards," *New York Times,* 24 May 1989.

22. *Buck* v. *Bell,* 274 U.S. 200 (1927).

23. "Proposal for Woman's Sterilization Draws Protest," *New York Times,* 25 September 1988.

24. Felicity Barringer, "Sentence for Killing Newborn: Jail Term, Then Birth Control," *New York Times,* 18 November 1990.

25. Rhonda Copelon, "The Chilling Truth About a 'Human Life' Amendment," *Ms.,* May 1979, 92.

26. "Court Calls Viable Fetus a Person," *New York Times,* 25 April 1985.

27. Alan L. Otten, "Women's Rights vs. Fetal Rights Looms as Thorny and Divisive Issue," *Wall Street Journal,* 12 April 1985.

28. Stephen Goode, "A Mother's Body, a Fetus's Fate," *Insight,* 27 June 1988, 54.

29. Goode, "A Mother's Body, a Fetus's Fate," 54. *See also* Christine Vandevelde, "The Equalizers," *Savvy,* April 1988, 62.

30. Goode, "A Mother's Body, a Fetus's Fate," 54.

31. Richard L. Madden, "Comatose Woman's Fetus Is Focus of Dispute," *New York Times,* 8 March 1987.

32. Eric Schmitt, "Doctors Perform Abortion on Comatose L.I. Woman," *New York Times,* 12 February 1989.

33. "Patient in Abortion Suit Has Baby," *New York Times,* 30 December 1990.

34. Paul Jacobs, "Pregnant Women Cautioned on Caffeine," *Los Angeles Times,* 5 September 1980.

35. "Mother Who Gives Birth to Drug Addict Faces Felony Charge," *New York Times,* 17 December 1988.

36. Isabel Wilkerson,"Woman Cleared After Drug Use in Pregnancy," *New York Times,* 3 April 1991.

37. Jan Hoffman, "Pregnant, Addicted—and Guilty?" *New York Times Magazine,* 19 August 1990, 34.

38. Wilkerson, "Woman Cleared After Drug Use in Pregnancy."

39. Wilkerson, "Woman Cleared After Drug Use in Pregnancy."

40. Marcia Chambers, "Are Fetal Rights Equal to Infants'?" *New York Times,* Week in Review Section, 16 November 1986.

41. "Punishing Pregnant Addicts: Debate, Dismay, No Solution," *New York Times,* Week in Review Section, 10 September 1989.

42. "Punishing Pregnant Addicts."

43. "Punishing Pregnant Addicts."

44. Anne Wyman, "Treatment vs. Punishment for Drug-Addicted Mothers," *Radcliffe News,* Summer 1990, 7.

45. Tamar Lewin, "Protecting the Baby: Work in Pregnancy Poses Legal Frontier," *New York Times,* 2 August 1988.

46. Vandevelde, "The Equalizers" (see n. 29), 58.

47. Quoted in Marcia Rockwood, review of *Crystal Eastman on Women and Revo-*

lution, ed. Blanche Wiesen Cook, *Ms.,* December 1978, 82.

48. Linda Greenhouse, "Court Backs Right of Women to Jobs with Health Risk," *New York Times,* 21 March 1991.

49. Greenhouse, "Court Backs Right of Women to Jobs with Health Risk."

50. Smuts, *Women and Work in America* (see chap. 3, n. 15), 145.

51. Peter T. Kilborn, "Who Decides Who Works at Jobs Imperilling Fetuses?" *New York Times,* 2 September 1990.

52. Jane Gross, "Anti-Abortion Revival: Homes for Unwed Mothers," *New York Times,* 23 July 1989.

53. Michael deCourcy Hinds, "Abortion Foes' Centers Guiding Lives After Births," *New York Times,* 13 May 1990.

54. Gross, "Anti-Abortion Revival." *See also* Jane Gross, "On Abortion, More Doctors Are Balancing Practice and Ideology," *New York Times,* 8 September 1991.

55. Ellen Willis, "Teen Lust," *Ms.,* July/August 1987, 193–94.

56. Kathryn E. McGoldrick, M.D., "The Safest Contraceptive: Saying 'No!' " *On the Issues,* vol. 5, 1985.

57. "Agent Hired in Fight to Prevent Abortion of 11-Year-Old Girl," *New York Times,* 10 June 1982.

58. Philip J. Hilts, "Birth-Control Backlash," *New York Times Magazine,* 16 December 1990, 70.

Chapter Twelve: The Temptation of Political Expediency: Antipornography

1. Hinds, "Abortion Foes' Centers Guiding Lives After Births," (see chap. 11, n. 53).

2. Joann S. Lublin, "Where Does the Women's Movement Go Now?" *Wall Street Journal,* 29 June 1982.

3. Lublin, "Where Does the Women's Movement Go Now?"

4. Lublin, "Where Does the Women's Movement Go Now?"

5. Susan Brownmiller, *Against Our Will: Men, Women, and Rape* (New York: Simon & Schuster, 1975), 395.

6. Dorothy Townsend, "Women Win 2½-Year Battle: Firm to Ban Violence on Album Covers," Los Angeles Times, 9 November 1979.

7. Townsend, "Women Win 2½-Year Battle."

8. Diana E. H. Russell with Laura Lederer, "Questions We Get Asked Most Often," in *Take Back the Night: Women on Pornography,* ed. Laura Lederer (New York: William Morrow and Company, Inc., 1980), 29.

9. Lois Gould, "Do Feminists Need Anita Bryant?" *San Francisco Chronicle,* 7 July 1977.

10. Susan Jacoby, "Hers," *New York Times,* 26 January 1978.

11. Joan Kennedy Taylor, "Women Against Pornography?" *Libertarian Review,* December 1979, 8–9. *See also* Lindsy Van Gelder, "When Women Confront Street Porn," *Ms.,* February 1980, 62ff. and Barbara Basler, "5,000 in Times Square Hold Rally Against the Pornography Industry," *New York Times,* 21 October 1979.

12. Quoted in Susan Brownmiller, "And the First Amendment Is in the Middle: Feminism Confronts Pornography," *Los Angeles Times,* 5 August 1979.

13. Paula Cizmar, "N.Y. Women Take Back the Night," *Mother Jones,* September/October 1979, 6.

14. Van Gelder, "When Women Confront Street Porn" (see n. 11).

15. Ellen Willis, "Lust Horizons: Is the Women's Movement Pro-Sex?" Village Voice,

17–23 June 1981, 1, 36–37.

16. Walter Goodman, "Battle on Pornography Spurred by New Tactics," *New York Times,* 3 July 1984.

17. Goodman, "Battle on Pornography Spurred by New Tactics."

18. Letter from Catharine A. MacKinnon, *New York Times Book Review,* 11 March 1990, 34.

19. Richard Stengel, "Sex Busters," *Time,* 21 July 1986, 18.

20. "Excerpts from Final Report of Attorney General's Panel on Pornography," *New York Times,* 10 July 1986.

21. Stengel, "Sex Busters," 14.

22. *Beauharnais* v. *Illinois,* 343 U.S. 250 (1952).

23. *New York Times Co.* v. *Sullivan,* 376 U.S. 254 (1964).

24. *Abrams* v. *United States,* 250 U.S. 616 (1919).

25. *Schenck* v. *United States,* 249 U.S. 47 (1919).

26. *Cantwell* v. *Connecticut,* 310 U.S. 296 (1940).

27. *Terminiello* v. *Chicago,* 337 U.S. 1 (1949).

28. *Roth* v. *United States,* 354 U.S. 476 (1957).

29. *Miller* v. *California,* 413 U.S. 15 (1973).

30. Marty Zupan, "Civil Libertarians Cry Wolf," *Reason,* July 1986, 15.

31. *Davis* v. *Beason,* 133 U.S. 333 (1890).

32. "Excerpts From Final Report of Attorney General's Panel on Pornography."

33. James Brown, "Media Fails to 'Question Authority,' " *Free Press Network,* vol. 8, no. 5 (November/December 1989): 4.

34. Stengel, "Sex Busters," 17.

35. Stengel, "Sex Busters," 21.

36. Stengel, "Sex Busters," 18, 21.

37. See Joan Kennedy Taylor, "Pornography and the Free Market," *Libertarian Review,* June 1978, 27-31.

38. Quoted in Taylor, "Pornography and the Free Market."

39. Linda Bird Francke, "Running Scared on Abortion," *New York Times,* 6 May 1978; reprinted, "Op-Ed at 20," *New York Times,* 30 September 1990.

Chapter Thirteen: The Temptation of Political Expediency: Social Feminism

1. Patricia McCormack, "A Gathering for Liberation," *Los Angeles Times,* 30 November 1979.

2. Betty Friedan, "Feminism Takes a New Turn," *New York Times Magazine,* 25 November 1979, 102, 106.

3. Friedan, *The Second Stage* (see chap. 1, n. 22), 228.

4. Friedan, *The Second Stage,* 229.

5. McCormack, "A Gathering for Liberation."

6. Friedan, *The Second Stage,* 335.

7. Nan Robertson, "Betty Friedan Ushers in a 'Second Stage,' " *New York Times,* 19 October 1981.

8. Quoted in Megan Marshall, "What Women Want in the 1980s . . ." *New Republic,* 20 January 1982, 32.

9. Marshall, "What Women Want in the 1980s . . ." 33.

10. Austin C. Wehrwein, "What Now, NOW?" *Boston Globe,* 12 October 1982.

11. Bernard Weinraub, "Feminists Turn to Economic Issues for '80," *New York Times,* 23 October 1979.

12. Gus Tyler, "Supplementary Statement," in *Women, Work, and Wages: Equal Pay for Jobs of Equal Value,* ed. Donald J. Treiman and Heidi Hartmann (Washington: National Academy Press, 1981), 107.

13. Ernest J. McCormick, "Minority Report," in Treiman and Hartmann, *Women, Work, And Wages,* 118.

14. Robert Pear, "Women Vow to Push Pay Equity Fight After Losing Court Ruling," *New York Times,* 6 September 1985.

15. news release, "Women's Economic Conference Challenges Policy Assumptions," issued by National Conference on Women, the Economy and Public Policy, 14 June 1984.

16. "Women in the Workplace: A Roundtable Discussion," *Manhattan Report,* vol. 4 no. 4, 1984, 16.

17. "Women in the Workplace," 13.

18. "More Gains for Women," *Time,* 14 September 1987, 64.

19. Sylvia Ann Hewlett, *A Lesser Life: The Myth of Women's Liberation in America* (New York: William Morrow & Company, 1986), 158, 165.

20. Hewlett, *A Lesser Life,* 14–15.

21. Hewlett, *A Lesser Life,* 14.

22. Tamar Lewin, "Maternity Leave: Is It Leave, Indeed?" *New York Times,* Business Section, 22 July 1984, 23.

23. Lewin, "Maternity Leave," 23.

24. Letter from Isabelle Katz Pinzler and Joan E. Bertin, *New York Times Book Review,* 8 June 1986, 33.

25. "Court Upholds Job Protection for Pregnant Women," *New York Times,* Week in Review Section, 18 January 1987.

Chapter Fourteen: Back to Our Roots: How We Might Grow

1. Letter from Joseph D. Grano, *New York Times Magazine,* 8 December 1985, 166.

2. Midge Decter, "The Intelligent Woman's Guide to Feminism," *Policy Review,* no. 16, Spring 1981, 45–53.

3. Decter, "The Intelligent Woman's Guide to Feminism," 45.

4. Dowling, *The Cinderella Complex* (see chap. 5, n. 8), 36–37.

5. Shelby Steele, "On Being Black and Middle Class," *Commentary,* vol. 85, no. 1 (January 1988): 44.

6. Steele, "On Being Black and Middle Class," 42–43.

7. Steele, "On Being Black and Middle Class," 47.

8. Robert B. Reich, "Secession of the Successful," *New York Times Magazine,* 20 January 1991, 42.

9. L. A. Kauffman, "NOW for Something Completely Different," *Progressive,* March 1984, 32.

10. Paula Rayman, "The Meaning of Work in Women's Lives," *Radcliffe Quarterly,* June 1990, 14.

11. Quoted in Vivian Gornick, "Women Who Did Something," review of *Elizabeth Cady Stanton: Susan B. Anthony: Correspondence, Writings, Speeches,* ed. and with a Critical Commentary by Ellen Carol DuBois, *New York Times Book Review,* 18 October 1981, 40–41.

12. Gornick, "Women Who Did Something," 41.

Index